The Word before the Powers

The Word
before the Powers

An Ethic of Preaching

CHARLES L. CAMPBELL

Westminster John Knox Press
LOUISVILLE • LONDON

Scripture quotations from the New Revised Standard Version of the Bible are copyright © 1989 by the Division of Christian Education of the National Council of the Churches of Christ in the U.S.A. and are used by permission.

Grateful acknowledgment is made to the following authors and publishers for kind permission to reprint from the following materials:

Quotations by Martin Luther King Jr. are reprinted by arrangement with the Estate of Martin Luther King Jr. c/o Writers House as agent for the proprietor. Copyright Martin Luther King Jr., 1963, copyright renewed 1991 Coretta Scott King. (Excerpts from the "I Have a Dream" sermon copyright 1963 Martin Luther King Jr., copyright renewed 1993 Coretta Scott King.) Excerpts from *The Grapes of Wrath* by John Steinbeck, copyright 1939, renewed © 1967 by John Steinbeck. Used by permission of Viking Penguin, a division of Penguin Putnam Inc. Excerpts from *Engaging The Powers* by Walter Wink, copyright © 1992 Augsburg Fortress (www.fortresspress.com). Reprinted by permission. Excerpt from *An Ethic for Christians and Other Aliens in a Strange Land* by William Stringfellow, 1973, W Publishing Group, Nashville, Tennessee. All rights reserved. Reprinted by permission. Excerpts from *At This Time In This Place: the Spirit Embodied in the Local Assembly* by Michael Warren, 1999, Trinity Press International, Harrisburg, PA. Used by permission. Excerpt from a sermon titled "The Liturgy of Our Lives" by Jane E. Fahey. Used by permission. Excerpt from a sermon titled "Dinner with Amos" by Theodore J. Wardlaw. Used by permission. Selections from a sermon titled "The Woman Who Just Said 'No.'" by Anna Carter Florence. Used by permission.

Book design by Sharon Adams
Cover design by Design Point Inc.

First edition
Published by Westminster John Knox Press
Louisville, Kentucky

This book is printed on acid-free paper that meets the American National Standards Institute Z39.48 standard. ∞

PRINTED IN THE UNITED STATES OF AMERICA

02 03 04 05 06 07 08 09 10 11 — 10 9 8 7 6 5 4 3 2 1

Library of Congress Cataloging-in-Publication Data

Campbell, Charles L., 1954-
  The Word before the powers : an ethic of preaching / Charles L. Campbell.
    p. cm.
  Includes bibliographical references (p.) and indexes.
  ISBN 0-664-22233-1 (pbk.)
    1. Preaching. 2. Powers (Christian theology)—Biblical teaching. 3. Violence—Biblical teaching. 4. Nonviolence—Biblical teaching. I. Title.

BV4221 .C35 2002
251—dc21

2002071314

For Lydia and Thomas

Contents

Acknowledgments

This book has been working on me for a long time, and many people have played a role in bringing it to completion. My close friend and colleague Stan Saunders first pointed me to Walter Wink's work. A short time later, Ed Loring, a partner at the Open Door Community in Atlanta, directed me to the writings of William Stringfellow. At the same time the Open Door Community itself, through its ministry to homeless people and prisoners, was introducing me to the powers on the streets of Atlanta and in the prisons of Georgia. In this crucible of reading and experience the book began to take shape.

My reflections were greatly enriched by the insights and questions of students in my "Principalities, Powers, and Preaching" classes, taught both at Columbia Seminary and in Jamaica. The Jamaican pastors in particular broadened my understanding of the demonic powers and helped me discern more clearly my own complicity with "Babylon." My good friend Joyce Hollyday, who team-taught this course with me on two occasions, became an important conversation partner, teaching me much about the powers and our resistance to them.

Invitations to give lectures at Duke Divinity School, Lutheran Theological Seminary in Philadelphia, and my alma mater, Hendrix College, gave me the opportunity to develop and receive feedback on the material in this book. In addition, educational events for the Leadership Conference of the Presbyterian Health, Education, and Welfare Association and for pastors and educators in the Southern Conference of the Moravian Church provided occasions for extended conversation about this material. I am extremely grateful for the warm hospitality and constructive feedback I received from all these groups.

When Westminster John Knox Press accepted my book proposal, Stephanie Egnotovich agreed to take a "hands on" role as editor. As a result, this project has in many ways been a team effort. Throughout the process, Stephanie has known when to critique and push and when to support and celebrate. Her insights and expertise have improved the book from beginning to end. I cannot imagine a better working relationship with an editor, and I am more grateful to her than I can say.

Many others also assisted and supported me during the writing of this book. Columbia Theological Seminary granted me a sabbatical during which several of the chapters were written. My colleagues Stan Saunders, Rick Dietrich, Christine Yoder, and Charlie Cousar read portions of the manuscript and made many helpful suggestions. Anna Carter Florence, my wonderful homiletics colleague, not only offered regular encouragement but also read and commented on the entire manuscript. Anna Louise Murchison and David Knauert assisted enormously in the preparation of the final manuscript, putting together permissions requests and compiling the bibliography and indexes.

Finally, my deepest thanks go to my family. Dana, with whom I celebrated twenty-five years of marriage and friendship this year, not only loved and supported me through yet another time- and attention-consuming project but also read much of the manuscript and made invaluable editorial corrections. My children, Lydia and Thomas, who have suddenly become young adults, were exceptionally patient with their father's absentmindedness and preoccupation during the writing of this book. I dedicate the work to them as they move into adulthood and a new stage of their engagement with the powers.

Introduction

On the day after France surrendered to Nazi Germany during World War II, André Trocmé, the pastor of the Reformed congregation in the small village of Le Chambon sur Lignon in southern France, stepped into the pulpit and proclaimed: "The responsibility of Christians is to resist the violence that will be brought to bear on their consciences through the weapons of the spirit."[1] Over the next four years the villagers, most of them descendants of the Huguenots, did just that. In a remarkable display of faithfulness and courage, which cost several of the participants their lives, the approximately five thousand people in the village and surrounding hamlets provided sanctuary to over five thousand Jews, saving them from the massacre of the Nazi death camps.

In a documentary film titled *Weapons of the Spirit*, Pierre Sauvage, a Jewish man who was born and sheltered in Le Chambon during the war, tells the story of the small village. The film is stunning and surprising, for what stands out is not simply the faithful discipleship of the villagers but their interpretation of their actions. When asked by Sauvage how they came to make such a risky decision to provide sanctuary for the Jews, the villagers generally looked at their interrogator with a puzzled expression on their faces and replied with comments such as "It happened so naturally, we can't understand the fuss. It happened quite simply"; "I helped simply because they needed to be helped. . . . The Bible says to feed the hungry, to visit the sick. It's a normal thing to do." In one instance, when asked why she continued to provide sanctuary even after

---

1. *Weapons of the Spirit*, prod. and dir. Pierre Sauvage, 1 hr. 30 min., First Run Features, 1989, videocassette.

1

the German army had occupied southern France and the situation had become more dangerous, one woman replied, "I don't know. We were used to it."

These responses suggest the people of Le Chambon experienced no single, clear, dramatic "moment of decision"; they made no self-conscious ethical "analysis" of the situation according to some moral calculus, which they then followed with action. Rather, the villagers were simply "doing what came naturally." Their actions flowed from their character and the character of the community of which they were a part. As Philip Hallie wrote in his book about the people of Le Chambon, "We fail to understand what happened in Le Chambon if we think that *for them* their actions were complex and difficult. . . . For certain people, helping the distressed is as natural and necessary as feeding themselves. The Trocmés, the Theises, and others in Le Chambon were such people."[2] One is reminded of the "sheep" in Matthew 25:31–40. When told they have cared for the "Human One," they reply, "When was it that we saw you hungry and gave you food, or thirsty and gave you something to drink?" Caring for "the least of these" has become so much a part of who they are that, like the people of Le Chambon, they really have no idea they are doing anything extraordinary.

Sauvage's film about the people of Le Chambon stands in the background of this book. That village's resistance to Nazi Germany brings the ethical dimensions of preaching into sharp, dramatic focus, just as a lens may focus the diffuse rays of the sun into a sharp, clear point. Looking through the lens of Le Chambon's resistance, the three key components of the ethic of preaching developed in this book become clear. First, the ethical context of preaching is the activity of the principalities and powers. The situation in Le Chambon was, admittedly, a dramatic and extreme example of the encounter between the Word of God and the powers of death in the world. Nevertheless, in more subtle but no less deadly ways the principalities and powers of the world remain aggressive actors that shape human life today and provide the context of Christian preaching. When understood in the context of the powers' work, as I hope to show, preaching takes on fresh ethical significance for the church.

Second, the preaching of the Word is a critical practice of resistance to the work of the principalities and powers. Trocmé's sermon, which I quoted at the beginning of this introduction, not only proclaims a message of resistance but is itself an extraordinary act of nonviolent resistance to the powers. Trocmé countered the powers of violence and death in the world not with more vio-

---

2. Philip P. Hallie, *Lest Innocent Blood Be Shed: The Story of the Village of Le Chambon and How Goodness Happened There* (New York: Harper & Row, 1979; HarperPerennial ed., 1994), 284.

lence and death but with the Word of God, the "sword of the Spirit" (Eph. 6:17). And he engaged in this resistance not in one isolated sermon but in the weekly practice of preaching, including children's sermons, in the church at Le Chambon.[3] Preaching provided Trocmé and continues to provide the church today with a specific and distinctive ethical option in the face of the powers of domination and death: nonviolent resistance. This homiletical practice of nonviolent resistance, I suggest, is not only central to the preaching of Jesus—both Jesus' own preaching and our proclamation of Jesus' life, death, and resurrection—but also central to the ethical life of the community of faith.

Third, the powers are engaged by a *community* of resistance, which is shaped by a distinctive way of seeing the world and by peculiar practices and virtues. The community of Le Chambon had been built up over the years by peculiar memories and traditions that shaped their vision of the world. These memories and traditions included not only the stories of their faithful, persecuted ancestors, the Huguenots, but also the stories in the Bible. Preaching was one means of keeping these memories and this vision alive, as Philip Hallie has noted: "Behind a Huguenot sermon is the history of a besieged minority trying to keep its moral and religious vitality against great adversity. The sermons of the pastor are one of the main sources of that vitality."[4] Song was another way the memories continued to shape the vision and life of the community. As the people would regularly sing about their ancestors,

> May the spirit that gave them life
> Inspire their children.
> May the spirit that gave them life
> Inspire their children
> To follow their example.

This example involved a set of communal practices, particularly the practice of hospitality, which grew out of a deep sympathy for the victims of the principalities and powers. Long before Jewish people began arriving at their doorsteps, the Chambonnais had been welcoming persecuted people into their homes and had been formed in the virtues shaped by the practice of hospitality. Their vision of the world, their practices, and their virtues had so formed the character of the Chambonnais that they welcomed Jewish people into their homes as "the normal thing to do."

These three components shape the ethic of preaching developed in this

---

3. Some of Trocmé's children's sermons, which often function as subversive parables, have been collected in *Angels and Donkeys: Tales for Christmas and Other Times*, trans. Nelly Trocmé Hewett (Intercourse, Pa.: Good Books, 1998). See also Hallie, *Lest Innocent Blood*, 170–72, 92.
4. Hallie, *Lest Innocent Blood*, 172.

book: the work of the principalities and powers; the preaching of the Word as an act of nonviolent resistance to the powers; and the formation of Christian communities of resistance. These three components also give form to the book. In chapters 1 and 2, I present general characteristics of the principalities and powers and their work. In chapter 3, I examine Jesus' engagement with the powers through his life, death, and resurrection. The remaining chapters develop an ethic of preaching in the context of these powers. In chapter 4, I argue that preaching is a distinctive practice of nonviolent resistance, which has significant implications for the moral life of the church. In chapters 5 through 8, I explore three critical dimensions of character ethics and develop their concrete implications for preaching as a practice of nonviolent resistance: vision (chapters 5 and 6), practices (chapter 7), and virtues (chapter 8). By the end of the book, I hope to have set forth an ethic of preaching that will be helpful to those who seek to proclaim the gospel in the midst of the enormous challenges of the new century.

The position I develop draws heavily on the work of William Stringfellow and Walter Wink, which has had a profound impact on my life. The interpretation of the powers developed by these two courageous theologians not only makes sense *to* me; it has come to make sense *of* me—of my struggles, my sinfulness, my hope. In addition, their work has provided a critical theological framework for interpreting not only my experiences working with homeless people on the streets of Atlanta but also the enormous problems I encounter when I read the daily newspaper.[5] I thus turn to Stringfellow and Wink in a deeply personal rather than merely academic sense. As will become clear, my purpose is neither to engage their work critically nor even to add distinctive new insights to their reflections on the principalities and powers. Rather, my purpose is to set forth a clear, bold understanding of the powers' work and to develop an ethic of preaching within this framework.

As will also become clear, I write from a position of great privilege, and I write primarily for preachers who find themselves standing in the pulpits of middle-class, mainline congregations. I do not presume to speak to or for people who live on the margins of privilege and power, though I hope my reflections may be of some help in these contexts. Although I write from a position of privilege, however, this book has been shaped profoundly by voices of people who wrestle with the powers from situations of oppression. In particular, over the past few years homeless people and gay, lesbian, bisexual, and

---

5. In *The Word on the Street: Performing the Scriptures in the Urban Context* (Grand Rapids: Wm. Eerdmans Publishing Co., 2000), which I coauthored with Stanley Saunders, I have given an account of my experiences among homeless people on the streets of Atlanta.

transgender people have been my teachers and have changed my life. They have helped me glimpse more fully the powers' deadly work in the world, as well as my own complicity in that work. For their honesty and courage I am profoundly grateful. This book owes as much to them as to Stringfellow and Wink.

What follows, then, represents not merely an academic exercise (despite all the footnotes). Rather, it is a reflective pause in the midst of my ongoing struggle with the powers and my continuing journey as a disciple, preacher, and teacher. I hope my reflections will prove valuable for others who find themselves on similar journeys.

1

"Not against Enemies of Blood and Flesh"

"How can one close one's eyes at the fact that the demons themselves have taken over the rule of the world, that it is the powers of darkness who have here made an awful conspiracy."

Dietrich Bonhoeffer[1]

In 1932, amid the gathering storm of World War II, Dietrich Bonhoeffer drew on the imagery of Ephesians 6 and penned these prescient words. In so doing, the German theologian foreshadowed a resurgence of interest in the New Testament understanding of the principalities and powers during the second half of the twentieth century.[2] As Bonhoeffer glimpsed early on, the century just ended brought a renewed appreciation for the activity of the "demonic" in the world. The atrocities of two world wars, the Holocaust, the nuclear arms race, totalitarian regimes, and ethnic cleansing have dashed modern hopes of human progress and challenged naive presuppositions about the powers of

---

1. Quoted in Bill Wylie-Kellermann, "Not Vice Versa. Reading the Powers Biblically: Stringfellow, Hermeneutics, and the Principalities," *Anglican Theological Review* 81, 4 (1999): 671.
2. Ibid. It is not my intention to provide a review of the literature, which has been done by other writers. For excellent overviews of this literature, see Walter Wink, *Naming the Powers: The Language of Power in the New Testament* (Philadelphia: Fortress Press, 1984); Marva Jenine Sandbe Dawn, "The Concept of 'The Principalities and Powers' in the Works of Jacques Ellul" (Ph.D. Diss., University of Notre Dame, 1992; Ann Arbor, Mich.: University Microfilms #9220014), 36–83; and Marva J. Dawn, *Powers, Weakness, and the Tabernacling of God* (Grand Rapids: Wm. B. Eerdmans Publishing Co., 2001), 1–34.

evil. Even an internationally renowned physicist, reflecting on the development of the first atomic bomb, could not avoid speaking of demonic powers: "When once you sell your soul to the devil," Freeman Dyson commented, "then there's no going back on it."[3]

More recently, the "manic" growth and activity of technology and global capitalism have stirred similar reflection on the activity of the principalities and powers in the world.[4] Further, the relentless and resilient force of racism, which continues to rise up in "ever more beguiling forms and predatory guises," has generated reflection on the demonic powers that seem to govern the world.[5] The intransigence of other "isms," from classism to sexism to heterosexism, has likewise called attention to the legion of powers that oppress people and hold them captive.[6]

In response to these events and developments, biblical scholars and theologians have returned to ancient insights into the workings of the principalities and powers as a profound means of interpreting our times. The language of the New Testament has been reclaimed in order for the church to see the contemporary world with new depth and realism. And as this new century

3. Quoted in *The Day after Trinity: J. Robert Oppenheimer and the Atomic Bomb*, prod. and dir. Jon Else, 1 hr. 28 min., Pyramid Home Video, 1980, videocassette.

4. Wes Howard-Brook and Anthony Gwyther have argued that global capitalism is the contemporary form of the beast in the book of Revelation; see *Unveiling Empire: Reading Revelation Then and Now* (Maryknoll, N.Y.: Orbis Books, 1999), 236–77. On global capitalism, see also William Greider, *One World, Ready or Not: The Manic Logic of Global Capitalism* (New York: Simon & Schuster, 1997); Naomi Klein, *No Logo: Taking Aim at the Brand Bullies* (New York: Picador USA, 1999). On technology as a power, see the numerous sociological and theological works by Jacques Ellul, most well known among them *The Technological Society*, trans. John Wilkinson (New York: Alfred A. Knopf, 1964). For a thorough analysis of Ellul's work within the framework of the principalities and powers, see Dawn, "'The Principalities and Powers.'" For another analysis of the "power" of technology, see Neil Postman, *Technopoly: The Surrender of Culture to Technology* (New York: Alfred A. Knopf, 1992; Vintage Books Edition, 1993).

5. William Stringfellow addressed racism as a power earlier in this century. See the helpful discussion in Wylie-Kellermann, "Not Vice Versa," 672–74. For another discussion of racism as a power, see Nibs Stroupe and Inez Fleming, *While We Run This Race: Confronting the Power of Racism in a Southern Church* (Maryknoll, N.Y.: Orbis Books, 1995), 123–29.

6. The books here are legion. For one helpful recent analysis, written with an eye toward people of privilege, see Mary Elizabeth Hobgood, *Dismantling Privilege: An Ethics of Accountability* (Cleveland: Pilgrim Press, 2000). For an exploration of these powers from a homiletical perspective, see Christine M. Smith, *Preaching as Weeping, Confession, and Resistance: Radical Responses to Radical Evil* (Louisville, Ky.: Westminster/John Knox Press, 1992). Many of the works cited throughout the rest of this book also examine these powers.

begins, with acts of unimaginable terrorism and the violent response of war, one senses that the exploration of the work of the principalities and powers will likely continue in the years ahead.[7]

ENCOUNTERING MONSTERS

At about the same time that Dietrich Bonhoeffer penned his prophetic words about the demonic powers in Germany, John Steinbeck, staring at the economic effects of the Great Depression and the Dust Bowl in the United States, wrote *The Grapes of Wrath*. In chapter 5 of his classic novel, Steinbeck provides one of American literature's most moving accounts of the work of the powers. He invites his readers to experience, rather than simply to analyze, the powers at work:

> The owners of the land came onto the land, or more often a spokesman for the owners came. They came in closed cars, and they felt the dry earth with their fingers, and sometimes they drove big earth augers into the ground for soil tests. The tenants, from their sun-beaten dooryards, watched uneasily when the closed cars drove along the fields. And at last the owner men drove into the dooryards and sat in their cars to talk out of the windows. The tenant men stood beside the cars for a while, and then squatted on their hams and found sticks with which to mark the dust.
>
> In the open doors the women stood looking out, and behind them the children—corn-headed children, with wide eyes, one bare foot on top of the other bare foot, and the toes working. The women and the children watched their men talking to the owner men. They were silent.
>
> Some of the owner men were kind because they hated what they had to do, and some of them were angry because they hated to be cruel, and some of them were cold because they had long ago found that one could not be an owner unless one were cold. And all of them were caught in something larger than themselves. Some of them hated the mathematics that drove them, and some were afraid, and some worshiped the mathematics because it provided a refuge from thought

---

7. I concluded the writing of this book in the months after the terrorist attacks on the World Trade Center and the Pentagon. While these events (and I suspect the events that will follow) call for reflection within the framework of the principalities and powers, I have intentionally chosen not to focus on them. I do not want to limit my discussion to one set of events apart from the ongoing work of the powers in numerous areas of life. I do hope the reflections in this book will aid pastors and preachers as they continue to wrestle with the interpretation of terrorism and the United States's response to it.

and from feeling. If a bank or a finance company owned the land, the owner man said, The Bank—or the Company—needs—wants—insists—must have—as though the Bank or the Company were a monster, with thought and feeling, which had ensnared them. These last would take no responsibility for the banks or the companies because they were men and slaves, while the banks were machines and masters all at the same time. Some of the owner men were a little proud to be slaves to such cold and powerful masters. The owner men sat in the cars and explained. You know the land is poor. You've scrabbled at it long enough, God knows.

The squatting tenant men nodded and wondered and drew figures in the dust, and yes, they knew, God knows. If the dust only wouldn't fly. If the top would only stay on the soil, it might not be so bad.

The owner men went on leading to their point: You know the land's getting poorer. You know what cotton does to the land; robs it, sucks all the blood out of it.

The squatters nodded—they knew, God knew. If they could only rotate the crops they might pump blood back into the land.

Well, it's too late. And the owner men explained the workings and the thinkings of the monster that was stronger than they were. A man can hold land if he can just eat and pay taxes; he can do that.

Yes, he can do that until his crops fail one day and he has to borrow money from the bank.

But—you see, a bank or a company can't do that, because those creatures don't breathe air, don't eat side-meat. They breathe profits; they eat the interest on money. If they don't get it, they die the way you die without air, without side-meat. It is a sad thing, but it is so. It is just so.[8]

Finally, after some discussion, the owners get to the point and inform the tenant farmers that they will have to get off the land. One tractor, it turns out, can do the work of a dozen families. When the farmers protest that they are poor and have worked the land for generations, the owners reply,

We know that—all that. It's not us, it's the bank. A bank isn't like a man. Or an owner with fifty thousand acres, he isn't like a man either. That's the monster.

Sure, cried the tenant men, but it's our land. We measured it and broke it up. We were born on it, and we got killed on it, died on it. Even if it's no good, it's still ours. That's what makes it ours—being born on it, working it, dying on it. That makes ownership, not a paper with numbers on it.

We're sorry. It's not us. It's the monster. The bank isn't like a man.

Yes, but the bank is only made of men.

No, you're wrong there—quite wrong there. The bank is something

8. John Steinbeck, *The Grapes of Wrath*, Penguin Great Books of the Twentieth Century (New York: Penguin Books, 1999), 31–32.

else than men. It happens that every man in a bank hates what the bank does, and yet the bank does it. The bank is something more than men, I tell you. It's the monster. Men made it, but they can't control it.[9]

As Steinbeck depicts so poignantly, the principalities and powers are superhuman creatures with a spirit and life of their own, beyond the control of human beings. They are aggressive actors in the world, shaping human life in profound ways. Not simply personal, spiritual beings "up in the heavens" somewhere, the powers are embodied and active in concrete, structural realities such as Steinbeck's Bank. In short, the powers comprise that "something larger than ourselves" within which many of us often feel trapped and against which we often feel powerless, whether we hate or fear or worship that "something." The powers create the sense that we live in "a machine in which everyone is caught . . . [but] that no one owns."[10] They elicit comments such as "Nobody really wants homelessness, but millions of people are homeless, and we can't seem to do anything about it"; or "Few people desire war, but the piles of bodies and warheads just keep growing"; or "It doesn't matter whom I vote for, nothing's really going to change"; or "I feel like I'm just being swept along by forces beyond my control." As Jacques Ellul has put it, "The powers add a 'plus' and a 'different' factor to our history. . . . Beyond factors that may be understood and analyzed, not everything can be accounted for. . . . The residue is a spiritual power, an *exousia*."[11]

Like Steinbeck, the writers of the New Testament understood these powers. Their everyday lives were shaped by all kinds of forces impinging upon them, and the realities of these powers permeate their writings.[12] In the rest of this chapter and the next one, I examine these forces that the New Testament writers refer to as the principalities and powers.[13] Although numerous

---

9. Ibid., 33. Walter Wink pointed me to this chapter of Steinbeck's novel. See Walter Wink, *Engaging the Powers: Discernment and Resistance in a World of Domination* (Minneapolis: Fortress Press, 1992), 50.

10. Michel Foucault, *Power/Knowledge: Selected Interviews and Other Writings, 1972–1977*, ed. Colin Gordon, trans. Colin Gordon, Leo Marshall, John Mepham, Kate Soper (New York: Pantheon Books, 1980), 156; quoted in David Toole, *Waiting for Godot in Sarajevo: Theological Reflections on Nihilism, Tragedy, and Apocalypse* (Boulder, Colo.: Westview Press, 1998), 179.

11. Jacques Ellul, *The Subversion of Christianity*, trans. Geoffrey W. Bromiley (Grand Rapids: Wm. B. Eerdmans Publishing Co., 1986), 175.

12. Wink, *Naming the Powers*, 7.

13. Throughout this book, the biblical translations are from the New Revised Standard Version, with one important exception. In the NRSV, the words for "principalities" and "powers" (*archai* and *exousiai*) have been translated as "rulers" and "authorities," which does not capture the superhuman character of these powers. In some of the texts cited in this book, I retain the language of "principalities and powers," which comes from the King James Version.

issues surround the interpretation of these powers in the New Testament, I focus on the following general characteristics: the powers are legion; the powers are material and spiritual; the powers are created by God; and the powers are fallen. Within this larger theological framework, I develop more specific characteristics of the powers' goals and strategies.

THE POWERS ARE LEGION

One of the most generally agreed-upon characteristics of the principalities and powers in the New Testament is their multiplicity.[14] The numerous terms for the powers in the New Testament pile up and interact with one another; they are paired together and occur in series, running together and blending into one another until the reader is almost overwhelmed by the torrent. A simple glance at the diversity of terms and phrases in the New Testament suggests the multiplicity of the powers: principalities, powers, authorities, dominions, names, world rulers, thrones, angels, elemental spirits, demons, princes, strongholds, spirit of the air, serpent, dragon, lion, beast, Beelzebub, Satan, Devil.[15]

In addition, a cursory glance at how the terms pile up in various texts suggests their dynamic, even interchangeable relationship with one another:

> God put this power to work in Christ when he raised him from the dead and seated him at his right hand in the heavenly places, far above all rule and authority and power and dominion, and above every name that is named, not only in this age but also in the age to come. (Eph. 1:20–21)

> He is the image of the invisible God, the firstborn of all creation; for in him all things in heaven and on earth were created, things visible and invisible, whether thrones or dominions or rulers or powers. (Col. 1:15–16)

> And the beast that I saw was like a leopard, its feet were like a bear's, and its mouth was like a lion's mouth. And the dragon gave it his power and his throne and great authority. (Rev. 13:2)[16]

---

14. William Stringfellow, *An Ethic for Christians and Other Aliens in a Strange Land* (Waco, Tex.: Word Books, 1973; 3d paperback ed., 1979), 77.

15. See Wink, *Naming the Powers*, 8; Stringfellow, *Ethic for Christians*, 77–78; Hendrik Berkhof, *Christ and the Powers*, trans. John H. Yoder (Scottdale, Pa.: Herald Press, 1977), 13–15.

16. See also Romans 8:38; Ephesians 6:12; 1 Peter 3:22. As becomes clear in what follows, the importance of the powers in the New Testament is not limited to the epistles and Revelation but is evident in the Gospels as well, even where the specific terminology is not present. The presence and activity of the powers are not limited to those places where certain terms are used.

As Walter Wink notes, "The language of power in the New Testament is imprecise, liquid, interchangeable, and unsystematic."[17]

Few people have captured the multiplicity of the powers or related them to contemporary social realities more richly than William Stringfellow. He enumerates the powers through a deluge of examples:

> The very array of names and titles in biblical usage for the principalities and powers is some indication of the scope and significance of the subject for human beings. And if some of these seem quaint, transposed into contemporary language they lose quaintness and the principalities become recognizable and all too familiar: they include all institutions, all ideologies, all images, all movements, all causes, all corporations, all bureaucracies, all traditions, all methods and routines, all conglomerates, all races, all nations, all idols. Thus, the Pentagon or the Ford Motor Company or Harvard University or the Hudson Institute or Consolidated Edison or the Diners Club or the Olympics or the Methodist Church or the Teamsters Union are all principalities. So are capitalism, Maoism, humanism, Mormonism, astrology, the Puritan work ethic, science and scientism, white supremacy, patriotism, plus many, many more—sports, sex, any profession or discipline, technology, money, the family—beyond any prospect of full enumeration. The principalities and powers *are* legion.[18]

Stringfellow's list captures well the "potent, mobile, and diverse" character of the powers; and that is the place to begin.[19]

At a more philosophical level, David Toole has linked this understanding of the powers with Michel Foucault's profound understanding of power relations. Although he does not use the New Testament language of the powers, Foucault, Toole argues, highlights the dynamic, mobile, decentralized character of power at work in the world. Power is omnipresent,

> not because it has the privilege of consolidating everything under its invincible unity, but because it is produced from one moment to the

---

17. Wink, *Naming the Powers*, 9. In addition to capturing the multiplicity of the powers, Wink demonstrates that the plurality of New Testament terms captures various dimensions of power: the person-in-office (*archōn*, "ruler"); the institutionalization of power through office, position, or role (*archē*, "principality"; also *thronos*, "thrones"); the justifications, legitimations, and sanctions undergirding the exercise of power (*exousia*, "power"); the power or force, particularly in the New Testament the spiritual force, by which power is maintained (*dynamis*); and the realm or expanse of territory over which a power rules (*kyriotēs*, "dominions"). All of these aspects of power include human, structural, and spiritual dimensions. The language of power in the New Testament thus provides a rich framework for social analysis. See ibid., 13–35.
18. Stringfellow, *Ethic for Christians*, 78.
19. Ibid., 79.

next, at every point, or rather, in every relation from one point to another. Power is everywhere; not because it embraces everything, but because it comes from everywhere.[20]

The New Testament writers capture a similar sense of the multiplicity and omnipresence of power relations in their lists of the powers, which aggressively impinge on human life from every imaginable angle: things visible and invisible, thrones, dominions, rulers, powers, authorities.[21]

The result is chaos, as the rival powers struggle for survival and dominance. Again in the words of Stringfellow:

> [People] are veritably besieged, on all sides, at every moment simultaneously by these claims and strivings of the various powers, each seeking to dominate, usurp, or take a person's time, attention, abilities, effort; each grasping at life itself; each demanding idolatrous service and loyalty. In such tumult it becomes very difficult for a human being even to identify the idols which would possess him [or her].[22]

The powers are legion. And the primordial chaos spills over into the creation.[23]

THE POWERS ARE MATERIAL AND SPIRITUAL

A more contested issue in the interpretation of the powers in the New Testament revolves around the material and spiritual aspects of the powers and their work.[24] On the one hand, some interpreters identify the powers almost exclusively with human institutions and structural realities; they place little or no emphasis on a "spiritual" dimension and certainly do not consider the powers as independent spiritual beings. William Stringfellow at times seems to fall

---

20. Michel Foucault, *The History of Sexuality*, vol. 1: *An Introduction*, trans. Robert Hurley (New York: Vintage Books, 1990), 93; quoted in Toole, *Godot in Sarajevo*, 177; see also 220–22.

21. Pablo Richard notes that the image of the beast in Revelation 13:1–2 embodies the complexity of the powers at work in the world. See Pablo Richard, *Apocalypse: A People's Commentary on the Book of Revelation*, trans. Phillip Berryman (Maryknoll, N.Y.: Orbis Books, 1995), 107. For a helpful analysis of the ways in which various powers interact in oppressing people and holding them captive, see Hobgood, *Dismantling Privilege*.

22. Stringfellow, *Ethic for Christians*, 90.

23. Ellul, *Subversion of Christianity*, 176. The beast in the book of Revelation emerges from the sea, the site of primordial chaos (Rev. 13:1).

24. For a thorough examination of this issue, see Wink, *Naming the Powers*.

into this camp, as the above quotations suggest, although he clearly recognizes that the creaturely powers are characterized by a mysterious "something more."[25] John Howard Yoder also places an emphasis on the structural character of the powers, though he too recognizes this "something more" in his emphasis on the values inherent in structures.[26]

Other interpreters, mostly in the evangelical camp, strongly emphasize the spiritual reality of the powers and even assert their existence as independent, spiritual beings at work in the world. Arguing against those who would understand the principalities and powers in a structural way, John Stott sums up this approach:

> All three references to the principalities and powers in Ephesians also contain a reference to the heavenly places, that is, the unseen world of spiritual reality. It is a stubborn fact, as if Paul were deliberately explaining who the principalities and powers are, and where they operate. Indeed, the six stages in the developing drama of the principalities and powers—their original creation, their subsequent fall, their decisive conquest by Christ, their learning through the church, their continued hostility, and their final destruction—all seem to apply more naturally to supernatural beings than to structures, institutions, and traditions.[27]

[handwritten margin note: Only Spiritual vs. only Structural]

More popularly, the novels of Frank Peretti, such as his best-selling *This Present Darkness*, present the powers as independent spiritual beings at work in the world.[28]

In what follows I take a third, rather pragmatic approach between these two extremes. On the one hand, I do not want to deny the existence of "spiritual beings" at work in the world. I have heard too many stories from pastors in Jamaica about demon possession and exorcisms to dismiss such possibilities on the basis of a modern, Western, materialistic worldview. I do not want to deny the independent existence and activity of spiritual powers—even spiritual beings—in the world. When confronted by such mysteries, I return to the

---

25. Stringfellow, *Ethic for Christians*, 78–80. Stringfellow also emphasizes the spiritual impact of the powers on human beings, as becomes clearer below in my discussion of death.

26. John Howard Yoder, *The Politics of Jesus* (Grand Rapids: Wm. B. Eerdmans Publishing Co., 1972), 138–42. Dawn places these approaches under the hermeneutical category of "analogy"; the powers are analagous to institutions and structures in contemporary society. See Dawn, "'The Principalities and Powers,'" 72–74.

27. John R. Stott, *God's New Society: The Message of Ephesians* (Downers Grove, Ill.: InterVarsity Press, 1979), 273; quoted in Dawn, "'The Principalities and Powers,'" 76. Dawn understands this hermeneutical approach as one of "direct application" (76–78).

28. Frank E. Peretti, *This Present Darkness* (Westchester, Ill.: Crossway Books, 1986).

well-known words of J. B. S. Haldane: "Now, my suspicion is that the universe is not only queerer than we suppose, but queerer than we can suppose."[29]

While not denying such spiritual realities, however, I focus on the activity of the powers as they are spiritually at work in and through concrete, material institutions, structures, and systems in the world. This is how the powers shape the lives of most of the people to whom I preach. I thus emphasize the central spiritual dimension of the powers, but not as spiritual beings existing and working independently of material structures in the world. Again, I do not mean to deny the possibility of such spiritual activity; I simply intend to refrain from speculating about it in order to focus instead on the activity of the powers that seems most significant and imposing in my context.

Anyone familiar with Walter Wink's work will recognize that I am affirming a version of the position he develops in his well-known trilogy on the powers and in his more recent popular volume *The Powers That Be: Theology for a New Millennium*.[30] From his thorough study of the language for the powers in the New Testament, which continually wavers back and forth between earthly, material aspects of power and heavenly, spiritual aspects, Wink comes to adopt a compelling both/and approach. The spiritual dimension of the powers remains central, but Wink does not treat this dimension apart from its material and structural embodiment. In the activity of the powers there is an inseparable link between the material and the spiritual. As Wink writes, the *spiritual* powers are not separate heavenly or ethereal entities but "the inner aspect of material or tangible manifestations of power."[31] In their fullest manifestation,

---

29. Cited in John Bartlett, *Familiar Quotations*, ed. Emily Morison Beck, 15th ed. (Boston: Little, Brown & Co., 1980), 821. For a structural account of the powers from a Caribbean perspective, see Burchell Taylor, *The Church Taking Sides* (Kingston: Bethel Baptist Church, 1995).

30. Walter Wink, *The Powers That Be: Theology for a New Millennium* (New York: Doubleday, 1998). In addition to his *Naming the Powers* and *Engaging the Powers*, see also Walter Wink, *Unmasking the Powers: The Invisible Forces That Determine Human Existence* (Philadelphia: Fortress Press, 1986).

31. Wink, *Naming the Powers*, 104; see also 105. Often in the New Testament, as Wink notes, these two dimensions of the powers are depicted *spatially*: what happens on earth happens simultaneously in heaven. In the book of Revelation, in particular, this spatial imagery is the primary means of portraying the material and spiritual dimensions of the powers. Wink develops his position within a larger emphasis on a new "integral worldview," which moves beyond modern materialistic interpretations of the world without returning to ancient or "spiritualistic" views or a theological view that concedes the material realm to science while claiming a spiritual realm for theology. Within the integral worldview, the material and spiritual interpenetrate each other and always exist together. See Wink, *Engaging the Powers*, 3–10. In my more pragmatic approach, I do not need to begin with that larger worldview, but rather simply affirm that the the spiritual and material dimensions of the powers work together on human beings.

the powers "are simultaneously the outer and inner aspects of one and the same indivisible concretion of power."[32] The spiritual dimension, to borrow Ellul's language, is the "plus" that must be named and engaged along with the earthly institutions.

Wink's emphasis on the inseparable link between the material and spiritual dimensions of the powers thus guides my reflections. His basic definition of the powers concisely captures this relationship:

> The "principalities and powers" are the inner and outer aspects of any given manifestation of power. As the inner aspect they are the spirituality of institutions, the "within" of corporate structures and systems, the inner essence of outer organizations of power. As the outer aspect they are political systems, appointed officials, the "chair" of an organization, laws—in short, all the tangible manifestations which power takes. Every Power tends to have a visible pole, an outer form—be it a church, a nation, or an economy—and an invisible pole, an inner spirit or driving force that animates, legitimates, and regulates its physical manifestation in the world. Neither pole is the cause of the other. Both come into existence together and cease to exist together.[33]

In short, the powers "comprise all of social, political, and corporate reality, in both visible and invisible manifestations."[34]

Wink thus offers a helpful way of taking the spiritual reality of the powers seriously without divorcing the powers from the institutional and structural embodiments through which they shape human life. For Wink, this spiritual dimension of the powers is a critical focus of the church's work: "The church's peculiar calling is to discern and engage both the structure *and the spirituality* of oppressive institutions."[35] As the writer of Ephesians puts it, capturing both the material and spiritual dimensions of the powers, "Our struggle is not against enemies of blood and flesh, but against the principalities, against the powers, against the cosmic powers of this present darkness, against the spiritual forces of evil in the heavenly places" (Eph. 6:12).[36]

There is another way of discerning the spiritual dimension of the powers. This dimension comes into prominence not only when we look at the nature of the powers themselves but when we look at their impact on human lives.

---

32. Wink, *Naming the Powers*, 107.

33. Ibid., 8.

34. Walter Wink, "Stringfellow on the Powers," in *Radical Christian and Exemplary Lawyer*, ed. Andrew W. McThenia, Jr. (Grand Rapids: Wm. B. Eerdmans Publishing Co., 1995), 26.

35. Wink, *Engaging the Powers*, 84; italics mine.

36. As Wink interprets them, the "heavenly places" are the spiritual dimensions of material realities. See his *Naming the Powers*, 84–89.

The powers shape the spirit of human beings and the spirit of our life together in profound ways. In their *effects*, they operate not simply at the material or physical level but often most profoundly at the spiritual level of human life.[37]

An interesting ambiguity in the English translation of the words of André Trocmé's sermon, which I quoted in the Introduction, captures well the spiritual influence of the powers: "The responsibility of Christians is to resist the violence that will be brought to bear on their consciences through the weapons of the spirit." The sentence is somewhat confusing. On the one hand, in light of Ephesians 6:12, it is clear that Christians are to resist the violence of the Nazis "through the weapons of the spirit." At the same time, however, the violence of the Nazis will be brought to bear not just on their bodies but "on their consciences"; the Nazis themselves will use not just physical weapons but "weapons of the spirit" to shape the people's consciences according to the ways of violence. Both the attack and the resistance of which Trocmé speaks take place not just at the material level but in the realm of the spirit.

The powers, as Trocmé indicates, work on people not just through material force but through spiritual influence. They do "not simply capture us from without but also from within."[38] The powers exercise a subtle, invisible influence on human beings until the spirit of the powers becomes internalized and people are self-disciplined to do the powers' bidding, like the "cold" bankers in *The Grapes of Wrath*, whose spirits have succumbed to the will of the Monster. In dealing with the powers, we are dealing with power in its spiritual dimensions.

In Matthew's version of the Beatitudes, Jesus himself begins with a recognition of this spiritual dimension of the powers' work: "Blessed are the poor in spirit, for theirs is the kingdom of heaven" (Matt. 5:3). This beatitude, with its emphasis on the spirit, has often been interpreted as somehow in conflict with Luke's version, "Blessed are you who are poor" (Luke 6:20). Within the framework of the material and spiritual character of the powers, however, the two beatitudes are not necessarily contradictory. Matthew does not necessarily move us away from the concrete, material realities of "the poor" to a different focus on "spirituality." Rather, Matthew may offer an even more profound grasp of the poor than does Luke, one that reckons with both the material and spiritual dimensions of the powers at work in the world.

Matthew's version of Jesus' words suggests that the deepest and most debilitating form of poverty occurs when the material, institutional oppression of poor people becomes internalized in their spirit. A homeless man worn down

---

37. Wink, *Engaging the Powers*, 96–104.
38. Toole, *Godot in Sarajevo*, 179.

by months or years on the streets begins referring to himself as a "bum" or "wino"—names that the powers use to keep him in his place—and he loses any spark of resistance. People in housing projects, repeating the slogans of the powers, blame themselves for their poverty and give up hope. A colonized people who internalize the image of themselves presented by the colonizers become a docile people. Here are the "poor in spirit" of whom Jesus speaks.[39] The powers no longer have any need to control them by force; the poor have become captive at the level of their spirit. People are oppressed not simply by the "heavy hand" of the powers but by "a more subtle power that works in us from within."[40] With this beatitude, Jesus reminds us that the work of the powers occurs not just at the material, institutional level but even more profoundly in the realm of the spirit. And Jesus reminds the church that the powers must be addressed in this spiritual dimension.

Possibly no more powerful account of the spiritual workings of the powers can be found than in Toni Morrison's novel *The Bluest Eye*.[41] The central metaphor of the story, blue eyes, becomes a metaphor for the spiritual oppression of a young African American girl, Pecola. In service to the power of white racism, a legion of other powers—from the entertainment and publishing industries, to the educational system, to the media, to the toy manufacturers, to the ideology of beauty—oppresses the spirit of a young black girl, who comes to see herself as ugly. Even her relationship to God—her prayer life—becomes spiritually captive to these powers: "Each night, without fail, she prayed for blue eyes. Fervently, for a year she had prayed."[42] As Morrison depicts, the principalities are at their most destructive in the spiritual oppression they wreak in so many lives.

Howard Thurman has written more analytically about the reality that Morrison depicts in her novel, focusing on the institutionalized "power" of segregation:

> The psychological effect of segregation . . . is the critical issue. For segregation dramatizes a stigma and becomes a badge of inferiority. A group segregated systematically over many generations experiences a decisive undermining of self-respect. For the sensitive, it means a constant, persistent resentment that is apt so to disease the personality that mental health is critically attacked.

---

39. For a helpful examination of this matter, see Paulo Freire, *Pedagogy of the Oppressed*, trans. Myra Bergman Ramos (New York: Continuum Publishing, 1981); see also Wink, *Engaging the Powers*, 99–104. While it is not only the "the poor" who can be "poor in spirit," it is important not to overlook the materially poor in a rush to spiritualize this beatitude.
40. Toole, *Godot in Sarajevo*, 178; see also 171–79.
41. Toni Morrison, *The Bluest Eye* (New York: Holt, Rinehart and Winston, 1970).
42. Ibid., 46.

> For the less sensitive there is ever the possibility of the acceptance of segregation, with its concomitant conscious admission of inferiority, of humiliation, of despair. Those who are despised, or who are treated systematically as if they were despised, are apt eventually to despise themselves.[43]

The spiritual effects of a power such as white racism are not just limited to the oppressed, however. The privilege that comes to white people can destroy their spirit in a different way.[44] In her book *Dismantling Privilege*, Mary Elizabeth Hobgood has examined the effects of racism on those who "enjoy" the privileges that come with being white. Most importantly, she notes that white privilege leads to moral bankruptcy:

> Because white status depends on denying the deepest parts of the relational self, our humanity is impoverished, and our capacity to be moral—in right relationship with others—is diminished. White supremacy produces trauma, pain, fear, ignorance, mistrust, and unshared vulnerability, and for this reason, white moral character is warped and undermined. Our integrity is necessarily damaged in environments that systematically promote discrimination, harassment, exploitation, and misery. Our integrity is damaged when, as participants in white culture, we are divorced from our deepest longings and capacities for creativity, and when we do not know how to intervene.[45]

---

43. Howard Thurman, "The Will to Segregation," in *Peace Is the Way: Writings on Nonviolence from the Fellowship of Reconciliation,* ed. Walter Wink (Maryknoll, N.Y.: Orbis Books, 2000), 166. Today some African Americans look more positively on separateness as a way of empowering identity. Nevertheless, Thurman offers a critical insight into the spiritual effects of the power of racism. In light of Thurman's comments, it is not surprising that Pecola, a very sensitive young girl, goes crazy by the end of *The Bluest Eye*.

44. For a powerful statement of the privileges that white people enjoy in a society governed by the "invisible system" of white racism, see Peggy McIntosh, "White Privilege: Unpacking the Invisible Knapsack," *Peace and Freedom* (July–August, 1989): 10–12. This article is an excerpt from McIntosh's essay "White Privilege and Male Privilege: A Personal Account of Coming to See Correspondences through Work in Women's Studies," Working Paper 189 (Wellesley, Mass.: Wellesley College Center for Research on Women, 1988).

45. Hobgood, *Dismantling Privilege*, 58. Hobgood also discusses other ways in which privilege harms the spirits of white people: alienation from the erotic and the natural world, from "spontaneity, playfulness, and creativity"; arrogance in believing that the white racial lens is the measure of all things; lack of friendship, intimacy, and the loss of community; immaturity and incompetence (58–59). Many of these spiritual losses are the result of the combined efforts of the powers of consumer capitalism and racism, which work hand in hand. Stringfellow also speaks of the "demoralization" of people of privilege held captive by the powers. See Stringfellow, *Ethic for Christians*, 28–30. For a discussion of the spiritual effects of the commodification of persons in consumer capitalism, see John F. Kavanaugh, *Following Christ in a Consumer Culture (Still)* (Maryknoll, N.Y.: Orbis Books, 1991), 38–61.

As Hobgood recognizes, the spiritual work of the principalities and powers is extensive, affecting people of "privilege" as well as those who are more visibly and obviously oppressed.

The powers, then, are legion. And they have a spiritual as well as a material dimension. As such, they are a pervasive influence on human life, surrounding human beings and influencing us in subtle, invisible ways, infiltrating and shaping our spirits like the air we breathe. Walter Wink has captured the pervasiveness of this "power of the air," mentioned in Ephesians 2:1–2:

> The *exousia* of the air . . . is . . . the invisible dominion or realm created by the sum total of choices for evil. It is the spiritual matrix of inauthentic living. It is the "surround" constellated by fields of forces in rebellion against God. It is nothing other than what Paul called "the spirit of the cosmos" (1 Cor. 2:12), a pseudo-environment that ascribes to itself absoluteness and permanence and thus, by simply appearing to be, wins from all who submit to it their total and unwitting obedience. It is, in short, what we mean today by such terms as ideologies, the *Zeitgeist*, customs, public opinion, peer pressure, institutional expectations, mob psychology, jingoistic patriotism, and negative vibes. These constitute the "power of the air," the invisible but palpable environment of opinions, beliefs, propaganda, convictions, prejudices, hatreds, racial and class biases, taboos, and loyalties that condition our perception of the world long before we reach the age of choice, often before we reach the age of speech. It "kills" us precisely because we "breathe" it in before we even realize it is noxious. Like fish in water, we are not even aware that it exists, much less that it determines the way we think, speak, and act.[46]

In light of Wink's insights, a comment by one of the scientists who helped develop the first atomic bomb at Los Alamos makes chilling sense. Reflecting on why he did not cease work on the bomb after Germany was defeated, even though all his personal beliefs should have led him to quit, Robert Wilson commented, "It simply was not in the air."[47]

THE POWERS ARE CREATED BY GOD

Although the negative aspects of the powers have become obvious in the preceding sections and are the focus of much that follows, the New Testament understanding of the powers, most scholars agree, is shaped by a story that includes several important theological affirmations.[48] To begin with, the pow-

---

46. Wink, *Naming the Powers*, 84.
47. Else, prod. and dir., *Day after Trinity*.
48. Part of this "story"—the fallenness of the powers—is discussed in the next chapter.

ers are created by God.[49] Colossians 1:15–17, which, like the Gospel of John, emphasizes the role of Christ in creation, is the primary statement of the origin of the powers in God's creative purposes:

> He [Jesus Christ] is the image of the invisible God, the firstborn of all creation; for in him all things in heaven and on earth were created, things visible and invisible, whether thrones or dominions or rulers or powers—all things have been created through him and for him. He himself is before all things, and in him all things hold together.

Not only are the principalities and powers created by God through the "cosmic" Christ, but they also have their purpose and their "coherence" or "order" in the life-giving purposes of God embodied in the way of Jesus.

Several important affirmations are implicit in this theological claim that the powers are created by God. First of all, the powers are creatures of *God*. Although this mystery is difficult for many of us to grasp, the powers are not the creation of human beings; they are not simply the institutional or structural consequences of human thought, activity, and organization.[50] While human beings are obviously involved in the genesis of particular institutions, something more than human initiative comes into play.[51] Like human beings themselves, the powers also are creatures of God, with "their own existence, personality, and mode of life."[52] This affirmation thus disabuses human beings of the illusion that we either create or control the powers. Moreover, it stands as a reminder that *only God* can finally redeem the powers.

Second, the powers are *creatures of God*. They have no existence independent of God's purposes. They cannot claim autonomy from their creator:

> Even in their apostasy and dereliction from their created vocation, the Powers are incapable of separating themselves from the principle of coherence. When subsystems idolatrously violate the harmony of the whole by elevating their own purposes to ultimacy, they are still no more able to achieve autonomy than a cancer can live apart from its host. Like a cancer, again, they are able to do evil only by means of the processes imbedded in them as a result of their good creation.[53]

The "rest of the story," dealing with Jesus Christ's work in relation to the powers, is covered in chapter 3.

49. This affirmation distinguishes a Christian understanding of the powers from that of John Steinbeck, who says the Bank was made by human beings.
50. Stringfellow, *Ethic for Christians*, 79–80.
51. Wylie-Kellermann, "Not Vice Versa," 678.
52. Stringfellow, *Ethic for Christians*, 79.
53. Wink, *Engaging the Powers*, 66–67; see also Yoder, *Politics of Jesus*, 43–44.

In short, no matter how evil the powers become, they are not outside God's sovereign purposes. Not only can God use the powers for good, but ultimately God *can* redeem them.[54]

Third, the powers are part of God's *good* creation. They have been created for the vocation of sustaining human life in society. Human society requires structures and institutions and systems; they are essential to the social character of our life together, and we cannot live without them. As John Howard Yoder has argued,

> Most of the references to the "Powers" in the New Testament consider them as fallen. It is important therefore to begin with the reminder that they were part of the good creation of God. Society and history, even nature, would be impossible without regularity, system, order—and this need God provided for. The universe is not sustained arbitrarily, immediately, and erratically by an unbroken succession of new divine interventions. It was made in an ordered form and "it was good." The creative power worked in a mediated form, by means of the Powers that regularized all visible reality.[55]

The structures and institutions of the world—political, economic, social—including the spirit or driving force that animates them, are part of God's *good* creation. Consequently, the goal cannot be to destroy them but rather to redeem them—to call them back to the vocation for which they were created.

Finally, as the Colossians text makes abundantly clear, the fact that the powers are part of God's good creation does not involve an uncritical obedience to the status quo. In fact, quite the opposite is the case. By affirming that the powers were created in, through, and for Christ, and by asserting that the powers "hold together" in him, the author of Colossians establishes a critical standard of expectation and judgment in relation to the powers. Where the powers function in ways that contradict the way of Jesus Christ, resistance is required. Where the powers desert their vocation of sustaining human life in community, they must be called back to that vocation in the name of the one in whom, through whom, and for whom they were created. Rather than suggesting an independent "order of creation" that must be obeyed no matter what, Colossians affirms the Lordship of Christ as a constant judgment on and invitation to the powers of the world.[56] As Wink writes, "The point of the Colossians

---

54. Yoder, *Politics of Jesus*, 143–44.
55. Ibid., 143; see also Wink, *Engaging the Powers*, 66.
56. Romans 13:1–7 has frequently been interpreted in such a "status quo" fashion, but this interpretation is certainly not what a close reading of the text suggests. First of all, "being subject" to "governing authorities" is not the same as "obedience" to them. Jesus Christ accepted "subordination" to the governing authorities in his execution on

hymn is not that anything goes, but that no matter how greedy or idolatrous an institution becomes, it cannot escape the encompassing care and judgment of the One in and through and for whom it was created."[57]

The powers, then, are created by God; they are part of the world that God pronounced "good." As has already become clear, however, one cannot speak of the powers as part of God's good creation without in the same breath noting their rebellion against God's purposes and their betrayal of their vocation. Although the powers are created good by God, human beings experience them primarily as fallen.

---

the cross. However, as becomes clear in chapter 3, Jesus' life was one not of obedience but rather of resistance to the authorities; indeed, even his crucifixion was an act of resistance. In addition, the context of Romans 13, often overlooked because of the Bible's current chapter divisions, is the love of *enemies*—thus making the governing authorities *enemies* of believers. Verses 1–7 are framed by the commandment to owe no one, even enemies, anything but love (12:21 and 13:8). Where the "governing authorities" make demands contrary to the love embodied in Jesus, nonviolent resistance is required. Finally, as Walter Wink has argued, the Greek word for "resist"—*anthistēmi*—used in 13:2, as in Matthew 5:39, refers to *violent* resistance. See Wink, *Engaging the Powers*, 185. See also Yoder, *Politics of Jesus*, 193–214; Karl Barth, *The Epistle to the Romans*, trans. Edwyn C. Hoskyns, paperback ed. (London: Oxford University Press, 1968), 475–92.

57. Wink, *Engaging the Powers*, 67.

2

The Rebellious Powers

Although created good by God, the powers live in rebellion against God's purposes.[1] They have repudiated their vocation. Instead of serving God's will and sustaining human life in society, the powers make idols of themselves and place their own desires above God's purposes for humanity and creation. In their rebellion they crucified Jesus (1 Cor. 2:6–8), and they seek to separate us from the love of God (Rom. 8:37–39). As William Stringfellow writes, "The principality, insinuating itself in the place of God, deceives humans into thinking and acting as if the moral worth or justification of human beings is defined and determined by commitment or surrender—literally, sacrifice—of human life to the survival interest, grandeur, and vanity of the principality."[2] Whether taking the form of the state, the institution, the ideology, or the dollar, the powers seek to claim the ultimate and complete loyalty of human beings, as if the meaning and value of life itself were grounded in serving their ends. They do everything in their power to create the illusion that they, not God, are the divine regents in the world. The beast in the book of Revelation first and foremost seeks to receive the *worship* of human beings.[3] Idolatry is the fundamental sin of the fallen powers.[4]

---

1. In addition to the works cited to this point, see Albert H. van den Heuvel, *These Rebellious Powers* (New York: Friendship Press, 1965).
2. William Stringfellow, *An Ethic for Christians and Other Aliens in a Strange Land* (Waco, Tex.: Word Books, 1973; 3d paperback ed., 1979), 81; see also 80–82.
3. See, for example, Revelation 13:4, 12, 15.
4. For a discussion of the idolatry demanded by consumer capitalism, see John F. Kavanaugh, *Following Christ in a Consumer Culture (Still)* (Maryknoll, N.Y.: Orbis Books, 1991), 37, 54–61.

In their fallen state, the powers have thus become relentlessly aggressive against all life, particularly human life in society.[5] The relationship between human beings and the powers has become inverted from God's original intention. Rather than serving the ends of human life, the powers now exercise dominion over human beings, restricting, controlling, and consuming human beings "in order to sustain and extend and prosper their own survival."[6] The powers, in short, have become demonic. In Steinbeck's terms, they have become monsters. And, like the landowners and bankers in *The Grapes of Wrath*, human beings have become these monsters' captives and slaves, whether we serve gladly as acolytes to the powers or simply acquiesce to our captivity in silence or helplessness.

In making themselves idols and taking dominion over human beings, the fallen powers are driven by several concerns. Most basically, the powers seek to *survive*.[7] Their fundamental concern is their own survival, and nothing must get in the way of that.[8] Everything else is expendable: human beings, compassion, humanity, the land, preaching—everything. For the powers, finally, the only morality that matters is their own survival, and they will use any means necessary to ensure that survival. The Bank, as Steinbeck depicts, cannot live without profits, and the Bank will do anything to get what it needs to survive. This same drive, as Stringfellow notes, characterizes all the powers: "The principalities have great resilience; the death game which they play continues, adapting its means of dominating human beings to the sole morality which governs all demonic powers so long as they exist—survival."[9] Anyone who has ever tried to make radical changes in an institution—including the church—is well aware of this resilience.

This quest for survival contributes to the chaos the powers bring into the world. While the powers may cooperate with one another at times in their own self-interest, they remain rivals who compete with each other for survival and preeminence. Multifarious powers make their diverse and conflicting claims

---

5. In using the traditional term *fallen*, which is employed by many who have written about the powers, I do not mean to affirm a chronological point in time at which the "fall" of the powers took place. I use the term to refer to a *quality* of the powers. The powers are characterized by their rebellion against the purposes for which they were created.

6. Stringfellow, *Ethic for Christians*, 84; see also 82–83.

7. I am speaking in this section about the powers' quest for survival at all costs in their power and domination. This kind of quest should be distinguished from the necessary efforts of many oppressed people to survive. For such people, survival is an essential and positive value.

8. On the priority of survival in a consumer capitalist system, see Kavanaugh, *Following Christ*, 37.

9. Stringfellow, *Ethic for Christians*, 93.

upon people, each one seeking to ensure its own continued existence. It is no wonder people feel pulled in so many directions, almost torn apart by the powers' competing, often contradictory, calls for loyalty and service. Survival drives the legion of powers in the world, and the consequence is conflict and chaos.

In addition to their desire to survive, the powers also seek to *dominate*. As Walter Wink has persuasively argued, the quest for domination drives the powers. Indeed, the total configuration of powers is best characterized, in Wink's terms, as the Domination System:

> The Powers are not that system; they are merely the individual institutions and structures deployed under the overall aegis of the Domination System. The Domination System is what obtains when an entire network of Powers becomes hell-bent on control. The Domination System is, so to speak, the system of the Powers, in a satanic parody of God, who might be called the System of the systems. The Domination System is thus equivalent to what the Bible so often means by the terms "world," "aeon," and "flesh."[10]

This system is characterized by power exercised *over* others, by control *of* others, by *ranking* as the primary principle of social organization, by *hierarchies* of dominant and subordinate, winners and losers, insiders and outsiders, honored and shamed.[11]

Steinbeck again captures well this quest for domination that drives the powers. Not only are the tenant farmers under the domination of the Bank—and the more encompassing "spirit of capitalism" that drives it—but the owners and bankers themselves have become mere instruments of the Bank's purposes; they have become captives and tools of the Bank, who act for the Bank's goals whether they like it or not. Every human being in Steinbeck's novel is caught in the Domination System. Some, like the farmers, are directly, physically oppressed by the System. Others, like the owners and bankers, have been seduced by the promises and rewards of the System and have become either numb ("cold") to what they are doing or powerless to resist.

---

10. Walter Wink, *Engaging the Powers: Discernment and Resistance in a World of Domination* (Minneapolis: Fortress Press, 1992), 49.
11. Ibid., 33–104. As Wink elsewhere writes, "This overarching network of Powers is what we are calling the Domination System. It is characterized by unjust economic relations, oppressive political relations, biased race relations, patriarchal gender relations, hierarchical power relations, and the use of violence to maintain them all" (Walter Wink, *The Powers That Be: Theology for a New Millennium* [New York: Doubleday, 1998], 39). On consumer capitalism as a system of domination, see Kavanaugh, *Following Christ*. The "Commodity Form of life," as Kavanaugh calls it, is shaped by precisely these characteristics.

This situation is no fiction limited to a Steinbeck novel. A few years ago, I was part of a group that was briefly placed under arrest in Atlanta. We were sitting in a downtown park after the 11 P.M. closing time and got caught in a police "sweep," through which the city was seeking to clear the park of homeless people. As we protested our arrest, the police officer finally silenced us and said, "Look, I really don't like having to do this. I *personally* don't want to arrest you. *I'm just a tool of the city.*" This is how the powers seek to dominate human beings: they turn people into mere "tools" of their purposes.

Within this pervasive system, a *spirit* of domination comes to pervade the whole social order, often without our even being aware of it. As the Roman Catholic pastoral theologian Michael Warren has pointed out, dominant and subordinate—"winners" and "losers"—become the primary metaphors that shape human life together.[12] And as was noted earlier, those who are oppressed begin to internalize their oppression.[13] The System deludes people into thinking not only that they deserve their positions but that this social order is the only one possible. The Domination System becomes the "air we breathe"; other alternatives become almost unimaginable.

Even ethics itself can be captured by this System, as Sharon Welch has demonstrated in her book *A Feminist Ethic of Risk*.[14] Welch argues that the dominant mode of contemporary ethical reflection, usually shaped by the "winners," has involved an "ethic of control." Such an ethic defines responsible ethical action as that which can control the future and produce results.[15] This ethical need to control or dominate the outcome of events can lead to unimaginable evil—often in the name of "good."[16] Such an ethical spirit, for example, justified the development of atomic weapons and countenanced the escalation of the arms race.[17] So deep does the Domination System run that it shapes even the very ethical thought that seeks to engage it.

Both the powers' need to survive and their quest for domination find their ultimate expression in *violence,* which takes systemic as well as interpersonal forms and involves psychological and spiritual, as well as physical, dimensions.[18] As Wink notes, the foundational myth—the real spirituality—of the Domination System is the "myth of redemptive violence," which comes to

---

12. Michael Warren, "Culture, Counterculture, and the Word," *Liturgy* 6 (Summer 1986): 90.
13. See Wink's discussion in *Engaging the Powers*, 96–104.
14. Sharon Welch, *A Feminist Ethic of Risk* (Minneapolis: Fortress Press, 1990).
15. Ibid., 3.
16. Ibid., 2–3.
17. Ibid., 2–6.
18. Defining "violence" is exceedingly difficult. I will refrain from attempting a concise definition, though I hope the breadth and nuances of my understanding become

shape not simply the activity of the powers but human interactions as well.[19] According to this myth, which traces its lineage back to the Babylonian story of creation, the way to bring order out of chaos is through violence.[20] Violence becomes the ultimate solution to human conflicts, as one of the farmers in *The Grapes of Wrath* states so well. Infuriated by the actions of the Bank, the farmer can envision only one solution: "Who can we shoot?" Later the farmer watches helplessly, gun in hand, as a tractor tills his front yard and tears down his porch. In a single image Steinbeck not only captures the powerlessness of guns against the principalities but also reveals the myth of redemptive violence that has been enacted throughout human history.[21]

Moreover, as Wink thoroughly details, this myth pervades American culture, from Popeye cartoons to children's comics to video games to popular movies (e.g., *The Lion King, Star Wars*) to foreign policy to the death penalty. The myth has, in fact, become the ethos of American society, into which virtually all children, particularly boys, are socialized from an early age.[22] We should thus not be surprised when even teenagers turn to guns as the appropriate—even the only imaginable—means for dealing with their "enemies." We should likewise not be surprised when our society responds in increasingly violent ways, such as capital punishment, toward violent criminals. The well-known question about the death penalty captures the cycle of violence perpetuated by this myth: "Why do we kill people who kill people to show that killing people is wrong?"

Events surrounding several mass murders in the United States during the 1990s provide a chilling confirmation of Wink's insights about the pervasive-

---

clear in what follows. Most fundamentally, I assume that any form of domination over people involves an element of violence. Ken Butigan and Patricia Bruno provide a helpful, broad definition of violence in their book *From Violence to Wholeness: A Ten Part Program in the Spirituality and Practice of Active Nonviolence* (Las Vegas: Pace e Bene Franciscan Nonviolence Center, 1999). Violence, they write, is "emotional, verbal or physical behavior that dominates, diminishes, or destroys ourselves and others. Violence crosses boundaries without permission. Violence disrupts authentic relationships. Violence separates us from others. It defiles the human person and desecrates the image of God. It is a process of economic, gender, racial, social or cultural domination" (3).

19. See Wink, *Engaging the Powers*, 13–31.

20. In the Babylonian creation myth, the god Marduk brings order out of chaos by killing his mother, Tiamat, and then fashioning the world from her dead corpse. See James B. Pritchard, *Ancient Near Eastern Texts Relating to the Old Testament*, 3d ed. (Princeton, N.J.: Princeton University Press, 1969), 60–72; Wink, *Engaging the Powers*, 14.

21. John Steinbeck, *The Grapes of Wrath*, Penguin Great Books of the Twentieth Century (New York: Penguin Books, 1999), 38–39. The Bank, of course, also ultimately relies on violence to sanction its actions toward the farmers (38).

22. Wink, *Engaging the Powers*, 22.

ness of the myth of redemptive violence in American society. The night of the Columbine High School murders, I watched a news report on television in which President Bill Clinton made a passionate plea for all of us to teach children nonviolent ways to deal with conflict. Shortly after the president's speech, however, the "special report" on Columbine was interrupted by another "special report" announcing that NATO's bombing of Belgrade had resumed. The report reminded me of the closing scene in William Golding's *Lord of the Flies*, in which a uniformed naval officer, guns in tow, chides the boys on the island for their violent, warlike behavior.[23] Golding's own comments on the conclusion of his novel cast a disturbing light on the sequence of events I witnessed on television:

> The whole book is symbolic in nature except the rescue in the end where adult life appears, dignified and capable, but in reality enmeshed in the same evil as the symbolic life of the children on the island. The officer, having interrupted a man-hunt, prepares to take the children off the island in a cruiser which will presently be hunting its enemy in the same implacable way. And who will rescue the adult and his cruiser?[24]

Further confirmation of adult enmeshment in the myth of redemptive violence came a couple days later when I read in the newspaper that Charlton Heston, the president of the National Rifle Association, had responded to the killings at Columbine High by saying that if there had just been *more guns* at the school, the killings could have been prevented. Heston's words were echoed several months later after more shootings occurred at a church in Texas. According to news reports, many Texans concluded that the answer to mass violence is more concealed weapons. One church member commented, "I'm going to get my concealed permit today. If one person had a concealed handgun at that service, there's a 90 percent chance the shooting could have been stopped before it started."

More recently, shortly after the terrorist attack on the World Trade Center and the Pentagon, Zell Miller, my senator from Georgia, commented, "I say bomb the hell out of them. If there's collateral damage, so be it. They certainly found our civilians to be expendable."[25] Miller's response was a gut-level reaction to these horrific events that revealed the depth of the myth of redemptive violence in our lives. This foundational myth, which shapes the

---

23. William Golding, *Lord of the Flies* (New York: Putnam, 1954), 182.
24. Quoted in Gil Bailie, *Violence Unveiled: Humanity at the Crossroads* (New York: Crossroad, 1995), 65.
25. *Atlanta Constitution*, September 13, 2001, A3.

spirituality of the Domination System, pervades American society. Who, indeed, will save the adults and our cruisers?

Violence, however, cannot be limited simply to dramatic actions or comments that embody the myth of redemptive violence. Violence operates broadly and at many levels throughout the Domination System; all relationships characterized by domination are also characterized by violence, whether that violence is purportedly "redemptive" or not.[26] William Stringfellow has noted the encompassing nature of violence in the world of the powers, arguing that violence characterizes any actions or systems that lead to death rather than life:

> Violence describes all of the multifarious, inverted, broken, distorted and ruptured relationships characteristic of the present history of the world. Violence is the undoing of Creation. Violence is the moral confusion and practical chaos which, so long as time lasts, disrupts and displaces the truth and peace of Creation, which the Bible denominates the Fall. Violence is the reign of death in this world and violence is the name of all and any of the works of death.[27]

The powers of death that oppress and hold captive minds and spirits, as well as those that inflict physical harm, also trade in the tools of violence. Pecola, the African American girl who prays each night for blue eyes in Toni Morrison's novel *The Bluest Eye*, is as much a victim of violence at the hands of the powers of death as are people killed in wars.

Exploring this deep, spiritual level on which the powers of death operate, John Kavanaugh has argued that violence comes to characterize human interaction in a system shaped by the spirit and institutions of consumer capitalism. In such a system, people become commodities—objects—and violence becomes the ultimate expression of this objectification.[28] As Kavanaugh writes,

---

26. By trying to encompass all violence within the myth of redemptive violence, Walter Wink, despite speaking of violence as the spirituality of the Domination System, limits the character of violence. While violence is related to domination and control and in that sense seeks to "redemptively" maintain order, I am not convinced that all violence takes the form of "redemptive violence" in the way Wink argues. Just as Wink critiques René Girard's theory of the scapegoat as too limited to account for all violence, Wink's theory of redemptive violence must be viewed as similarly limited (see Wink, *Engaging the Powers*, 153). No single myth can account for the various forms of violence. Wink's emphasis on redemptive violence is nevertheless important when I turn to the work of Jesus, whose work of redemption overturns the violence of the Domination System and its central myth.

27. Stringfellow, *Ethic for Christians*, 127.

28. Kavanaugh, *Following Christ*, 50.

Once a man or woman, be he or she oppressor or oppressed, whether dressed in silk or sprawled in a Calcutta slum, whether on a battlefield or in a delivery room, whether bourgeoisie or proletariat, whether criminal, president, or both, is perceived as a thing or in terms of the commodity, he or she is thereby rendered replaceable. The fetus is a "blob of protoplasm." The criminal is "scum and vermin." The brain damaged are "vegetables." The poor are "like animals." The Iraqi is "the enemy." The wealthy or police are "pigs." The "enemy" is an obstruction—quantifiable, repeatable, manipulable, expendable, the legitimate object of our hatred and violence. Only on this level of understanding can the questions of violence in the street or among nations, on death row or in hospitals, be adequately addressed as fragmented symptoms of a totality which itself so often escapes our attention and critique.[29]

The powers driven by the commodifying spirit of consumer capitalism, Kavanaugh suggests, shape the ways in which people "see" the world and provide the larger framework within which individual acts of violence need to be understood.[30] As he concludes, "We are actually educated and trained to behave and think like things and to relate to each other as things. Thing-knowledge and thing-behavior in turn support and legitimate violence and domination as the resolution to human problems of power and possession."[31] The spirit of violence in the Domination System runs very deep indeed.

The end of this system is *death*. Ultimately, the powers are the powers of death.[32] In their rebellion the principalities and powers finally become demonic, having such dehumanizing purposes that they must be said to be governed by the power of death.[33] Quite simply, the powers seek to put to death any who would resist their will to survival and domination. Death is their ultimate power and sanction.

Death, like violence, must be understood in a very broad sense. As the biblical writers grasped, death is a reality far broader and deeper than mere

---

29. Ibid., 45. Kavanaugh goes on to examine the consequences of the objectification of women in sexual violence (47–53). While Kavanaugh examines how this commodification of persons shapes human interactions, William Greider demonstrates the ways in which laborers in the global capitalist system become commodities to be exploited— another concrete expression of violence. See William Greider, *One World, Ready or Not: The Manic Logic of Global Capitalism* (New York: Simon & Schuster, 1997).
30. Kavanaugh, *Following Christ*, 46.
31. Ibid., 57.
32. Stringfellow, *Ethic for Christians*, 81.
33. Ibid., 32. *Demonic*, as Stringfellow uses the term, does not simply mean "evil." Rather, the demonic involves death and fallenness; it is a state of separation from life, bondage to death, and alienation from God. See William Stringfellow, *Free in Obedience* (New York: Seabury Press, 1964), 62–64.

physical death. If necessary, of course, the powers will crudely and directly resort to physical death—as they did at the cross.[34] When someone threatens their reign and cannot be dealt with in other ways, the powers will resort to execution. The assassinations of Gandhi and Martin Luther King Jr. provide contemporary examples of how the powers wield physical death when necessary.

As William Stringfellow has demonstrated, however, the "deadly" work of the powers usually takes more subtle forms—political, social, personal, and especially moral.[35] This death involves the death of our humanity, the death of our compassion, the death of the creation God intends us to be. We become servants or acolytes of the powers, doing what we hate but unwilling or unable to resist. We go along. We give up. We stay busy. We become numb. And in so doing, we die, like the owners and bankers in *The Grapes of Wrath*, who had become "cold," or the policeman in Woodruff Park, who was just a "tool of the city." In subtle ways, Stringfellow writes, the powers seek to kill our "moral conscience." And when they succeed, the powers have no need to resort to persecutions or imprisonment, for people are already morally captive.[36]

Steinbeck provides a powerful image of the death that occurs when people become captive to the powers. Describing the tractor driver who comes to till the land of the tenant farmers, Steinbeck writes:

> The man sitting in the iron seat did not look like a man; gloved, goggled, rubber dust mask over nose and mouth, he was a part of the monster, a robot in the seat. The thunder of the cylinders sounded through the country, became one with the air and the earth, so that earth and air muttered in sympathetic vibration. The driver could not control it—straight across country it went, cutting through a dozen farms and straight back. A twitch at the controls could swerve the cat', but the driver's hands could not twitch because the monster that built the tractor, the monster that sent the tractor out, had somehow got into the driver's hands, into his brain and muscle, had goggled him and muzzled him—goggled his mind, muzzled his speech, goggled his perception, muzzled his protest. He could not see the land as it was, he

---

34. In 1 Corinthians 2:6–8, Paul is clear that the "rulers of this age" crucified Jesus. On these "rulers" as more than simply human beings, see Walter Wink, *Naming the Powers: The Language of Power in the New Testament* (Philadelphia: Fortress Press, 1984), 40–45.

35. Stringfellow uses "death" in the broadest possible sense: "Thus, in this book, when the name of death is used, I intend that it bear *every* definition and nuance, *every* association and suggestion, *every* implication and intuition that *anyone* has *ever* attributed to death, and I intend that the name of death, here, bear all meanings simultaneously and cumulatively" (*Ethic for Christians*, 69).

36. Stringfellow, *Ethic for Christians*, 106.

could not smell the land as it smelled; his feet did not stamp the clods or feel the warmth and power of the earth. He sat in an iron seat and stepped on iron pedals. He could not cheer or beat or curse or encourage the extension of his power, and because of this he could not cheer or whip or curse or encourage himself.[37]

Captive to the power of technology, which has been placed in the service of a profit-driven capitalist economy, the driver of the tractor has lost his humanity; he has become, in Kavanaugh's terms, a "thing"—part of the machine, part of the monster, unable to resist. He has, in the words of Stringfellow, lost the ability to "live humanly." He is, in short, dead. And this death, whether it be physical death or the death of our humanity, is the ultimate work of the fallen powers.

STRATEGIES OF THE POWERS

As has become evident by now, the rebellious powers accomplish their deadly purposes through various strategies, some of them obvious and direct, others subtler. Although these strategies, like the powers themselves, are legion, at least nine need to be considered by preachers.

1. *Negative sanctions*. These kinds of sanctions threaten people with negative consequences if they do not conform to the will of the powers. Most extreme among these sanctions is the threat of physical death—often violent death. Embodied most graphically by the beast in the book of Revelation, the threat of physical death is the final sanction of the powers and their most dramatic strategy for keeping human beings "in line." Ultimately, the powers play on the human fear of death in order to keep people complicit with their purposes. It is thus not surprising that Paul mentions death as the final enemy that will be destroyed (1 Cor. 15:26).

    Other negative sanctions also come into play. Although less dramatic than physical death, these sanctions can be very compelling: the loss of a job, ostracism by peers, the lack of "security." The tractor driver in *The Grapes of Wrath* goes along with the "powers that be" in order to put food on his family's table. The tangible and understandable threat of starvation and homelessness drives him to turn against his neighbors and "sell his soul" to the monster.

2. *Rewards and promises*. The powers work not only through threats but also by means of seduction. In the book of Revelation, this strategy of the powers is embodied in the figure of the whore, who seduces people into

---

37. Steinbeck, *Grapes of Wrath*, 35.

idolatry and accommodation to the ways of the empire.[38] Some of these seductive rewards are obvious: a nice house, a sport-utility vehicle, membership in the country club, a good college for the kids, financial security, popularity, influence. Particularly in a consumer culture, the powers promise these kinds of rewards if one just "goes along" and doesn't "rock the boat." Indeed, no matter how demonic the powers may be, they inevitably claim to provide some rewards to at least some people in order to justify their reign in the world. Even a tyrannical government will claim that it is providing its citizens with "internal order" or with security from outside threats.

In addition to these specific kinds of rewards, the powers, at a deeper and more ominous level, promise people a kind of "salvation" through identification with something larger than their own lives. As Wink writes, "Overwhelmed by the incomprehensible size of corporations, bureaucracies, universities, the military, and media icons, individuals sense that their only escape from utter insignificance lies in identifying with these giants and idolizing them as the true bearers of their own human identity."[39] In particular, our jobs can be the source of this kind of "salvation," which may help to explain the "workaholism" that drives so many people in our society today. The results can be deadly, far beyond mere hypertension or heart attacks. Writing about the environmental crisis, Richard Gottlieb notes how people contribute to the destruction of the earth because of their deep need to find identity and importance in a job that is bigger than themselves:

> As it was in the Holocaust, so it is in the environmental crisis: people desperate for a sense of personal identity can take part in public work that brings ruin to the world. Our drive to have the kind of work that makes us feel important is thus spiritually significant, and perhaps much more dangerous, than the familiar problems of personal greed or attachment.[40]

The powers, then, not only grant us specific rewards for our complicity but promise us salvation through identification with something larger than our individual lives, which often feel small and meaningless. As a consequence, people often become willing "tools" of the powers.

3. *Isolation and division*. This third strategy often provides fertile ground for the promise of salvation offered by the powers.[41] The need for identifi-

---

38. This image, while graphic, is degrading to women and reflects a patriarchal system. An alternative image needs to be found, without losing the reality of the powers' strategy of seduction.
39. Wink, *Powers That Be*, 60. See also Wink, *Engaging the Powers*, 29.
40. Roger S. Gottlieb, *A Spirituality of Resistance: Finding a Peaceful Heart and Protecting the Earth* (New York: Crossroad, 1999), 68; see also 59–102.
41. James Scott refers to this strategy as the "logic of atomization" in *Domination and the Arts of Resistance: Hidden Transcripts* (New Haven, Conn.: Yale University Press, 1990), 64.

cation with a "power" greater than oneself is much stronger when an individual has been isolated from other communities and feels small and insignificant.[42] Isolated individuals are often particularly fragile and manipulable. Consequently, the powers seek to isolate people from one another and encourage people to compete with each other. Modern individualism, embedded in what Kavanaugh calls the "commodity form of life," serves as a powerful tool of the powers, alienating people from one another and making them more susceptible to both the threats and the promises of the powers.[43]

In addition to isolating individuals, the powers foster and use divisions among people. "Divide and conquer" is one of their primary strategies. The tenant farmers in *The Grapes of Wrath* are stunned when the unknown tractor driver takes off his goggles and mask and is seen to be one of their neighbors: "Why, you're Joe Davis's boy!" the farmers exclaim.[44] People who should be making common cause in resisting the powers are instead set against each other. Similar divisions exist today. As many social analysts have noted, the current economic arrangements remain in place in part because the "powers that be" have managed to create racial divisions between white workers and workers of color, who should be allies in the struggle against economic injustice. Promoting hostility between racial groups keeps them divided, both nationally and internationally. Even as these groups share common positions at the bottom of the economic ladder, their disunity enables the global economy to function smoothly.[45]

Another means of division involves scapegoating. A person or a group, usually a marginalized one, becomes the scapegoat on whom the sins of the society are placed. Today in U.S. cities, for example, homeless people have become scapegoats. The presence of homeless people on city streets provides a sharp, visible reminder of the injustice inherent in the capitalist economic system. Rather than address this underlying economic reality, however, the powers blame homeless people not only for their own plight but for the problems in the cities as well. Political and economic powers have joined together to remove these people from the streets by passing laws that criminalize homelessness, by running homeless people out of town, or by putting them in jail. The sins of the society are thereby loaded onto the backs of one group, just as the sins of Israel were placed on the "scapegoat" (which, like homeless people and like Jesus on the cross, was then sent out of the city into the wilderness).[46] Although such scapegoating makes certain groups feel better about

42. Wink, *Engaging the Powers*, 29.
43. On the ways in which the commodity form of life—the form of life shaped by consumer culture—breaks down relationships, see Kavanaugh, *Following Christ*, 7–10, 38–53.
44. Steinbeck, *Grapes of Wrath*, 36.
45. Mary Elizabeth Hobgood, *Dismantling Privilege: An Ethics of Accountability* (Cleveland: Pilgrim Press, 2000), 52.
46. See Leviticus 16:20–22.

themselves and their society, it does not solve the problem of homelessness but instead perpetuates the violent, divisive goals of the Domination System. Such division helps consolidate the powers' control over human lives.[47]

4. *Demoralization*. In the face of the powers, the problems often seem so huge and the possibilities for change so remote that many people simply give up in despair. The powers wear people down until they have no more energy to resist. The powers, Stringfellow writes, have

> wrought a fatigue both visceral and intellectual in millions upon millions of Americans. By now truly *de*moralized, they suffer no conscience and they risk no action. Their human interest in living is narrowed to meager subsisting; their hope for life is no more than avoiding involvement with other humans and a desire that no one will bother them. They have lost any expectations for society; they have no stamina left for confronting the principalities; they are reduced to docility, lassitude, torpor, profound apathy, and default. The demoralization of human beings in this fashion greatly conveniences the totalitarianism of the demonic powers since the need to resort to persecutions or imprisonment is obviated, as the people are already morally captive.[48]

The media contribute to this kind of demoralization, as cultural critic Neil Postman has argued. For example, by reporting nightly on huge problems around the world that most people can do little or nothing about, the television news media contribute to the feeling of powerlessness that many people experience. Overwhelmed by the extent of global problems, people simply give up and, possibly as a means of self-protection, become numb to what they view nightly on television.[49]

---

47. The irony of scapegoating is that it serves to create unity in the powerful majority but is actually a strategy of division. Much of the work on scapegoating draws on the writing of René Girard; see, for example, *The Girard Reader*, ed. James G. Williams (New York: Crossroad, 1996), 9–29, 97–141. For discussions of Girard's work, see Wink, *Engaging the Powers*, 144–55; Bailie, *Violence Unveiled*; and Robert G. Hamerton-Kelly, *Sacred Violence: Paul's Hermeneutic of the Cross* (Minneapolis: Fortress Press, 1992).
48. Stringfellow, *Ethic for Christians*, 106. On the despair of both the "materially successful" and the "dispossessed," see Douglas John Hall, "Despair as Pervasive Ailment," in *Hope for the World: Mission in a Global Context*, ed. Walter Brueggemann (Louisville, Ky.: Westminster John Knox Press, 2001), 83–93. As Sharon Welch notes, despair is "cushioned" by privilege for affluent and middle-class people—a luxury that poor people do not have (*Feminist Ethic of Risk*, 15).
49. Neil Postman, *Amusing Ourselves to Death: Public Discourse in the Age of Show Business* (New York: Viking/Penguin Books, 1985). Postman argues that by providing such an enormous quantity of news on which no action can be taken, the media have altered the "information-action ratio" (67–68).

Under the guise of providing important information, the media in this instance act as one of the powers that demoralize people and stifle any energy for resistance.

In a consumer culture, as John Kavanaugh has argued, the powers can achieve this kind of demoralization through seduction as well as repression. Seduced by the consumer value system—reinforced, again, by the media—people often lose their identity "in an amalgam of the accoutrements of mass civilization." Having no deep roots in God, no sense of responsibility for anything higher than personal consumption and survival, people easily become demoralized. Indeed, according to Kavanaugh, the system depends on this kind of demoralization in order to keep people in conformity with its values and priorities.[50] By demoralizing people in this way, the powers squelch resistance before it ever begins.

5. *Diversion.*[51] The powers will do almost anything to divert people from noticing what they are up to. Although various forms of entertainment serve as principal tools of diversion,[52] one key form diversion takes today is busyness. Busyness has, in fact, become a primary way in which the principalities divert us from seeing and responding to the realities of death in the world. When people become too busy to notice or care about anything beyond their daily routines, the powers have diverted one more potential challenge to their dominion in the world. As one woman recently commented to me, "By the end of the day, when I can finally sit down at home, I'm too tired to care about anything else going on in the world." Such busyness is not simply an unfortunate aspect of contemporary life. It is one way in which people are held captive by the powers.

6. *Public rituals.* In countless ways, from large, public events to everyday interactions, the Domination System manages to ritualize relationships of dominant and subordinate. In the New Testament period this ritualization often occurred around meals. Meals were intentionally arranged to honor some people and shame others. Certain people received places of honor and extravagant food, while others were intentionally given lesser seats and a less appealing meal. Many of these meals were held in public view so that passersby could witness the disparities, publicly reinforcing the power arrangements.[53] Meal practices today may serve a similar ritual function. With whom do we eat? Where do we eat? What foods

---

50. Kavanaugh, *Following Christ*, xxvi.
51. Stringfellow, *Ethic for Christians*, 105–6. Stringfellow includes scapegoating as a means of diversion.
52. See Postman, *Amusing Ourselves to Death*. Stringfellow singles out professional sports as a primary form of diversion. His words certainly ring true in Atlanta, where, amid serious urban problems, a major public emphasis is placed on new sports facilities, professional athletic teams, and, just a few years ago, the Olympics (Stringfellow, *Ethic for Christians*, 90–91, 105).
53. I am indebted to my New Testament colleague Stanley P. Saunders for this information.

do we eat? And what kinds of power arrangements are being reinforced by these rituals, which are at times quite public? Similar public rituals that enact and reinforce the "public transcript" of power relations in the Domination System occur in countless everyday interactions between people of different races, genders, and classes.[54] In fact, the church's ritual life often enacts this "public transcript." When men alone or heterosexuals alone stand in positions of ritual authority, the church becomes complicit in the ritual enactment of the Domination System.

The powers also act through the ritualization of public protest. The powers co-opt protest by transforming it into a tame public ritual, which the powers themselves can often even appear to support.[55] At the church I attend, for example, we have a Palm Sunday parade every year in downtown Atlanta. We seek to remember that radical event in which Jesus came into Jerusalem challenging the powers of the world by enacting a parody of worldly power. Rather than enter the city in a chariot with an army, as one might have expected, Jesus came humbly riding on a donkey. And the entire city was shaken politically by this event.[56] In our contemporary parade, however, we not only get a parade permit from the city but take advantage of police escorts provided by the city. While we do provide a valuable public witness in the midst of the city, no one in Atlanta is "shaken" by the parade. An event that once offered a radical challenge to the powers has now become a harmless public ritual managed by the city.

On a larger scale, the nation has co-opted and tamely ritualized the remembrance of Martin Luther King Jr. through the creation of a harmless national holiday in his honor. As Vincent Harding, African American scholar and social activist, has written:

> Now that King seems safely dead, now that he has been properly installed in the national pantheon—to the accompaniment of military bands, with the U.S. Marine Corps chorus singing "We Shall Overcome," and the cadenced marching of the armed forces color guards—we think we know the man's impact and influence. Didn't President Reagan sign a bill authorizing a national holiday honoring this teacher of nonviolence?
>
> And didn't Coca-Cola make available one of its corporate jets to fly King's family members and friends from one celebration to another? What more impact and influence could we want?
>
> Even those of us who feel drawn to King—and who now

---

54. For a valuable examination of the "public transcript" and the ways in which daily rituals support it, see Scott, *Domination*, 45–69.
55. Stringfellow, *Ethic for Christians*, 104–5.
56. Matthew 21:1–11. The Greek word translated "in turmoil" in the NRSV (*eseisthē*, v. 10) is related to the word for earthquake in Matthew 28:2 (*seismos*)—thus my translation, "shaken"; see also Matthew 27:51, 54.

seek to stand as far as possible from the cruel ironies of such
national hero-making—are not immune to amnesia.[57]

The powers transform King's work into a harmless ritual that causes us to
forget his radical challenge to the United States's racial, economic, and military policies. Such is the danger of ritualization at the hands of the powers.

7. *Surveillance.* Often used in conjunction with negative sanctions, such as
the threat of arrest or unemployment, surveillance is a critical tool in the
powers' efforts to ensure conformity to their ways. An ancient strategy,
surveillance has increased exponentially through the use of modern technology. Computer technology collects and records data on the mundane
details of our everyday lives, from our telephone calls to our workplace
activities to our consumer purchases. Omnipresent cameras record our
comings and goings not only in stores, banks, schools, and the workplace
but even in public areas and city parks.[58] A few years ago at a church
"block party" held on the street in front of the Georgia state capitol
building, a security guard accosted several of us because we were sitting
on a small rock wall along the sidewalk in front of the capitol. Surprised
by the sudden appearance of the security guard, we noticed for the first
time the security cameras scanning the area, probably intended to keep
homeless people from loitering there, and we realized we had been under
surveillance the entire time. The threat of such surveillance keeps people
in conformity to the will of the powers.

In today's consumer society, such surveillance does not rely simply on
negative sanctions. Surveillance is also employed by marketers to seduce
people into particular patterns of consumption. Invisible observers continually track the "digital footprints" of our purchases and preferences,
gathering personal consumer data such as itemized telephone bills, credit
card exchanges, bank withdrawals, and Web activity in order to influence
consumer behavior. Based merely on our zip code, marketers can give us
a printout of our "attitudes, probable household inventory, leisure-time
activities, media habits, and consumption patterns" in hundreds of different categories.[59] This information then becomes the basis for income-
and lifestyle-specific advertising, which lures us into particular consumer
choices. In both oppressive and seductive ways, then, the powers use surveillance to ensure conformity to their ways.[60]

---

57. Vincent Harding, "We Must Keep Going: Martin Luther King and the Future of
America," in *Peace Is the Way: Writings on Nonviolence from the Fellowship of Reconciliation,* ed. Walter Wink (Maryknoll, N.Y.: Orbis Books, 2000), 194. The use of King's
image in recent commercials raises similar issues.
58. Stringfellow, *Ethic for Christians,* 102. I have seen surveillance cameras in at least
one of the city parks in Atlanta.
59. Michael Warren, *At This Time, in This Place: The Spirit Embodied in the Local Assembly* (Harrisburg, Pa.: Trinity Press International, 1999), 105.
60. My account of electronic surveillance draws on David Lyon, *The Electronic Eye: The
Rise of Surveillance Society* (Minneapolis: University of Minnesota Press, 1994). As many

8. _Language and image_. Particularly significant for preachers, the powers use language and image to delude and capture the minds and hearts of human beings. As Stringfellow argues, the verbal is "definitive in all the ploys of the principalities"; Babel becomes the prevailing form of existence, by which he means "the inversion of language, verbal inflation, libel, rumor, euphemism and coded phrases, rhetorical wantonness, redundancy, hyperbole, such profusion in speech and sound that comprehension is impaired, nonsense, sophistry, jargon, noise, incoherence, a chaos of voices and tongues, falsehood, blasphemy."[61]

In the place of truthful speech we encounter the propaganda of the state, the exaggerations of Madison Avenue, the doublespeak of politicians and advertisers, the false claims of expertise by bureaucrats, the code language of racism, and the diversions of the entertainment industry. In the midst of this constant "babel," truth and falsehood get confused, image replaces reality, and words are devalued. Confusion reigns—and we become caught in the web of the powers.[62]

Advertisements for new technological "advances" such as e-mail, cell phones, and laptop computers provide a striking example of the deceptive ways in which the powers use language to make us captives. This technology, we are promised, will "set us free" from our offices and make possible more leisure time to do the things we enjoy. What has happened, however, is just the opposite. We have become captives to technology. We now cannot _escape_ from "the office," because we take it with us wherever we go. The deceptive language of freedom has been used to lure us into further bondage.

Such "babel," at a deeper level, drains important symbols, particularly religious symbols, of their depth and power.[63] The powers _must_ make significant religious language and symbols impotent as quickly as possible,

---

people have noted, the mere threat or suspicion that one is under surveillance is often enough to ensure conformity. Michel Foucault's influential discussion of the Panopticon, an architectural design for the ideal prison developed in the eighteenth century by the utilitarian philosopher and social reformer Jeremy Bentham, has highlighted this dimension of surveillance. See Michel Foucault, _Discipline and Punish: The Birth of the Prison_, trans. Alan Sheridan (New York: Vintage Books, 1979), 195–228. One of the earliest popular accounts of surveillance, which has also been influential in contemporary reflection, is George Orwell's novel _Nineteen Eighty-four_. For a discussion of "Orwellian" and "panoptic" approaches to electronic surveillance, see Lyon, _Electronic Eye_, 57–80.

61. Stringfellow, _Ethic for Christians_, 98, 106.

62. For Stringfellow's detailed discussion of the verbal ploys of the powers, see _Ethic for Christians_, 98–106. For a helpful videotape that explores how the English language has been inflated and manipulated to distort, obfuscate, and cover up meaning, see _Doublespeak_, 28 min., Films for the Humanities, 1993, videocassette. For a stinging critique of the loss of the power of "word" in modern society, largely because of its replacement by image, see Jacques Ellul, _The Humiliation of the Word_, trans. Joyce Main Hanks (Grand Rapids: Wm. B. Eerdmans Publishing Co., 1985).

63. Neil Postman, _Technopoly: The Surrender of Culture to Technology_ (New York: Alfred A. Knopf, 1992; Vintage Books Edition, 1993), 164.

undermining their sacred connotations in any way possible, for, as Postman has noted, "the elevation of one god requires the demotion of another."[64] Because language shapes the way in which we see the world, the trivializing of Christian language and symbol is one effective way to "demote" the God of the Christian faith.

The powers accomplish this trivialization by the repeated use of such symbols, as well as through their use in indiscriminate contexts and for trivial purposes.[65] The cross is reduced to a popular fashion accessory. Christmas becomes an occasion for commerce to employ a wide range of Christian symbols in the service of consumerism. The name of God is invoked to sell frankfurters. In this effort the powers of technology and consumerism work hand in hand, as the media overload people with countless commercials, ads, and billboards, many of which contribute to this sacred "symbol drain."[66]

No company has perfected this trivializing of sacred symbols and religious yearnings more effectively than Coca-Cola, which boasts the world's most recognizable trademark. Coca-Cola accomplishes this not primarily by using traditional religious symbols in its advertising but by creating a grand religious vision associated with its product. Tapping into deep-rooted human aspirations, Coca-Cola, through its massive advertising, has actually replaced traditional symbols by transforming Coke itself into a religious icon. Jesus does not appear in ads but rather comes to be defined by Coke's slogan and logo: red-and-white bumper stickers declare that Jesus is the "real thing."

Welsh theologian and BBC producer Iwan Russell-Jones has examined the ways in which Coca-Cola offers consumers a "vision of humanity restored, Babel reversed, Pentecost released from a can of Coke."[67] It is a religious vision that seeks to encompass the entire world. Ironically, it is a vision of "harmony" in the service of Coca-Cola's efforts to dominate the economic and cultural landscape.

"Coke adds life." "It's the real thing—the taste of your life." "I am the future of the world, I am the home of every nation." "I'd like to buy the world a Coke." Such slogans, Russell-Jones argues, tap into deep-rooted beliefs and aspirations of people around the world. "They have truly become part of our history, the text of our lives, the nursery rhymes of our children. We know them better than Scripture, they are dearer to us than the hymnody of the church."[68] They offer us, indeed, "The World of Coca-Cola," as the company's museum in Atlanta is named. And in the process they give us a symbolic world as shallow and unnourishing as the nutritionless product the company markets.

---

64. Ibid., 165.
65. Ibid., 165–70.
66. Ibid., 164–65, 170. As Postman notes, a conservative guess is that the average American will view close to 2 million television commercials by the age of sixty-five; and this doesn't include radio commercials, newspaper and magazine ads, or billboards (170).
67. Iwan Russell-Jones, "The Real Thing?" *And Straightaway* (Fall 1993): 3–4.
68. Ibid., 4.

Russell-Jones further notes our captivity to this "world":

> Why does no one cry "blasphemy"? Is it because we are blind
> to what has happened to us? Is it because our much vaunted
> sophistication and ironic detachment is incapable of protect-
> ing us from the seduction of images, the idolatry of con-
> sumption? The advertisers know who we are. They know
> where our loyalties really lie. They have made us in their own
> image, and we cannot conceive what it would be like to lead
> lives that bear any other likeness. The world we inhabit is
> indeed the world of Coca-Cola.[69]

As Michael Warren has summarized the impact of such a symbol
drain, "Images and ways of imagining can subvert a religious consciousness, erode its core the way termites can eat away at the core of
wood hard enough to defy a saw."[70] Of all the actions of the powers,
these efforts to make life shallow and trivial may be the most destructive of all.

In addition to deceiving us, creating chaos, and draining our symbols,
language and images also shape our imaginations—how we see the world.
And how we see the world shapes how we live in it.[71] Our lives, in short,
are formed by the fundamental metaphors and images into which we are
socialized, which become institutionalized in patterns of interaction
between persons.

As I noted earlier, Michael Warren has explored how certain images
serve as lenses through which we view the world, and he has argued that
the image of domination and subordination has become a comprehensive
metaphor through which many in our society see and live in the world.[72]
This image tends to break personal and social reality into the basic categories of "superior" and "inferior." It comes to expression in popular
speech, in which individuals are categorized as "losers" and "winners,"
with the winners being those who successfully dominate and come out
"on top."[73] "We're number one!" becomes not just a popular slogan
shouted at sporting events but a declaration of the competitive character
of many of our lives. Through such comprehensive metaphors, reinforced daily by visual imagery, the Domination System reinforces its
power, and the powers create the illusion that their way is the way of life.
Through the language and images that shape our world, the ways of the
System become the "air we breathe," and alternatives become almost
unimaginable.

---

69. Ibid.
70. Warren, *At This Time*, 34.
71. Ibid., 36, 32. Warren particularly examines how our imaginations are formed by
images of domination (34–37) and the ways in which "style" comes to replace depth
and substance (37–38).
72. Warren, "Culture, Counterculture, and Word," 90.
73. Ibid.

9. *Secrecy.* The "shadow side" of language and images, secrecy is the final strategy employed by the powers.[74] Just as the principalities understand the power of language and images, so they also grasp the power that comes with secrecy. Tobacco companies keep secret their long-term knowledge of the health hazards of smoking. The military keeps secret the harm done to countless soldiers and civilians through the use of depleted uranium weapons.[75] Voices of Native Americans and slaves, which do not serve the reigning national myth, are silenced in official histories.[76] Coca-Cola even vaunts the formula for its soft drink as a "closely guarded secret." Such secrecy renders us powerless against manipulation by propaganda or other "babel."[77]

Secrecy and silence, in fact, can become a helpful barometer regarding the powers that really hold us captive. When secrecy and silence are demanded, we must be vigilant about identifying the powers at work. Congregations should take note in particular of those areas of their life in which silence is required. In most churches, for example, secrecy reigns around economic matters. Each church member is ensured privacy regarding income, investments, and giving. There is no talk about such matters; it is off limits, in complete contradiction to the vision of the church in the opening chapters of Acts. Similarly, preachers need to be aware of the topics that are "off limits" in the pulpit. Here, too, economics is often at the top of the list. Nothing will get a preacher in trouble faster than breaking the silence and speaking the truth about economic realities in the global economy. Such areas of silence in the church should always give preachers pause. Where secrecy reigns and truthtelling is forbidden, the principalities and powers are often at work to keep people captive to the ways of death.

The fallen principalities and powers, then, use a legion of strategies to further their idolatrous purposes of survival, domination, and death. Against the onslaught of these powers, human resistance seems almost fruitless, if not impossible. For Christians, however, the story does not end with the rebellious activity of the powers and the helplessness of human beings before them. In his life, death, and resurrection Jesus has engaged and overcome the powers, setting people free for lives of faithful resistance. And a primary means of this resistance is preaching, the "sword of the Spirit, which is the Word of God."

---

74. Stringfellow, *Ethic for Christians*, 101–2.
75. John Catalinotto and Sara Flounders, eds., *Metal of Dishonor: Depleted Uranium: How the Pentagon Radiates Soldiers and Civilians with DU Weapons*, rev. ed. (New York: Depleted Uranium Education Project International Action Center, 1999).
76. See Ched Myers, *Who Will Roll Away the Stone? Discipleship Queries for First World Christians* (Maryknoll, N.Y.: Orbis Books, 1994), 117.
77. Stringfellow, *Ethic for Christians*, 101.

3

Jesus and the Powers

The activity of the principalities and powers provides the context for Jesus' ministry, including his preaching, and offers an essential lens through which to understand his crucifixion and resurrection. As Walter Wink has noted, Jesus' entire ministry challenges the powers, and the gospel itself is "a context-specific remedy for the evils of the Domination System."[1] In his ministry, Jesus engages the Domination System at both the material and spiritual levels. He resists the powers and offers an alternative to their order of survival, domination, and violence. The powers respond to this threat in a predictable way: they crucify Jesus, putting to death the one who threatens them. Through his crucifixion, however, Jesus unmasks the powers as the powers of death, not life. And through his resurrection, Jesus overcomes the powers of death, sets human beings free from the fear of death, and promises the final and complete redemption of creation, including the powers themselves. A brief examination of Jesus' ministry, crucifixion, and resurrection will flesh out this story of Jesus' engagement with the principalities and powers and lead to a discussion in chapter 4 of the ethical significance of Jesus' preaching.[2]

---

1. Walter Wink, *Engaging the Powers: Discernment and Resistance in a World of Domination* (Minneapolis: Fortress Press, 1992), 48.
2. My discussion of Jesus' ministry is suggestive rather than exhaustive. I am trying to highlight the ways in which the central practices of Jesus' ministry—preaching and teaching, table fellowship, exorcism, and healing—present a thoroughgoing challenge to the principalities and powers of the world. I am not saying that this is the *only* way to understand Jesus' ministry. Nor do I deny those texts that may run counter to the

RESISTING THE POWERS: THE TEMPTATION

In the Synoptic Gospels, Jesus' engagement with the powers begins with his temptation in the wilderness, immediately after his baptism. In the temptation stories, particularly as developed by Matthew and Luke, Jesus' mission begins to take shape. His ministry will be one of resistance to the principalities and powers of the world. In addition, Jesus' temptation is inescapably linked to his crucifixion, highlighting the fact that Jesus' ministry of resistance leads to his execution by the powers.

In his temptation Jesus confronts and resists "the devil," or "Satan," who is the spirit of the Domination System.[3] The devil represents the driving force that moves and shapes the work of the particular powers and of the Domination System as a whole. Consequently, the devil's temptations hold before Jesus the central priorities of the powers, which I delineated in chapter 1. In the wilderness Jesus encounters the Domination System in all its power and is tempted to take the path of survival, domination, violence, and idolatry.

In the temptation stories, Jesus' response to these temptations is a resounding no. His obedience and faithfulness primarily take the form of *resistance*. At the beginning of the Gospel story we do not learn the positive direction of Jesus' ministry. Rather, we simply learn what Jesus will *not* do. We discover the kind of Messiah he will *not* be, the means he will *not* take, the ends he will *not* pursue. The mission of Jesus, into which he has just been baptized, begins with resistance to the powers; it begins with a "No!" to the powers and priorities that drive the world and lead to death.[4]

In his obedience to God, Jesus says no to three particular temptations of the devil, which represent the fundamental priorities of the powers of the world.[5]

---

picture I am trying to paint. Nevertheless, I do think most of the New Testament can be read fruitfully within the framework I am developing. For a more extended account of Jesus' ministry as an engagement with the powers, on which much of this chapter depends, see Wink, *Engaging the Powers*, 107–37; and Ched Myers, *Binding the Strong Man: A Political Reading of Mark's Story of Jesus* (Maryknoll, N.Y.: Orbis Books, 1988). For a recent homiletical Christology with similar emphases, see L. Susan Bond, *Trouble with Jesus: Women, Christology, and Preaching* (St. Louis: Chalice Press, 1999), 109–50. See also the earlier works of David Buttrick: *Preaching Jesus Christ: An Exercise in Homiletic Theology* (Philadelphia: Fortress Press, 1988) and *The Mystery and the Passion: A Homiletic Reading of the Gospel Traditions* (Minneapolis: Fortress Press, 1992).
3. Wink, *Engaging the Powers*, 9, 57, 58, 90.
4. Stringfellow has argued that Christian resistance to the principalities and powers also begins with such a "No." See William Stringfellow, *An Ethic for Christians and Other Aliens in a Strange Land* (Waco, Tex.: Word Books, 1973; 3d paperback ed., 1979), 155.
5. I use the story of Luke as my focus, though similar things could be said of Matthew's account of the temptation (See Luke 4:1–13; Mt. 4:1–11).

First, Jesus refuses to use his power to secure his own *survival*. Jesus is famished, and the devil invites him to turn "this stone" (singular in Luke 4) into bread. The devil, representing a fundamental drive of the powers, invites Jesus to use his power to meet his own needs, to ensure his own survival. Responding, as he will each time, with a text from Deuteronomy, Jesus replies, "One does not live by bread alone." Like the people in the wilderness who lived on manna, Jesus affirms that dependence on God and obedience to God are more important than securing one's own survival. People can in fact suffer "death by bread alone," as is evident in our consumer society.[6] Jesus says no to making his own survival the top priority and to using his power to meet his own needs.

Second, the devil invites Jesus to use his power to establish a political empire grounded in the ways of the world—the ways of *domination* and *violence*.[7] Jesus can have all worldly power, which, disturbingly, has been given over to the devil, if he will simply worship the devil and follow the way of the Domination System. "All of the kingdoms can be yours," the devil tells Jesus, "if you will just lord your power over others and take up the sword of the nations. Take charge of the biological weapons, deploy some troops, command the implementation of a 'Star Wars' missile defense system. All the kingdoms can be yours—if you will just use the world's means of power: domination and violence."

But again, Jesus says no. To serve the devil in this way would be idolatry (something the powers, particularly the nation, always seek from people). To take this path would set Jesus on the way of the world rather than the way of God. So Jesus refuses to take the path of domination and violence. In fact, his "No!" to this path runs throughout the temptation story. The only "weapon" Jesus uses (and will ever use) against the Domination System is the Word. The only "sword" Jesus will take up is the "sword of the Spirit, which is the word of God" (Eph. 6:17). Jesus does not use his power to destroy even the devil by means of violence or domination. Rather, he lives with the confidence expressed in Martin Luther's great hymn "A Mighty Fortress Is Our God": "The prince of darkness grim, We tremble not for him; His rage we can endure, For lo! His doom is sure, One little word shall fell him." Jesus says no to the path of violence and domination.

The devil then turns to Scripture for the final temptation, reminding us

---

6. Jesus does not say that people do not need bread but that they do not live by bread *alone*. Jesus' resistance at this point is not meant to undermine the legitimate need for bread that millions of people in the world confront today. That kind of survival is quite different from the temptation of the powers. On the ways in which the consumer society and the commodification of existence lead to death, see John F. Kavanaugh, *Following Christ in a Consumer Culture (Still)* (Maryknoll, N.Y.: Orbis Books, 1991), 3–19; 38–53.

7. The order of the temptations is different in Matthew and Luke; the second and third temptations are reversed in the two Gospels.

that even Scripture can be used by the powers in opposition to the will of God. Quoting Psalm 91:11–12, the devil tempts Jesus to use God for his own ends, to make God an instrument for his own success and popularity.[8] By jumping off the temple and having God's angels protect him before the eyes of all the people, Jesus could give the people dramatic proof of who he is; he could give them the kind of Messiah they want and could avoid misunderstanding and rejection. "Come on, Jesus," the devil taunts, "God will protect you; the Scriptures say so. Use God just this once as a means to your personal goals." This avenue is one the powers take all the time. How often, for example, do nations call on God in the midst of war and seek to make God a servant of their own goals in order to ensure popular support? And how often does the capitalist system claim divine sanction, even within the churches? This is one of the ways in which the powers make idols of themselves—by subordinating the living God to their own ends.[9] But again, Jesus says no to this kind of idolatry. He will not test God in this way; he will not try to use God for his own ends.

Luke concludes the story with a foreboding word: "When the devil had finished every test, he departed from him until an opportune time" (4:13). This rather ominous conclusion to the story provides a critical link between the temptation and the cross. The "opportune time" when the devil will return is the time of Jesus' passion and crucifixion, when the Domination System will not simply test Jesus with words but attack him with actions. The final verse in Luke's temptation story thus stands as a warning: don't try to understand the cross apart from the particular story of Jesus that runs from temptation to crucifixion. There is an essential narrative connection between Jesus' life and his death. The cross cannot be plopped down out of the blue as a magical transaction between God and individual sinners. Rather, Jesus' resistance to the powers of the world leads to his crucifixion and gives the cross its distinctive meaning.

In the temptation stories, the drama of the gospel is foreshadowed both by the powers and by Jesus. On their part, the powers must crucify Jesus because of the "No!" he speaks to their way. Intent on their own *survival* at all costs, the powers must crucify the one who threatens their authority. Committed to *domination* by the sword, the powers must put to death the one who challenges their most basic values. Making *idols* of themselves by using God for their own

---

8. For Luke, this is the climactic temptation, possibly because of the devil's use of Scripture or because this temptation—using God for one's own ends—is the core temptation underlying the other two.

9. Although he takes a somewhat different approach, Ched Myers argues that this temptation is fundamentally one of idolatry. See Ched Myers, *Who Will Roll Away the Stone? Discipleship Queries for First World Christians* (Maryknoll, N.Y.: Orbis Books, 1994), 140.

ends, the powers must crucify one who names their pretensions and serves God alone. On his part, Jesus takes up the way of the cross in the wilderness; by rejecting the way of survival, domination, violence, and idolatry, he takes the first step down the path to crucifixion. If Jesus had chosen the way of survival, he would have avoided crucifixion. If he had chosen the way of violent domination, he would not have succumbed to the cross. And if he had chosen to use God for his own ends—placing effectiveness over faithfulness—he would have never ended up at Golgotha.

In the temptation story we glimpse the fundamental conflict—the conflict between the way of God and the way of the powers, between the way of life and the way of death—that eventually, at an "opportune time," will end on the cross. The crucifixion is no accident and no magical transaction isolated from the life and ministry of Jesus. The cross is a direct consequence of Jesus' resistance to the powers of death in the world.

JESUS' MINISTRY AND THE POWERS

Preaching

In his ministry after the temptation, Jesus continues the path of resistance that leads to the cross; at virtually every turn he proclaims and embodies an alternative to the ways of the Domination System. Just as Jesus had relied on the Word in the wilderness, so, when he returns from the wilderness, he immediately begins proclaiming a new order breaking into the world (Matt. 4:17, 23; 5:1–7:28; Mark 1:14–15; Luke 4:16–30). Although Jesus uses language traditionally associated with hierarchy and domination—"kingdom of God/heaven"—both his proclamation and his ministry turn that language on its head, undermining its association with violence and domination while retaining the political character of the gospel. In his words and deeds, Jesus challenges and subverts the Domination System at every turn.[10]

In his opening sermons—the Sermon on the Mount (Matt. 5:1–7:27) and the sermon at Nazareth (Luke 4:16–30)—Jesus boldly announces the new reality that has "come near" in him. He speaks the Word that he will "perform" in his life and ministry.[11] In the Beatitudes (Matt. 5:3–12), which open

---

10. This section draws heavily on the work of Wink and Myers.
11. As the first chapter of the Gospel of John makes clear, there is a unity between Jesus' words and life. Jesus not only proclaims the Word but *is* the Word. Just as God created the world through a word (Genesis 1), so the "new creation" breaks into the world through the Word (John 1).

the Sermon on the Mount and announce the new eschatological order that provides the context for the practical instruction in the rest of the sermon, Jesus reverses the priorities of the Domination System. In a series of eschatological blessings (not moral imperatives), Jesus proclaims that beatitude in the new order belongs not to those who lord their power over others through violent domination but to the "poor in spirit," "those who mourn," "the meek," "the merciful," "the pure in heart," "the peacemakers," and even "those who are persecuted for righteousness sake." The Beatitudes, in fact, provide a "systematic and explicit repudiation of the Domination System."[12] In making these pronouncements, Jesus not only envisions a new order; he also sets that new reality loose in the world. Nothing can ever be the same again.

In the rest of the sermon, Jesus delineates the concrete practices of the new community that lives in this new reality, what Wink calls "God's Domination-Free Order."[13] In this new community, reconciliation takes priority over vengeance (Matt. 5:21–26); women are no longer treated as objects or property (5:27–32); love of enemies and nonviolent resistance replace violent domination of the "other" (5:38–48);[14] religious practices do not become the source of superiority and competition (6:1–18); the desire for wealth is not the driving motivation of life (6:19–34).[15] Socially, politically, religiously, and economically, Jesus subverts the Domination System and the spirit that drives it.

In his opening sermon in Luke, sometimes called the "Nazareth Manifesto," Jesus likewise announces a new order that "is being fulfilled" in the very proclamation and hearing of his words. Taking up the mantle of the prophet and drawing on Isaiah 61, Jesus proclaims good news to the poor, release to the captives, recovery of sight to the blind, freedom to the oppressed, and the year of the Lord's favor (Luke 4:18–19). All of these pronouncements should be taken literally as words for those who are physically in need of healing and ache for liberation from oppression and captivity. At the same time, however, Jesus' words confront the powers in the spiritual dimensions of their work. As

---

12. Wink, *Engaging the Powers*, 112.
13. Ibid., 107–37. Ched Myers, highlighting the economic dimensions of this order, speaks of God's "Great Economy." See Myers, *Who Will Roll the Stone?* 168–70.
14. As Walter Wink has persuasively argued, the actions in 5:38–42 ("turning the other cheek," "giving the cloak also," and "going the second mile") are not acts of passivity but acts of nonviolent resistance (*Engaging the Powers*, 175–89).
15. These economic practices are essential elements of nonviolence. As René Girard has argued, acquisitive, mimetic rivalry and desire lie at the heart of society's violence. See René Girard, *The Girard Reader*, ed. James G. Williams (New York: Crossroad, 1996), 9–65. In Matthew 6:19–34, Jesus replaces such desire with trust in God and pursuit of life in God's new order. See also Kavanaugh's discussion of the link between violence and the commodity form of life in *Following Christ*, 43–53.

I noted in chapter 1, the powers seek to hold people captive to their idolatrous, dominating ways. But Jesus announces release from this captivity. The powers seek to take away our vision—our imagination—so that we live under the delusion that their way is the only way, and we are unable even to conceive an alternative. But Jesus announces new sight—new imagination—for those whom the powers have blinded. The powers, particularly in our capitalist system, create domination through the commodification of reality and the accumulation of wealth. But Jesus, placing persons before capital, proclaims the jubilee year, in which wealth will be redistributed and people will live free of the drive to accumulate that distorts human life and serves as a source of human violence.[16]

And Jesus doesn't stop there. In his reflections that follow, he subverts all notions of religious or ethnic superiority that hold people captive and cause them to denigrate and oppress "outsiders." In telling the stories—directly from the people's Scripture—of the widow at Zarephath and Naaman the Syrian, Jesus invites his hearers to see the mercy of God at work in the "other"—even the enemy. He undercuts one of the main sources of domination and violence in the world: ethnic and religious superiority, which continues to wreak its havoc through contemporary movements for "ethnic cleansing" and acts of religious violence, from Serbia to Palestine to Northern Ireland to New York City.[17] Not surprisingly, at this point his hearers' "captivity" to the Domination System becomes evident. They seek to get rid of this one who undercuts their assumptions of superiority. Just as Jesus' challenge to the Domination System will later lead the powers to crucify him, so here, right at the beginning of the story, Jesus' message draws forth the response of mob violence.

In his Nazareth Manifesto as in the Sermon on the Mount, Jesus proclaims the shape of the new order breaking into the world in his person. In both sermons he challenges "every conceivable prop of domination, division, and supremacy," and he offers an alternative to the way of violent domination in the world.[18] Later in Luke, Jesus sets out the domination-free character of his new community as its fundamental difference from the "powers that be." At the Last Supper, Jesus' disciples reveal their own captivity to these powers by

16. The early Christians understood the jubilee character of Jesus' new order. Acts 2 and 4 describe the way in which the early Christian communities sought to bring that order into reality by the practice of redistributing goods (Acts 2:44–45; 4:32, 34–37).
17. For an extraordinary account of the relationship between ethnic and religious "belonging" and violence in the world today, see Michael Ignatieff, *Blood and Belonging: Journeys into the New Nationalism* (New York: Farrar, Straus and Giroux, 1995).
18. Wink, *Engaging the Powers*, 110.

arguing over who among them will be the greatest. In response to their request, Jesus offers the disciples a concise, programmatic statement about the new community he is building:

> The kings of the Gentiles lord it over them; and those in authority over them are called benefactors. But not so with you; rather the greatest among you must become like the youngest, and the leader like one who serves. For who is greater, the one who is at the table or the one who serves? Is it not the one at the table? But I am among you as one who serves. (Luke 22:24–27)

At a shared meal, at which he gives his body and blood as "one who serves," Jesus teaches the disciples directly about the new, domination-free community he is creating in the midst of the Domination System. In fact, the meal itself becomes both the central image and the primary embodiment of the political, social, economic, and religious alternative Jesus offers to the powers of the world who "lord it over" others.

Table Fellowship

Jesus' last supper is no isolated event. Rather, it is the culmination of the radical "table ministry" he enacted throughout his life. Within the context of Jesus' story, it is no surprise that Jesus' final meal with his disciples provides the context for his strong challenge to the Domination System or that a meal serves as the image for the radical reversal of power he embodied throughout his ministry. Throughout his life, table fellowship provided one of the concrete practices through which Jesus challenged the powers of domination and violence in the world.

It is difficult for many of us today to appreciate the radical character of Jesus' table fellowship. As I noted in chapter 2, meals in Jesus' culture were public rituals with enormous religious and social significance. Table fellowship was an occasion not only to protect religious purity but also to reinforce social status—and these religious and social dimensions were often closely related. Meals were rituals of division, practices set up to distinguish between insiders and outsiders, clean and unclean, honored and shamed.

On the religious side, a good, observant Jew not only would avoid eating *foods* that were unclean but would avoid sharing table fellowship with *people* considered unclean. Table fellowship was the most intimate form of community, and sharing such intimacy with a person considered unclean would bring contamination upon oneself. "Righteous" people simply did not eat with "sinners." And in first-century Palestine, unlike in later Christianity, sinners were not people suffering a subjective state of guilt but groups of social outcasts:

people in one of the despised trades, such as tax collectors; those guilty of fla-
grant immorality, such as adulterers, prostitutes, extortioners, and murderers;
those who failed to keep the Law according to the standards of the religious
authorities; and those who were ethnically and religiously impure, such as
Samaritans and Gentiles.[19] Religious and social divisions went hand in hand
at the table.

One can sense the magnitude of this issue in the story of Peter and Cor-
nelius in Acts 10:1–48. It takes an extraordinary act of God and an extraordinary transformation of Peter to bring him to share "unclean" foods at table
with Gentiles. And, if Paul's account of Peter's table practices is accurate, even
that dramatic transformation was difficult for Peter to sustain within the context of Jewish tradition and expectations (see Gal. 2:11–21). Similarly, Paul's
struggle with food offered to idols suggests the critical role that table practices
played in the culture of early Christianity (1 Cor. 8:1–13).

No wonder the religious authorities reacted strongly when confronted with
Jesus' table fellowship (Mark 2:16). Through his meals with others, Jesus was
breaking down the divisions between clean and unclean and embodying an
alternative community in the midst of the world. Jesus not only declared all
foods clean, arguing that nothing that goes into a person can make him or her
unclean (Mark 7:14–23). Jesus also ate with *people* considered unclean. He
shared table fellowship with "tax collectors and sinners," with social outcasts
excluded from the community because of their uncleanness. Indeed, Jesus
apparently even ate with Samaritans. At the well in Sychar, he publicly
requested a drink of water from a lone Samaritan woman, who was possibly an
outcast even among her own people. After a lengthy conversation with the
woman, which itself shocked his disciples, Jesus stayed with the Samaritans
"for two days," presumably eating with them—at the very least, eating food
purchased from Samaritans (John 4:1–42). Table fellowship with sinners was
perhaps the central feature of Jesus' ministry.[20] Through such table fellowship,
Jesus broke down the divisions between clean and unclean, superior and inferior, and he embodied a sign of the new order breaking into the world. The
religious authorities who sought to protect the status quo were naturally
offended.

Such meal fellowship also challenged the larger culture of honor and shame
in the Roman world. As I noted in the previous chapter, in that culture meals—
particularly the evening meal—were some of the most important occasions for
social theater and ritual. A rich householder would often stage a dinner for
those whose favor he was seeking to gain. The meal was designed to display

---

19. Ibid., 115.
20. Ibid.

one's own wealth and status ostentatiously and to honor the guest for the sake of anticipated future rewards. An important element at many of these meals was the presence of persons of lesser honor and status, who would be seated in different spaces and served lesser-quality food, all as a way of shaming them in order to accentuate the honor of those in the chief seats. Often all this took place in dining areas open to the streets, so that passersby could witness and comment on the affair. Meals, in short, were occasions publicly to reinforce the social hierarchy in a culture of honor and shame.

The pressures of this system can be seen in the life of the early church, shedding light on the radical character of Jesus' table fellowship. In 1 Corinthians 11:17–34, Paul struggles precisely with the Corinthian Christians' accommodation to these cultural practices. In the community's meals, the poor receive little or nothing, while the rich not only get the best food but even get drunk—that is, have more than they need. The dominant culture's table rituals of honor and shame have captured the alternative table practices of the Christian community. The common meal has become a source of social and class division. And Paul, in his inimitable way, minces no words in his condemnation: "Now in the following instructions I do not commend you, because when you come together it is not for the better but for the worse. . . . When you come together it is not really to eat the Lord's supper" (11:17, 20).

The ground of Paul's critique is the table fellowship of Jesus, particularly his last supper with his disciples (1 Cor. 11:23–26). Paul understood that Jesus' table fellowship was an act of resistance to the culture's divisive, oppressive hierarchies of honor and shame. He understood that such practices, which stood at the heart of the culture, had implications for social and economic relationships. He understood that for Jesus the table was a place to enact the love at the heart of the new order he was bringing into the world.[21] The table was a jubilee table, at which the social patterns of domination and subordination were to be broken down and a new community embodied. Table fellowship was to be an enactment of the new life of the baptized community, in which "there is no longer Jew or Greek, there is no longer slave or free, there is no longer male and female" (Gal. 3:28). In short, Jesus' table fellowship, which Paul faithfully carries forward into the life of the early Christian community, was a practice of resistance in the face of the powers of the world that use everyday ritual practices to enslave human minds and hearts to the Domination System. In his table fellowship Jesus *enacted* the new, nonviolent, domination-free order that he *proclaimed* in his preaching and teaching.

---

21. At the Last Supper, Jesus even dipped bread with his enemy—the one who would betray him—just as throughout his ministry he had eaten with the religious authorities who became his enemies. This is radical table fellowship indeed.

Exorcisms and Healings

Jesus engaged in a similar kind of enactment through his exorcisms and heal-ings, which embodied the inbreaking of God's new creation into the world and demonstrated Jesus' authority over the powers of death at work in the world. Jesus' exorcisms are probably the most direct example of his engagement with the powers of death that hold people captive. As Walter Wink notes, "Exor-cism in its New Testament context is the act of deliverance of a person or insti-tution or society from its bondage to evil, and its restoration to the wholeness intrinsic to its creation."[22] Exorcisms deal with the spiritual captivity in which the powers hold people, institutions, and societies. Such exorcisms were a key characteristic of Jesus' messianic mission, which he passed on to his followers. They were a principal element of Jesus' apocalyptic struggle with the pow-ers.[23] In fact, Jesus' very presence called the demonic powers out into the open.[24] It is no coincidence, for example, that when Jesus first enters the syn-agogue, threatening the "space" of the religious authorities, a demon appears, representing the "scribal establishment, whose 'authority' undergirds the dominant Jewish social order" (Mark 1:21–28).[25]

Jesus' exorcisms are not simply personal but political.[26] Jesus confronts not simply individual demons but the larger social and political powers that hold people captive. He challenges the spirituality of the "structures of power and alienation in the social world."[27] Jesus' exorcism of the Gerasene demoniac (Mark 5:1–20), for example, involves casting out the spirit of Roman oppres-sion, which is embodied in a representative person. The demoniac is possessed by "Legion," a technical name for a Roman military division. In constantly breaking his chains among the tombs, the demoniac acts out the community's repressed longing to be freed from their oppression and the death it brings to them. At the same time, the demoniac provides a scapegoat for the pent-up violence of the community; he continually bruises himself with stones, repeat-edly enacting in his person the scapegoat mechanism whereby a society keeps its violence in check by channeling it onto a sacrificial victim—often by ston-ing. In short, the demoniac represents in an external form the spirit of oppres-sion and the repressed desire for freedom that possesses the entire community,

---

22. Walter Wink, *Unmasking the Powers: The Invisible Forces That Determine Human Existence* (Philadelphia: Fortress Press, 1986), 59. For Wink's fuller treatment of the demonic in *Unmasking the Powers*, see 41–68.
23. Myers, *Binding the Strong Man*, 143.
24. Wink, *Unmasking the Powers*, 59.
25. Myers, *Binding the Strong Man*, 141–42.
26. Stringfellow, *Ethic for Christians*, 144–46, 149–51.
27. Myers, *Binding the Strong Man*, 143.

and his presence among the people serves to maintain order in the community by keeping their violent resentment in check.

Jesus' exorcism of the Gerasene demoniac is thus a "public symbolic action" in which he confronts the powers of Roman imperialism that hold the community in their formidable grip.[28] Moreover, in this exorcism Jesus challenges the deeper violence of the scapegoat mechanism by setting free the one who had become the channel for the community's own violence. Not surprisingly, when they hear that the demoniac is now in his right mind, the people in the community are not pleased but ask Jesus to leave. Their possession is so deep that they cannot even imagine liberation from it; they have become more comfortable with their captivity to the empire than with the possibility of freedom. Without their scapegoat in place, moreover, there is the potential for chaos; for without a channel for their violence, which cannot be exerted against Rome, the possibility exists that the violence will erupt in uncontrolled ways within the community itself. Jesus' exorcism thus challenges not only the particular spirit of oppression that holds the people captive within the Roman Empire but also the spirit of violence that demands scapegoats.[29]

In the Gospel of Mark, according to Ched Myers, this exorcism, juxtaposed with Jesus' exorcism in the synagogue (Mark 1:21–28), represents Jesus' inaugural challenge to the powers. In Mark, Jesus prepares the "space" for his ministry with these two exorcisms, highlighting the character of his ministry as an engagement with the principalities and powers. When Jesus appears in the synagogue—the institutional space of the religious authorities—a demon appears and seeks to control him by getting his name. Similarly, when Jesus first appears on Gentile territory, a demon representing Roman imperial power again appears, seeking to control him by getting his name. The "powers that be," knowing the threat Jesus poses to the status quo, immediately seek to bring his work under their own authority. In both instances, Jesus exorcises these demonic powers as a symbolic political act. As Myers writes,

> Put in military terminology, [these two exorcisms] signal the decisive breach in the defenses of the symbolic fortress of Roman Palestine. The political and ideological authority of both the scribal establishment and the Roman military garrison—the two central elements

---

28. Ibid., 193.

29. This very brief account is based on more thorough accounts by Wink, *Unmasking the Powers*, 43–50; and Myers, *Binding the Strong Man*, 190–94. Wink, drawing on René Girard's interpretation of this story, develops the scapegoat theme more fully, while Myers focuses more on the exorcism as "political symbolic action." The two accounts seem to me to be complementary rather than contradictory. Despite their differences, both highlight the political and social dimensions of Jesus' exorcism.

within the colonial condominium—have been repudiated. The narrative space has been cleared for the kingdom ministry to commence in
full, both to Jew and gentile.[30]

At the very heart of Jesus' ministry were his exorcisms, which set people free
from the powers that held them captive, including the political and institutional
principalities that enslaved them at both the material and spiritual levels.

The early church understood the importance of exorcism in Jesus' ministry
and carried it forward in its own life. Exorcism became not simply an occasional rite for demonically possessed individuals but an essential aspect of the
rite of baptism. Just as the community meal carried forward Jesus' table fellowship as an ongoing act of resistance to the powers, so the church's entrance
rite carried forward Jesus' work of exorcism in setting people free from their
captivity to the Domination System. The early church understood that the
"world" (kosmos) lived in opposition to God.[31] Christians sensed the truth spoken by the devil, who tells Jesus in the wilderness that all the kingdoms of the
world have been "given over to me" (Luke 4:6). As the writer of 1 John summarized the insight of early Christian communities, "The whole world lies
under the power of the evil one" (1 John 5:19). Consequently, believers who
were reborn into the new creation through the waters of baptism first had to
have the demonic powers—the Domination System in all its fullness—"cast
out" of them.

After baptism, regular acts of exorcism continued, not just in dramatic form
but even in the ongoing prayer life of the community. The Lord's Prayer itself,
as William Stringfellow has pointed out, is an act of exorcism: "Whether many
who redundantly and ceremoniously recite the Lord's Prayer are cognizant of
it or not, the fact remains that the invocation of the name of God, followed at
the end of the prayer by the plea to 'deliver us from evil' or from 'the evil one,'
constitutes an act of exorcism."[32] The church understood itself as an alternative community living in resistance to the principalities and powers of the
world; it thus had to struggle constantly to live free from captivity to the "collective possession" of the society around it.[33]

Like his exorcisms, Jesus' healings were not simply actions on behalf of individuals but at a deeper level presented a challenge to the powers of death at
work in the world, which were not simply physical but social as well. Through
his healings Jesus not only restored people to physical health but restored out-

30. Myers, *Binding the Strong Man*, 194.
31. Wink, *Engaging the Powers*, 51–59.
32. Stringfellow, *Ethic for Christians*, 150. See Matthew 6:9–13.
33. On the reality of "collective possession," see Wink, *Unmasking the Powers*, 50–52,
64–68.

siders and unclean persons to community and social standing. When Jesus touched a leper, for example, he challenged a system of exclusion that created a living death for many people by isolating them from community.

Similarly, when Jesus interrupts his trip to Jairus's house to talk with a bleeding woman who has touched him and been healed, Jesus interrupts an entire social order based on domination and subordination (Mark 5:21–43). The healing of the woman is not simply physical but social. By stopping for the woman, Jesus gives priority not to the socially and religiously prominent leader of the synagogue but to one who is the ultimate outcast— religiously, economically, socially. He opens the space for her to tell her own story, and he declares that through her faith she has been the agent of her own healing. He calls her "daughter," affirming her full membership in the community of faith. And he makes her, of all people, an example of faith for the synagogue official. The woman is, in fact, raised from the dead just as truly as Jairus's daughter is raised later in the story. Such authority over the multiple powers of death in the world is the fundamental significance of Jesus' healings. In those healings, the reign of God breaks in to challenge the powers.

The Gospel of John captures well the significance of Jesus' healings in the story of the raising of Lazarus, Jesus' climactic healing in the Gospel (John 11:1–44).[34] In this story Jesus reveals what is implicit in all his healings—his authority over the power of death. In addition, through this story the political implications of Jesus' power over death become apparent. As a result of his raising Lazarus, the powers that be seek to kill both Jesus and Lazarus (John 11:53; 12:10). At first glance this response seems strange; Jesus' power over death should have been good news for everyone. As I noted in the first chapter, however, death is the ultimate sanction of the powers. When Jesus raises Lazarus, demonstrating his authority over death, he takes away the ultimate sanction the powers wield over people. If people no longer fear death, the powers lose their ultimate vehicle of control. Genuine freedom becomes a possibility. It is thus not surprising that the early disciples were arrested for proclaiming the _resurrection_ (Acts 4:1–3). There can be no greater threat to the powers than the resurrection of the dead, so they must (foolishly) seek to put to death the one who threatens their authority in this way.

Jesus' ministry thus involves a thoroughgoing challenge and alternative to the principalities and powers of the world. He lives free of the powers' clutches and enacts a radical alternative to their ways of domination and death. As Wink summarizes,

---

34. My interpretation relies on Stringfellow, _Ethic for Christians_, 49.

Looking back over Jesus' ministry, what emerges with bracing clarity is the comprehensive nature of his vision. He was not intent on putting a new patch on an old garment, or new wine in old skins (Mark 2:21–22 par.). He was not a reformer, bringing alternative, better readings of the Law. Nor was he a revolutionary, attempting to replace one oppressive power with another (Mark 12:13–17 par.). He went beyond revolution. His assault was against the basic presuppositions and structures of oppression itself.[35]

Because Jesus threatens the powers at such a profound level, they must act; the powers cannot sit by and allow such a threat to their survival and domination to exist. Consequently, they turn against him and seek to destroy him through the violent means which are their fundamental mode of operation: they seek to put him to death. In his death, however, Jesus actually enacts his most profound challenge to the powers—his challenge to their resort to violence.

THE CROSS AND THE POWERS

From the time he is born, when he is a threat to Herod's power, to his first sermon in Nazareth, when the people try to throw him off the cliff, to his healing of Lazarus, which results in the final plot against him, the powers seek ways to kill Jesus. When their survival and domination are threatened, the powers have one, ultimate response: do away with the threat through violence and death. Jesus is no exception.

The crucifixion is the work of the principalities and powers.[36] The New Testament goes to great lengths to make this point. The profound reality in the Gospels is that Jesus' death cannot be simplistically blamed on any one individual or group. Something larger is at work. Pilate, for example, seeks to release Jesus because he cannot discern that he has committed a capital offense. He seeks to "wash his hands" of Jesus' death. Nevertheless, Pilate con-

---

35. Wink, *Engaging the Powers*, 136.
36. The Christus Victor model of the atonement is the classic view that treats Jesus' death and resurrection in relation to the principalities and powers. My interpretation follows the general contours of this model. On the Christus Victor model of the atonement, see Gustaf Aulén, *Christus Victor: A Historical Study of the Three Main Types of the Idea of the Atonement*, trans. A. G. Herbert (New York: Macmillan, 1931). For contemporary treatments of the Christus Victor model, see J. Denny Weaver, "Atonement for the Nonconstantinian Church," *Modern Theology* 6 (July 1990): 307–23; and Gayle Gerber Koontz, "The Liberation of Atonement," *Mennonite Quarterly Review* 63 (April 1989): 171–92.

sents to Jesus' crucifixion. He is complicit, but, oddly, through his weakness rather than his strength. The political powers that impinge on his office hold him captive, and he goes along with them, in all probability to ensure his survival in office and the continuation of his rule.

Even the religious leaders cannot be simplistically blamed. Unquestionably, the religious authorities play an important role. But they themselves are captive to institutions and powers that are larger than they. They function not so much as individuals but, like Pilate, as the acolytes of the institutions they serve. And beyond them is the demonic "mob spirit" that takes over the crowd and cries out for Jesus' crucifixion.[37] In the entire passion narrative, something larger than individuals is at work; the powers of death in the world animate the events that lead to Jesus' crucifixion. The apostle Paul rightly sums up the role of the powers in Jesus' death: "None of the rulers of this age understood this [wisdom of God]; for if they had, they would not have crucified the Lord of glory" (1 Cor. 2:8).

Even as the powers close in on Jesus, however, he explicitly and consistently refuses to respond to them on their own violent terms. Jesus refuses to take the military option; he refuses to combat violent domination with more violent domination. Jesus intentionally chooses the way of nonviolence, for God's reign in the world—God's purpose of Shalom—cannot be fulfilled through violent means. Moreover, Jesus' refusal to take the violent option, which leads to his crucifixion, represents his most profound challenge to the powers of the world and his most crucial witness to and embodiment of God's reign.

As I noted earlier, Jesus' refusal to take the way of violence and domination begins in his temptation in the wilderness. The devil offers Jesus all the kingdoms of the world if he will simply take up the methods and means of the Domination System. Jesus refuses. Later, Satan appears again, in Caesarea Philippi, in the unlikely figure of Peter at precisely the moment that Jesus first predicts his coming passion (Mark 8:31–33). The idea of a crucified messiah is so wrenching, so out of character with the victorious military messiah expected by the people, that Peter rebukes Jesus for announcing that he will be killed by the powers that be. Jesus, however, rebukes Peter, saying, "Get behind me, Satan!" The temptation to take up the military option has raised its head through Peter, who is himself so captive to the Domination System that he can actually be called Satan. The spirit of the Domination System casts its net so widely and so thoroughly that even a disciple of Jesus cannot imagine an alternative to the way of domination and violence. Here, too, however, as in the wilderness, Jesus resists the temptation and takes another path.

---

37. On the powers and "mob spirit," see Wink, *Engaging the Powers*, 9.

The passion narrative itself traces Jesus' rejection of the way of violence and his challenge to the principalities and powers. At the beginning of the passion narrative, for example, Jesus triumphantly enters Jerusalem riding humbly on a donkey. In this carefully orchestrated piece of "street theater," Jesus enacts a parody of the world's understanding of power and domination, as well as a challenge to the religious community's expectations about the messiah.[38] He begins at the Mount of Olives, the traditional location from which people expected the final battle for Jerusalem's liberation would begin. From this traditional location, Jesus begins his "final campaign." When he sends out for provisions, however, things begin to get rather strange. The provisions he seeks are not the weapons of war but a donkey and a colt. Jesus goes to take possession of Jerusalem unarmed and on a donkey.

When Jesus does finally enter the city, he enjoys all the trappings of a great military procession for a triumphant national hero. The people get caught up in the event and do all the things a victorious military leader would expect. They spread palm leaves and cloaks before Jesus as a symbol of honor and acclaim. They shout, "Hosanna! Blessed is the one who comes in the name of the Lord." "God saves." "Long live the king!" And Jesus rides through the midst of the adoring crowds.

The whole time, however, he is turning the world's notions of power and rule and authority on their heads. His theater is a wonderful piece of political satire. In his "triumphal entry," Jesus lampoons all the powers of the world and their pretensions to glory and dominion, and he enacts an alternative to the way of the Domination System. He comes not as one who lords his authority over others but as one who rejects domination and comes as a servant. He comes not with pomp and wealth but as one identified with the poor. He comes not as a mighty warrior but as one who refuses to rely on violence. Jesus enacts the subversive, nonviolent reign of God in the midst of the city.

In the rest of the passion narrative Jesus continues on this same path. In the course of the story, Jesus explicitly and repeatedly rejects the military option; he rejects the use of violence to further God's purposes in the world. At the time of his arrest, a logical time to "fight back," Jesus rejects this option. In the Gospel of Matthew, for example, when one of the disciples takes a sword and cuts off the ear of the high priest's slave, Jesus rebukes him, saying, "Put your sword back into its place; for all who take the sword will perish by the sword." And it is not that Jesus could not have chosen the violent option; in the very next sentence he goes on to say, "Do you think that I cannot appeal to my Father, and he will at once send me more than twelve legions of angels? But

---

38. The image of "street theater" is taken from Myers, *Binding the Strong Man*, 294.

how then would the scriptures be fulfilled, which say it must happen in this way?" (Matt. 26:51–56). Jesus intentionally chooses the way of nonviolence, for the purposes of God cannot be fulfilled through violent means.

At his trial, Jesus also restates his refusal to resort to violent means in pursuit of God's ends. In the Gospel of John, responding to Pilate's inquiry as to whether he is the king of the Jews, Jesus replies, "My kingdom is not from this world. If my kingdom were from this world, my followers would be fighting to keep me from being handed over to the Jews. But as it is, my kingdom is not from here" (John 18:36). Jesus is not affirming an unearthly, "spiritual" kingdom off in heaven somewhere. Rather, Jesus announces a kingdom that is "in the world, but not of it." He announces that his reign does not rest on the violence on which the powers of the world depend. In fact, this distinction between violence and nonviolence is the central distinction between the "kingdoms of this world" and the reign that Jesus inaugurates.

Finally, the cross itself becomes a subversion of the world's understandings of power and dominion. Jesus' crown is a crown of thorns. His robe is one of mockery. His throne is a cross. And, in the most profound irony in the Gospels, the sign above his head on the cross reads "King of the Jews." The victim is enthroned. The victim of the world's injustice is ironically the ruler. The victim of the powers' quest for survival and domination at all costs is in fact the true monarch. The violence of the powers is thoroughly subverted as God identifies not with those who inflict the violence but with the one who is its victim. No longer can such scapegoating, unjust violence claim the sanction of God in the world.[39]

Moreover, hanging from his "throne," Jesus speaks words that embody his ultimate and most complete resistance to the Domination System: "Father, forgive them; for they do not know what they are doing" (Luke 23:34). Through these words, Jesus resists the *spirit* of domination at the deepest level. Even nonviolent resistance can participate in domination if it seeks a victory *over* others, but it is just such a victory over other persons that Jesus here rejects. His battle is not against persons but against the powers of the world that hold people captive and cause them to be complicit in domination, often when they do not recognize what they are doing. Jesus' battle, in the words of Ephesians 6:12, is not against "enemies of blood and flesh, but against the principalities and powers." So, on the cross, in his climactic moment of nonviolent resistance, Jesus seeks forgiveness for and reconciliation with the very enemies who participate in his

---

39. René Girard argues that the gospel story presents a challenge to sacrifice and the scapegoat mechanism by espousing the perspective of the victim rather than that of the persecutors. For a concise statement of Girard's argument, see René Girard, "Mimesis and Violence," in *The Girard Reader*, 9–19.

crucifixion. He refuses to use even nonviolent resistance as a way to oppose or dominate other people. The purpose of his resistance is to set people free from their captivity to and complicity with the powers; his goal is a community of people reconciled to each other and living in freedom from the powers. In his words from the cross, Jesus reminds us that even nonviolent resistance is not immune to the spirit of domination, and he rejects any form of resistance that seeks to dominate other people. On the cross, Jesus resists not simply the political and institutional manifestations of domination but also the *spirit* of domination that lives within us and represents our most profound captivity to the powers.[40]

In a passage that at first glance seems to contradict the spirit of what I have just written, the author of Colossians proclaims that in his crucifixion Jesus has overcome the powers. In Colossians 2:15 we read that Jesus "disarmed the principalities and powers and made a public example of them, triumphing over them."[41] The image is, ironically, one of a triumphant military procession, in which the victorious army leads the vanquished army through the streets. The enemy has been "disarmed," and they are now presented as a public example, showing forth their defeat. Turning this imagery of military domination on its head, however, the author affirms that this victory occurs *on the cross*. In his *crucifixion*, where he refuses to take the military option, Jesus overcomes the powers of death with the way of life.

Jesus' crucifixion exposes the lies and pretensions of the powers. He reveals them to be not divine regents of the world (despite their idolatrous claims) and not the agents of life in the world but rather opponents of God's way and purveyors of death. On the cross we see the principalities and powers graphically and publicly "paraded" before us as the powers of death. And once they are publicly exposed in this way, the powers are effectively "disarmed"; they can no longer delude us because the "mirrors" by which they have maintained their reign have been removed. They can no longer fool us with their promises and claims, for we have seen them for what they are. They have become emperors without any clothes. And we begin to be set free from their clutches and their power. On the cross Jesus has *already* overcome the powers and freed

---

40. For an insightful discussion of the ways in which even nonviolent resistance can seek domination, see Jim Douglass, "Civil Disobedience as Prayer," in *Peace Is the Way: Writings on Nonviolence from the Fellowship of Reconciliation*, ed. Walter Wink (Maryknoll, N.Y.: Orbis Books, 2000), 149–52.

41. Jesus does ultimately overcome the powers, but this "triumph," as Walter Wink notes, is one not of domination but of transformation. Jesus' nonviolent overcoming of the powers ultimately restores them to their original vocation (Walter Wink, *Naming the Powers: The Language of Power in the New Testament* [Philadelphia: Fortress Press, 1984], 50–55). In addition, this overcoming of the powers must be distinguished from any domination of other human beings, as was noted in the previous paragraph.

humanity from our enslavement to the Domination System and our captivity to the path of violence and domination.

Martin Luther King Jr.'s nonviolent campaigns provide a helpful illustration of what the author of Colossians affirms. When the white powers that be turned the hoses and dogs on the marchers—and the images were splashed across television—the reality of white racism was graphically and publicly "paraded" in front of all Americans. And King, deeply immersed in the gospel of Jesus Christ, knew exactly what he was doing: "Let them get their dogs," he shouted, "and let them get the hose, and we will leave them standing before their God and the world spattered with the blood and reeking with the stench of their Negro brothers." It is necessary, he continued, "to bring these issues to the surface, to bring them out into the open where everybody can see them."[42] And King was to some degree successful. Once exposed, racism began to lose some of its power over many people.

This is what happens on the cross. Jesus exposes the powers, and by exposing them, as we read in Colossians, he "disarms" them and frees us from their grip. As Gil Bailie has written, "The crucifixion both 'accomplishes' the decisive demystification of the demonic powers and inaugurates the historical epoch in which these powers—and the social and psychological structures based upon them—will undergo a progressive delegitimization, as the Crucified One gradually draws all humanity to himself."[43]

Jesus' crucifixion, then, is an act of nonviolent resistance to the principalities and powers of the world, an act of resistance in which Jesus stands in solidarity with all those who are victims of the powers. The way of the cross is the way of treason against the principalities and powers, in which Jesus challenges not only the idolatrous claims of the powers but also their reliance on violence to ensure their own survival and domination.[44] And when Jesus tells

---

42. Richard Lischer, *The Preacher King: Martin Luther King, Jr. and the Word That Moved America* (New York: Oxford University Press, 1995), 157. See also Wink, *Unmasking the Powers*, 64–68; Stringfellow, *Ethic for Christians*, 150–51. Wink and Stringfellow speak of such actions as public, "collective" exorcisms. In this sense, Jesus' crucifixion is a form of public exorcism.

43. Gil Bailie, *Violence Unveiled: Humanity at the Crossroads* (New York: Crossroad, 1995), 226. Bailie is commenting on John 12:31–32: "Now is the judgment of this world; now the ruler of this world will be driven out. And I, when I am lifted up from the earth, I will draw all people to myself." While I would take issue with Bailie's emphasis on gradual progress, his insight into the demystification of the powers is important. On the tension between progress and apocalyptic faith, see Ched Myers, *Who Will Roll the Stone?* 389–402.

44. Crucifixion was the punishment for treason. And Jesus first informs the disciples of his forthcoming passion immediately after they confess him to be the Messiah—a confession that itself is an act of treason against the empire. Publicly to confess Jesus as Messiah in the context of empire is, in fact, to take up the way of the cross.

his disciples to "take up your cross and follow me," he is calling the church to this way of nonviolent resistance. He is calling us not simply to bear the burdens of life or to practice ascetic self-denial but to take up the way of resistance to the Domination System. He is calling us not passively to accept violence or abuse but actively to resist the powers of domination without resorting to their violent means.[45] Jesus is calling us not to suffer for the sake of suffering but to bear the suffering that may come when we stand in solidarity with the victims of the powers and engage in nonviolent resistance against their oppression. By exposing the powers on the cross, Jesus takes the first step toward setting us free for this kind of discipleship.

RESURRECTION AND THE POWERS

Jesus overcomes the powers not only on the cross but also in his resurrection, as we read in Ephesians 1:20–23: "God put this power to work in Christ when he raised him from the dead and seated him at his right hand in the heavenly places, far above all rule and authority and power and dominion, and above every name that is named, not only in this age but also in the age to come." Here again, as in Colossians 1:15, Jesus has *already* overcome the powers. In this text, however, Jesus' victory comes not at the point of his crucifixion but at the point of his resurrection and ascension. When he is raised from the dead, Jesus overcomes the powers of death and is placed "far above" them. And he

---

45. Jesus' call to "take up your cross" is not, for example, a call for women to return to abusive situations and "bear" their abuse in the name of Jesus. Such an interpretation is a demonic distortion of the text—and a stark reminder that even Christian theology may be corrupted by the Domination System. The cross involves active resistance, though without resorting to violence. The way of the cross calls women in abusive situations to *resist* that abuse by publicly exposing the perpetrator of the abuse and taking the steps necessary to get free of such a relationship governed by the powers of death. On the use of the cross and doctrines of the atonement to perpetuate violence against women and other oppressed groups, see Joanne Carlson Brown and Rebecca Parker, "For God So Loved the World?" in *Christianity, Patriarchy, and Abuse: A Feminist Critique*, ed. Joanne Carlson Brown and Carole R. Bohn (New York: Pilgrim Press, 1989), 1–30; Nancy J. Duff, "Atonement and the Christian Life: Reformed Doctrine from a Feminist Perspective," *Interpretation* 53 (January 1999): 21–33; and Bond, *Trouble with Jesus*. While my approach does not address all the issues raised in these articles, I do hope to challenge uses of the cross that perpetuate abusive relationships. For an important examination of preaching in relation to domestic violence, see John S. McClure and Nancy J. Ramsay, eds., *Telling the Truth: Preaching about Sexual and Domestic Violence* (Cleveland: United Church Press, 1998).

overcomes the powers not by means of domination and death but by the power of new life.

Whereas the crucifixion exposes the lies and pretensions of the powers, the resurrection deals with their ultimate sanction and threat: death. The power of death has been overcome; death has lost its "sting" (1 Cor. 15:54–57). Whereas the crucifixion frees us from our illusions about the powers and their claims, the resurrection frees us from the fear of death. Not only can the powers no longer deceive us into thinking their way is the way of life; they also no longer can threaten us with their ultimate sanction, death. The resurrection not only confirms the way of the cross as the way of God but also sets the church free from the fear of death that so often prevents us from "taking up our cross" and following Jesus. In his crucifixion and resurrection, then, Jesus has *already* overcome the powers and set the church free from captivity to them. He has inaugurated the new creation in which Christians can begin to live even now.[46]

As a simple look around the world reveals, however, that is not the entire story. Although ultimately overcome in the cross and resurrection, the powers continue to go about their deadly work in the world, often with the intensity and violence of an injured beast. On the surface, the cross and resurrection seem to have changed very little; the new creation seems as far away as ever. If anything, the rage of the powers seems to have been intensified by Jesus' work, as the book of Revelation captures so well:

> Then I heard a loud voice in heaven, proclaiming,
> "Now have come the salvation and the power
>   and the kingdom of our God
>   and the authority of his Messiah,
> for the accuser of our comrades has been thrown down,
>   who accuses them day and night before our God.
> But they have conquered him by the blood of the Lamb
>   and by the word of their testimony,
> for they did not cling to life even in the face of death.
> Rejoice, then, you heavens
>   and those who dwell in them!
> But woe to the earth and the sea,
>   for the devil has come down to you
> with great wrath,
>   because he knows that his time is short!"
>
> (Rev. 12:10–12)

---

46. The Gospel of John highlights Jesus' inauguration of the "new creation." The book opens with the words of Genesis 1—the story of the first creation. At the point of Jesus' resurrection, the Gospel turns to imagery from Genesis 2 (a man and a woman in a garden) to signal the inbreaking of the new creation (John 20:11–18).

While the Domination System's spiritual power over believers has been broken in Jesus' death and resurrection,[47] the principalities and powers continue their deadly work. People continue to suffer at the hands of the powers, to do the bidding of the powers, and to live in captivity to their claims and promises and threats. Discipleship continues to be cruciform rather than triumphant. Even the church, set free from the powers in Jesus Christ, often chooses to live in the tomb of death, despite the fact that the stone has already been rolled away. In fact, as I noted in chapter 1, the horrors of the twentieth century have turned the church's attention back to the New Testament understanding of the principalities and powers. As theologians and biblical scholars put it, there is a stark "not yet," as well as an "already," to the new creation inaugurated by Jesus' life, death, and resurrection.

This "not yet" is evident in 1 Corinthians 15:24–28. In this text it is only at "the end"—the final fulfillment of God's purposes—that Jesus ultimately overcomes the powers: "Then comes the end, when he hands over the kingdom to God the Father, after he has destroyed every ruler and every authority and power" (v. 24).[48] Only when God's purposes have been brought to fulfillment will the deathly ways of the powers finally be overcome. Not surprisingly, as Paul notes, the last of these powers to be dealt with is death—the driving force and ultimate reality and sanction behind all of the powers' work (1 Cor. 15:26). As Paul recognizes, the struggle against the powers continues despite their having been overcome through the cross and resurrection. Christians live in the tension between this "already" and "not yet." That is, Christians live in the tension between two coexisting "worlds"—the new creation inaugurated by Jesus and the Domination System perpetuated by the powers. Christian discipleship, as Stringfellow puts it, is pursued in the conflict between the new Jerusalem and Babylon;[49] each moment Christians are called to take up the cross and practice the "social reversal" of the new creation.[50]

Christians, however, live in this tension and engage in this practice clinging to a promise: the powers will finally be redeemed. As beings created in,

---

47. This is the significance of the devil being cast out of heaven in Revelation 12. The spiritual ("heavenly") power of the devil (the spirit of the Domination System) over believers has been broken. Thus they are not afraid of death and give their testimony. Significantly, it is the blood of the Lamb *and* this testimony of believers that defeat the devil in Revelation 12.

48. As Wink notes, the "destruction" of the powers in this text involves not domination and violence but rather the transformation of the powers back to the vocation for which they were created. See Wink, *Naming the Powers*, 50–55.

49. See Stringfellow, *Ethic for Christians*, 25–64.

50. Myers, *Who Will Roll the Stone?* 401.

through, and for Christ, the powers will ultimately be transformed and brought back to their true vocation of sustaining human life in community. While there is no sense that human beings will ourselves transform or "Christianize" the powers, we do live with the promise and in the hope that God is at work to transform the powers and that God will fulfill that work through Jesus Christ. Clinging to this promise in the face of the powers of death, the church, and particularly the church's preaching, takes up the way of resistance.

4

An Ethic of Preaching:
Nonviolent Resistance

When most pastors consider the participants involved in preaching, the principalities and powers rarely receive serious attention, despite the enormous role they play in human life. Rather, three other participants usually shape the discussion: the preacher, the congregation, and God. While all three have been affirmed throughout the history of preaching, their roles in preaching have been conceived differently at different times. In some eras, as in the latter half of the nineteenth century, the preacher comes into prominence. The authority of the preacher takes center stage in one way or another, whether that authority comes from the office or the charisma of the person in the pulpit. At other times, such as during the neo-orthodox revolt against nineteenth-century liberalism, God—or the Word of God—becomes central in the preaching event. The preacher "steps aside" so the Word can do its work. Even the congregation receives slight attention because the preacher is not concerned about results or effectiveness. More recently, in reaction to both the neo-orthodox emphasis on the Word and the earlier dominance of the preacher's authority, homiletics has placed more emphasis on the congregation. "Congregation-centered preaching" has become a distinctive characteristic of much contemporary homiletical thought.[1]

Despite these varying emphases and configurations, the three major participants remain the same: preacher, congregation, and God. The significance of the principalities and powers for the practice of preaching goes largely

---

1. Beverly Zink-Sawyer, "'The Word Purely Preached and Heard': The Listeners and the Homiletical Endeavor," *Interpretation* 51 (October 1997): 342–57.

unnoticed.[2] Although often ignored, however, these powers shape human life in profound ways and deserve serious attention as the primary ethical context of Christian preaching. While this fact is not often considered today, it was recognized in earlier times. The activity of the powers, for example, significantly informs the understanding of preaching in the letter to the Ephesians. In the letter we read that "our struggle is not against enemies of blood and flesh, but against the principalities, against the powers, against the cosmic powers of this present darkness, against the spiritual forces of evil in the heavenly places" (Eph. 6:12). And in response to these realities, the writer of Ephesians proclaims, the church takes up one offensive weapon: "the sword of the Spirit, which is the word of God" (6:17). Preaching, in this view, involves a cosmic battle against the principalities and powers, which are actively at work in the preaching occasion.

Similarly, Martin Luther, the great reformer, emphasized the central role—indeed, the dangerous role—the principalities and powers play in preaching, as he noted in his commentary on Isaiah 40:6:

> How difficult an occupation preaching is. Indeed, to preach the Word of God is nothing less than to bring upon oneself all the furies of hell and of Satan, and therefore also of . . . every power of this world. It is the most dangerous kind of life to throw oneself in the way of Satan's many teeth.[3]

Few mainline preachers would describe the vocation of preaching in these dramatic terms. On one level, Luther's terminology seems antiquated; sophisticated contemporary preachers, shaped by the presuppositions of science and modernity, don't speak often about Satan—much less about Satan's many teeth. At a deeper level, however, Luther simply understands preaching as something more dramatic than the sermons we hear in many churches today. Preaching, for Luther as for Paul, involves an encounter between the principalities and powers and the "sword of the Spirit."

---

2. Several authors have taken seriously the role of the "principalities and powers" in preaching, though not in the detail in which I am doing. See, for example, David G. Buttrick, *Preaching Jesus Christ: An Exercise in Homiletic Theology* (Philadelphia: Fortress Press, 1988) and *The Mystery and the Passion: A Homiletic Reading of the Gospel Traditions* (Minneapolis: Fortress Press, 1992); L. Susan Bond, *Trouble with Jesus: Women, Christology, and Preaching* (St. Louis: Chalice Press, 1999). Christine Smith, though not drawing as directly on the language of "principalities and powers," has explored similar issues in her book *Preaching as Weeping, Confession, and Resistance: Radical Responses to Radical Evil* (Louisville, Ky.: Westminster/John Knox Press, 1992).
3. *WA*, 25, 253. Thanks to Justo Gonzalez and Judi Holley for translating the Latin. See also Heiko Oberman, "The Preaching of the Word in the Reformation," *Harvard Divinity Bulletin* 25 (October 1960): 9.

William Stringfellow lamented the loss of this encounter between the powers and the Word in the church in the United States. The "monstrous" ethical heresy in America, he wrote, lies in "thinking that the whole drama of history takes place between God and [human beings]. But the truth, Biblically and theologically and empirically, is quite otherwise: the drama of this history takes place among God and [human beings] and the principalities and powers."[4]

A similar lament could be raised in relation to preaching. With Stringfellow, I would argue that the monstrous *homiletical* heresy of recent years is the assumption that the whole drama of the gospel takes place between God and human beings.[5] The aggressiveness of the powers and the moral captivity of people have received inadequate attention. As a result, preaching becomes ethically naive and simplistic, unable to address the countless powerful forces that shape and destroy human life in the world. In the following chapters, I explore the homiletical implications that emerge when the activity of these powers becomes the primary ethical context in which preaching takes place. In this context, as I argue in this chapter, preaching itself becomes a practice with extraordinary ethical implications.

PREACHING AS A FUNDAMENTAL ETHICAL OPTION

What is the ethical significance of preaching in the face of the principalities and powers? That is the question for this chapter, and I pose it in a specific way. My concern at this point is not the *what* of preaching—what we speak, the message we proclaim—but the *that* of preaching—the basic fact that Jesus chose to preach and that the church has continued this practice through the ages. So the question becomes: Is a particular ethic inherent in the very practice of preaching itself?

This way of understanding the ethical implications of preaching is a reversal of the more traditional way in which I have previously explored the relationship between preaching and ethics. In the past I examined the implications of various approaches to ethics—particularly character ethics—for preaching.[6]

---

4. Quoted in Bill Wylie-Kellermann, "Listen to This Man! A Parable before the Powers," *Theology Today* 53 (October 1996): 304.

5. For a discussion of the individualistic character of much contemporary homiletical theory, see Charles L. Campbell, *Preaching Jesus: New Directions for Homiletics in Hans Frei's Postliberal Theology* (Grand Rapids: Wm. B. Eerdmans Publishing Co., 1997), 117–45.

6. See, for example, my articles, "Living Faith: Luther, Preaching, and Ethics," *Word and World* 10 (Fall 1990): 374–79 and "More than Quandaries: Character Ethics and Preaching," *Journal for Preachers* 16 (Pentecost 1993): 31–37. In the next chapter I take up this matter and argue that character ethics is in fact the best way to understand the ethical function of preaching amid the principalities and powers.

The driving question was "How does theological ethics inform the theory and practice of preaching?" And that's a valuable and important question; we can learn a lot about both ethics and preaching by pursuing it.

In this chapter, however, I am reversing the question and am exploring the significance of the practice of preaching for the church's ethic. Rather than ask how ethics informs preaching, I ask how the practice of preaching informs the church's ethical reflection and moral life. To put it another way, I am seeking an "ethic of preaching," understanding the genitive in this phrase as subjective. That is, in the "ethic of preaching" I develop, preaching is the subject and ethics is the object, not the other way around. The question is "Does the practice of preaching itself embody a particular ethic?"

This question has enormous implications, particularly for those in the Reformed tradition. This tradition affirms that the preaching and hearing of the Word represents one of the "marks" of the church—one of the practices that constitute the church as church. Where the preaching of the Word is absent, there is no church. The question I am posing in this chapter suggests a corollary to this affirmation: if there is an ethic inherent in the practice of preaching, then that ethic would also be a "mark" that constitutes the church as the church. Put in the form of a loose syllogism, the argument looks like this:

> If the practice of preaching is a "mark" that constitutes the church as church,
> And if there is a specific ethic inherent in the practice of preaching,
> Then that ethic inherent in preaching would also be a "mark" that constitutes the church as the community of faith.

If this logic is not flawed, then my question is an important one, particularly since my conclusions cut against the grain of much of Reformed ethics.

Is there an ethic inherent in the practice of preaching? Ephesians 2:17 provides a good starting point for addressing this question: "He came and preached peace to you who were far off and peace to those who were near." Commenting on this text in his book *He Came Preaching Peace*, John Howard Yoder writes, "What this biblical text originally meant was not that Jesus was a preacher in any ordinary sense of the word. It does not refer to his verbal ministry. Rather, it says that his life and death incarnated a message—that his total being in the world heralded the new state of things which it describes as 'peace.'"[7]

Yoder's statement is fine as far as it goes. Jesus did embody through his "total being in the world" a new state of things described as "peace"—

---

7. John H. Yoder, *He Came Preaching Peace* (Scottdale, Pa.: Herald Press, 1985), 11.

Shalom.[8] However, Yoder makes a critical mistake in drawing such a sharp distinction between Jesus' "verbal ministry" and his incarnation of a message in his life and death. Jesus' verbal ministry was in fact one of the primary ways in which Jesus incarnated his message. Jesus' preaching of the gospel cannot be isolated from the gospel itself; the act of proclamation was part and parcel of the gospel that Jesus enacted in the world. Indeed, Jesus' preaching was at the very heart of his "total being in the world," which heralded that new state of Shalom.

Yoder ignores the extraordinary implications of the affirmation in Ephesians: "Jesus came *preaching* peace." That sentence is not just a statement about the message Jesus proclaimed: the good news of God's domination-free order. That statement also refers to the *means* Jesus chose to embody and further that peaceable reign. Jesus did not choose the means of the Domination System. He did not choose coercion. He did not choose weapons or war—though some apparently hoped he would. He did not choose the way of domination—though, as I noted in the previous chapter, he was tempted with this option out in the wilderness. In short, he did not choose violence. From the temptation to the cross, the only sword Jesus wielded was "the sword of the Spirit, which is the word of God."

This choice represents a clear alternative to violent domination and coercion. This Word represents God's way of working in the world, as is manifest initially in the creation story. In Genesis 1, God creates through the word; God speaks the world into being. For Christians this affirmation has become a rather commonplace confession. However, such an understanding of creation represents a direct challenge to the violent myths of creation that shaped the cultural ethos in which Genesis was produced. In the Babylonian creation myth, the *Enuma Elish*, for example, creation is an act of violence. The god Marduk murders and dismembers Tiamat, the mother of the gods, who represents chaos, and forms the world from her corpse.[9] As Wink writes about the myth, "Order is established by means of disorder. Creation is a violent victory over an enemy older than creation. The origin of evil precedes the origin of things. Chaos

---

8. Shalom involves both peace and justice. It is the "positive peace" that Martin Luther King Jr. sought: "True peace is not merely the absence of some negative force—tension, confusion, or war; it is the presence of some positive force—justice, good will, and brotherhood" (Martin Luther King Jr., "Facing the Challenge of a New Age," in *Peace Is the Way: Writings on Nonviolence from the Fellowship of Reconciliation*, ed. Walter Wink [Maryknoll, N.Y.: Orbis Books, 2000], 180).
9. Walter Wink, *Engaging the Powers: Discernment and Resistance in a World of Domination* (Minneapolis: Fortress Press, 1992), 14. See James B. Pritchard, *Ancient Near Eastern Texts Relating to the Old Testament*, 3d ed. (Princeton, N.J.: Princeton University Press, 1969), 60–72.

(symbolized by Tiamat) is prior to order (represented by Marduk, god of Babylon). Evil is prior to good. Violence inheres in the godhead."[10]

In contrast, in the biblical story a good God creates a good creation not through violent means but through the Word. Neither evil nor violence is inherent in God or the creation (including human beings, created in God's image), but both enter the world through human sin.[11] From the very beginning, the Word of God is set over against violent domination. And just as God began the first creation through the Word, so, through Jesus, God inaugurates the new creation through the Word. The Gospel of John makes this connection clear, highlighting the inseparable connection between Jesus' person and his preaching: "In the beginning was the Word. . . . And the Word became flesh and lived among us" (John 1:1, 14). Just as the creation story in Genesis represents a nonviolent alternative to the Babylonian myth of creation, so Jesus enacts a nonviolent alternative to the principalities and powers, which perpetuate the myth of redemptive violence.

As Jacques Ellul has argued extensively, the very character of the Word as "word" represents an alternative to the means and implements of violence. The Word allows humans the freedom of decision, choice, and expression. The Word requires mutuality, the participation of the one speaking and listening; it refuses to make the "other"—the hearer—into an object or a commodity, which is characteristic of the powers of technology and capitalism. Rather, in always inviting response, the Word makes persons conscious of their opportunity to become subjects rather than objects.[12]

The Word does not coerce or control its outcome. It is thus a very fragile agent for pursuing truth in the world; it "evaporates as soon as it has been said," and the speaker cannot control the results.[13] God nevertheless works through the Word, and not through absolute constraints; and Jesus, as the incarnation of the Word, embodies this way not merely in his life but most specifically in his choice of preaching as the means to the reign of God.[14] Indeed, in the ambiguity surrounding his person and the ultimate rejection of

---

10. Wink, *Engaging the Powers*, 14.
11. Ibid. For a helpful discussion of violence in the Old Testament, written by a feminist scholar, see Johanna W. H. van Wijk-Bos, "Violence and the Bible," in *Telling the Truth: Preaching about Sexual and Domestic Violence*, ed. John S. McClure and Nancy J. Ramsay (Cleveland: United Church Press, 1998), 21–33. For another perspective, see Gil Bailie, *Violence Unveiled: Humanity at the Crossroads* (New York: Crossroad, 1995), 133–84. Bailie argues that the Old Testament is a "text in travail" in which the violence is almost always qualified and undermined by a counterword in the texts.
12. Jacques Ellul, *The Humiliation of the Word*, trans. Joyce Main Hanks (Grand Rapids: Wm. B. Eerdmans Publishing Co., 1985), 63–67, 38, 45.
13. Ibid., 40–41.
14. Ibid., 68.

his way, Jesus embodies the fragility of the Word as God's way in the world. Jesus' choice of preaching is thus consistent with his life and represents a profound challenge to the powers of violent domination, as well as to the particular form those powers take in a capitalistic, technological society.

Not only does Jesus' choice of preaching represent an alternative to violence; his *rejection of silence* does as well. Silence can be a form of violence (and domination and control), as Jane Tompkins has noted in her book on the genre of the Western, *West of Everything*.[15] According to Tompkins, Western novels and movies shed light on our contemporary culture of violence. More important, she argues, this genre presents silence and violence as direct alternatives to speech. As a conscious rejection of popular women's literature of the nineteenth century, the Western presented an alternative to the *wordiness* of nineteenth-century feminine culture; it offered an alternative to "organized religion and the whole women's culture of the nineteenth century and all the *sermons* and novels that went with them."[16] Male silence in the Western represents a rejection of women, who rely on *language*. In the genre, language is understood as ineffectual and is linked with a negative view of peace and cooperation as a way of solving conflicts.[17] The alternative to language, the companion of silence, is the gun. Tompkins summarizes this connection between silence and violence in her comments on Owen Wister's *The Virginian*:

> The temperance ladies talk and talk; that is *all* they do. It never comes to shooting. Meanwhile, they drive their husbands crazy with their cackle. Drive them to drink, which dulls the feelings men can't talk about. So the Virginian and Trampas (the enemy he passes on the road) hardly exchange a word. They cannot communicate; therefore, they will kill each other someday. Their silence signals their seriousness, their dignity and reality, and the inevitability of their conflict. Silence is a sign of mastery, and goes along with a gun in the hand. They would rather die than settle the argument by talking to each other.[18]

In light of Tompkins's insight, maybe we should not be surprised when a mass murder occurs and people comment about the murderer, "I don't know, he lived alone, kept to himself, and never talked to anybody."[19] In the Domi-

---

15. Jane Tompkins, *West of Everything: The Inner Life of Westerns* (New York: Oxford University Press, 1992).
16. Ibid., 66; italics mine.
17. Ibid., 54.
18. Ibid., 63–64.
19. Walter Brueggemann, "Preaching a Sub-Version," *Theology Today* 55 (July 1998): 202.

nation System, silence and violence often go together. And through his choice of preaching, Jesus rejects both.

From a different angle, Walter Brueggemann has also noted the connection between silence and violence.[20] Arguing that violence is the fundamental cultural narrative of our time, Brueggemann cites silence as one of the taproots of violence.[21] The Domination System pursues its way of death by silencing its victims and opponents, for silence is one of the ways in which the deathly status quo gets authenticated. As the gay and lesbian community has rightly acknowledged, "Silence is death." When people are silenced by the System, when they feel their voices will not be heard and do not matter, they not only are the victims of violence but also often become the breeding ground of further violence, as their pent-up oppression goes unexpressed and finally explodes.[22]

As an alternative to such silence, Brueggemann offers "speech that breaks the silence of violence and the violence of silence."[23] Truthful speech offers an alternative to the violence of oppressive systems that silence their victims and to the violent forms of resistance that discern no other options. Truthful speech becomes the means of nonviolent resistance to the Domination System. Jesus' preaching thus provides an alternative to silence—and to the violence that silence often endures and creates.

Jesus came *preaching* peace. The ethical significance of this affirmation cannot be overstated when it is understood in the context of the principalities and powers. For Jesus, preaching offered a distinct alternative to the means employed by the powers, the means of violent domination. Preaching, in contrast to the way of the Domination System, was the *means* that was ethically consistent with the *end* of God's Shalom. The very act of preaching—the choice of preaching as a means—represented a rejection of and alternative to the "myth of redemptive violence." Preaching itself was a practice of nonviolent resistance to the values and means of the Domination System.

Jesus came *preaching* peace. Other approaches would have been inconsistent with the Shalom of God that Jesus sought to embody and further in the world. Those means would have been at odds with the end for which he was working—the beloved community. We simply cannot get to God's domination-free

---

20. Ibid., 202–4. See also Walter Brueggemann, "Voice as Counter to Violence," *Calvin Theological Journal* 36 (2001): 22–33.

21. Brueggemann, "Preaching a Sub-Version," 203.

22. See the discussion of the Gerasene demoniac in chapter 3. Such pent-up oppression can lead to violence, including the violence of scapegoating. See James C. Scott, *Domination and the Arts of Resistance: Hidden Transcripts* (New Haven, Conn.: Yale University Press, 1990), 202–27.

23. Brueggemann, "Preaching a Sub-Version," 203.

order—a community of mutuality, justice, and peace—by means of violence and domination. We cannot "seek first the reign of God" through violent means. We cannot get to the "new state of peace" by becoming the evil we oppose.

As a number of people have noted, for example, in some ways Hitler won World War II because, in trying to defeat him, the United States took up his methods and became like him. The United States, after all, firebombed German cities and ultimately used the atomic bomb on Hiroshima and Nagasaki, becoming what it proclaimed it hated. And the nation has continued down that violent path ever since, leading the way in the arms race at virtually every stage.[24] In contrast, Jesus' preaching—his refusal to resort to coercion and violence—was itself an embodiment of the "new state of peace." Preaching was the means that was ethically consistent with the end of God's Shalom.

In fact, in the person of Jesus the distinction between means and ends no longer really holds. In the person of Jesus, means and ends are collapsed. Jesus not only works toward the end of God's new order; he embodies that order, making it a present reality. In him God's reign draws near to us. As Jacques Ellul puts it,

> For Christians there is no dissociation between the end and the means. . . . The point from which we ought to start is that in the work of God the end and the means are identical. Thus when Jesus Christ is present the Kingdom has "come upon" us. This formula expresses very precisely the relation between the end and the means. Jesus Christ in his Incarnation appears as God's means, for the salvation of [humanity] and for the establishment of the Kingdom of God, but where Jesus Christ is, there also is this salvation and this kingdom. . . . In the action of God, the means only appears as the realized presence of the end. The end, this Kingdom, which will "come" at the end of time, is already present when the divine means (the only, unique, Mediator) is present.[25]

Within this understanding of the relationship between means and ends, Jesus' choice of preaching as a "means" becomes even more significant. Jesus' preaching is one of the key ways in which he embodies the presence of God's Shalom in the world.[26]

---

24. Wink, *Engaging the Powers*, 197–99; William Stringfellow, *An Ethic for Christians and Other Aliens in a Strange Land* (Waco, Tex.: Word Books, 1973; 3d paperback ed., 1979), 125; Jacques Ellul, *Violence: Reflections from a Christian Perspective*, trans. Cecelia Gaul Kings (New York: Seabury Press, 1969), 29.

25. Jacques Ellul, *The Presence of the Kingdom*, trans. Olive Wyon (New York: Seabury Press, 1967), 79.

26. Proponents of nonviolence, including Gandhi and Martin Luther King Jr., have consistently emphasized the importance of the *means* being consistent with the *end*. As

Jesus came *preaching* peace. In choosing this means, Jesus takes up what Wink calls a "third way," which involves neither passivity nor violence.[27] On the one hand, preaching is not the way of passivity but the way of *resistance* to the powers. The image of the "sword of the Spirit" is no accident. Through his preaching, Jesus actively challenges and engages the powers of the world. In the face of the deception of the powers that hold people captive, Jesus speaks the truth, exposing the lies of the powers and offering people an alternative to their way. Through his preaching, Jesus not only refuses complicity with the powers but also proclaims his solidarity with all who are victims of the "System." By means of his truthful speech, Jesus seeks to set people free from the powers of death. Jesus offers the power of life. So Jesus preaches, even if it creates conflict, even if it leads to the cross. The way of preaching may be opposed to violence, but it is not the way of passivity.

On the other hand, the way of Jesus is also not the way of coerced belief or violent domination. Jesus does not become the evil he opposes. He does not take the path of violence. Rather, he limits himself to the "sword of the Spirit." He respects the freedom of those who listen to him, and he affirms their role as subjects responding to the Word, rather than objects to be controlled by the Word—even if it means he is rejected and crucified. Jesus sticks to preaching, for that is the means that is ethically consistent with the peaceable reign of God he inaugurates. Through his preaching, Jesus engages in a "third way" that avoids both passivity and violence. Pursuing this third way, Jesus actively engages the powers but at the same time breaks the "spiral of violence" that dominates the world. And it is this third way that overcomes the powers, breaks their ultimate ability to enslave us, and creates a space for resistance and newness.

Moreover, this understanding of preaching as an alternative to violent domination is not limited to Jesus. The apostle Paul also understood preaching as such an alternative.[28] Paul's transformation on the Damascus road can in fact be understood as a turn from the way of violence to the way of proclamation.

On the road to Damascus, as the story is related in Acts, Saul is "still breathing threats and murder against the disciples of the Lord" (9:1), having earlier approved of the stoning of Stephen (8:1). Caught up in his religious and ethnic

---

King wrote, "Constructive ends can never give absolute moral justification to destructive means, because in the final analysis the end is preexistent in the means" (Martin Luther King Jr., "My Pilgrimage to Nonviolence," in Wink, ed., *Peace Is the Way*, 65–66).

27. On Jesus' "third way," see Wink, *Engaging the Powers*, 175–93.

28. I am indebted to Kathryn Summers Bean, one of my former students, for this insight.

superiority, Saul pursues the way of violent domination. He seeks to destroy his enemies; through violent means, he seeks to bring an end to the chaos caused by the disciples of Jesus. At this point violence, for Saul, is redemptive—the way to bring order out of chaos. On his way to Damascus, however, he encounters the living Jesus, who comes to him as the persecuted one: "Saul, Saul, why do you persecute me? . . . I am Jesus, whom you are persecuting" (9:4–5). Saul is *spoken to* by the victim of his violence. And from this point his life is transformed.

This transformation shapes Paul's ministry in three ways. First, the barriers erected by his sense of religious and ethnic superiority come tumbling down. From this time on, Paul will be a missionary to the Gentiles in the name of Jesus. Reconciliation between Jew and Gentile (as well as between other groups—slave and free, male and female—divided by the Domination System) becomes the primary thrust of his ministry. Second, Paul's "social location" changes from that of the persecutor to that of the victim of persecution. Paul immediately takes his place among the Christians whom he had been persecuting. He receives his baptism, "ordination," and sight at the hands of one of those whom he had persecuted, Ananias. From this point on, Paul pursues his ministry from the vantage point of the victims. Finally, Paul turns away from the means of violence to the means of preaching. The story that begins with Saul "breathing threats and murder" ends with Paul proclaiming the gospel. Indeed, after his baptism, "ordination," and communion, Paul's first act of ministry is preaching (9:17–20). Preaching becomes the alternative to violence for the remainder of Paul's ministry. And, not surprisingly, the focus of Paul's preaching is "Christ crucified" (1 Cor. 1:23). The word of the cross becomes the center of Paul's message because the cross is the locus of Jesus' solidarity with the victims of domination, as well as the ultimate embodiment of Jesus' nonviolent resistance to the powers of the world that create the realities of domination and subordination, victimizer and victim.

The importance of this turn from violence to preaching becomes even clearer in Paul's own account of his transformation in the first chapter of Galatians. Paul begins with an emphasis on his violent persecution of his opponents: "You have heard, no doubt, of my earlier life in Judaism. I was *violently persecuting* the church of God and was trying to destroy it" (1:13).[29] Then, after telling about the interim period he spent in Arabia and Jerusalem preparing for his ministry, Paul describes the new point at which he arrived: "Then I went into the regions of Syria and Cilicia, and I was still unknown by sight to

---

29. The Greek word translated "violently" in the NRSV (*hyperbolē*) technically means "excessive"; the NRSV nevertheless rightly captures the connotations of the text.

the churches of Judea that are in Christ; they only heard it said, 'The one who formerly was persecuting us is now proclaiming the faith he once tried to destroy'" (1:21–22). Proclamation replaces persecution. Preaching replaces the way of violent domination. Paul's transformation mirrors the role of preaching in Jesus' ministry. Preaching is consciously the way of nonviolent resistance to the principalities and powers; it is the way to set people free from their captivity to the powers of sin and death in the world. Paul therefore emphasizes the role of the Word in setting people free from those powers. "For freedom," as he writes, "Christ has set us free" (Gal. 5:1).[30] After his encounter with Jesus on the Damascus road, Paul takes up Jesus' third way.

Preaching calls us to a similar reenactment of Jesus' third way in the world. Inherent in the practice of preaching—the *that* of preaching—is an ethic that rejects the way of violent domination and calls us to an alternative ethical option: the option of nonviolent resistance. To put it in other terms, the practice of preaching involves an *ethical performance* of the story of Jesus. As Nicholas Lash has argued, some texts begin to deliver their full meaning only when they are *performed*.[31] A play delivers its meaning only when it is performed by a company of actors. A musical score delivers its meaning when it is performed by a group of musicians. According to Lash, the story of Jesus is this kind of text. The Christian interpretation of this story requires its *performance*. That is, the Christian interpretation of Scripture is similar to the interpretation of *Macbeth* by a company of actors or the interpretation of "Take Five" by the Dave Brubeck quartet.

The primary poles in the interpretation of Scripture are not finally written *texts* (for example, the biblical text at one pole and theological texts or sermonic texts at the other). Rather, the poles in biblical interpretation are *patterns of human action*: on the one hand, "what was said and done and suffered, then, by Jesus and his disciples," and on the other, "what is said and done and suffered, now, by those who seek to share his obedience and hope."[32] Within this framework, the most important interpretation of the story of Jesus takes place in the performance of that story in the life of the Christian community.

The act of preaching plays a central role in the church's interpretive performance of Scripture. In this role, preaching embodies an essential, distinctive performance of the story of Jesus. Specifically, preaching enacts a concrete ethical performance of Jesus' third way—the way of active, nonviolent resistance to and engagement with the principalities and powers of the world. The

---

30. See also Romans 6:1–11.
31. Nicholas Lash, "Performing the Scriptures," in *Theology on the Way to Emmaus* (London: SCM Press, 1986), 37–46.
32. Ibid., 42.

preaching of the church reenacts this ethical option at the heart of the story of Jesus.

Preaching is thus a significant act of moral obedience to the way of Jesus; it is an act of discipleship. Like Jesus, who nonviolently embodied the reign of God and challenged the powers of the world, the preacher is called to engage in nonviolent resistance to the powers. Not only is the preacher's message—the *what* of preaching—shaped by the story of Jesus, but the very practice of preaching itself—the *that* of preaching—is a performance of that story, an embodiment of God's reign after the pattern of Jesus.

The faithful preacher does not remain silent but witnesses boldly, announcing the coming of God's reign in Jesus Christ, exposing the deadly, idolatrous ways of the powers, and envisioning an alternative world—the new creation. Indeed, the preacher may at times seem assertive, even pushy; for Christian preaching is not a form of passivity but an active engagement with the powers. As writer and television commentator Dorothy Samuel has noted, "The love demonstrated by St. Paul and Jesus and Gandhi and Martin Luther King was a tough, firm, outspoken honesty that demanded the best from people, a love more accurately described by the Quaker injunction, 'speak truth to power,' than by the passive acquiescence of 'never make anyone unhappy.'"[33]

Such truthful preaching may even create conflict, not only with the authorities outside the church but even among those within the church, who in many instances are as much the beneficiaries as the victims of the "powers that be." Peacemaking and conflict often go together, because genuine peacemaking requires truthtelling.[34] (Consider what happened to Jesus in his first sermon at Nazareth—the congregation tried to throw him off a cliff.) Jacques Ellul's comment about preaching provides a troubling reminder of this fact: "If you see the powers of the world so well disposed, when you see the state, money, cities accepting your word, it is because your word . . . has become false. For it is only to the extent that you are a traitor that the world can put up with you."[35] Preaching, as an enactment of the story of Jesus, does not involve passivity or avoid conflict.

As disciples of Jesus, however, faithful preachers not only reject passivity but also refuse to coerce belief or resort to violent domination, even in the face

---

33. Dorothy T. Samuel, "The Violence in Ourselves," in Wink, ed., *Peace Is the Way*, 241.
34. Stanley Hauerwas, "Peacemaking: The Virtue of the Church," in *Christian Existence Today: Essays on Church, World, and Living in Between* (Durham, N.C.: Labyrinth Press, 1988), 89–97.
35. Jacques Ellul, *The Meaning of the City*, trans. Dennis Pardee (Grand Rapids: Wm. B. Eerdmans Publishing Co., 1970), 37.

of conflict, disbelief, and rejection. Faithful preachers embrace a strange kind of powerlessness, like the powerlessness of Jesus on the cross. They finally must rely on God to make effective not only individual sermons but the very practice of preaching itself. Like the Word made flesh, the preacher's words depend on God for their effectiveness. Nevertheless, precisely by embracing this powerlessness—again, like Jesus on the cross—preachers resist and challenge the way of domination, coercion, and violence.

To put it another way, preaching involves what Sharon Welch calls an ethic of risk, rather than an ethic of control.[36] As I noted in chapter 2, an ethic of control defines responsible ethical action as that which can control the future and produce "results." To be responsible means that one can ensure the aim of one's action will be carried out. Such an ethic inevitably leads to violence as a means that can ensure "results." The arms race, Welch argues, is a direct result of this ethic of control.[37] An ethic of risk, however, does not define ethical action in terms of control. Rather, ethical actions are those that make possible further resistance to the powers. An ethic of risk, Welch argues, "begins with the recognition that we cannot guarantee decisive changes in the near future or even in our lifetime. The ethic of risk is propelled by the equally vital recognition that to stop resisting, even when success is unimaginable, is to die."[38] Faithfulness is more important than effectiveness or success. And this is good news for all of us who know that preaching often does not produce immediate results. As preachers, we always live by hope.

In the practice of preaching, then, the preacher is called to enact the way of Jesus in the world—the way of risky, nonviolent engagement with the powers. In moral obedience, shaped by the pattern established by Jesus, the preaching of the church takes the path of nonviolent resistance, rather than coercion or domination, in the face of those who oppose God's reign. Apart from all words spoken, the practice of preaching itself proclaims that the church does not resort to violence in the name of truth; rather, it witnesses. At the very point at which the church seeks to speak truth, the church also enacts its refusal to coerce belief by violent means. Indeed, in the act of witnessing to Jesus, the church reminds itself that a resort to violence is a contradiction of the one whom we preach and the beloved community we seek.

Preaching is an odd activity in a world in which people seek to get their way and impose their truths through violent means. Preaching is a strange, risky,

---

36. Sharon D. Welch, *A Feminist Ethic of Risk* (Minneapolis: Fortress Press, 1990).
37. Ibid., 23–47.
38. Welch, *Ethic of Risk*, 20. Like Stringfellow, Welch notes the wide range of forms this death can take: "the threat of physical death, the death of the imagination, the death of the ability to care."

even foolish means for the church to engage the powers and further our convictions; it is a countercultural practice in a world where attempts to control and manipulate the future through violence usually rule the day. But preaching is odd because it reenacts the odd way of Jesus in the midst of a violent world.

Moreover, as a "mark" of the church, the practice of preaching constitutes the community of faith as an odd and distinctive people. More specifically, the practice of preaching constitutes the church as a nonviolent community. Because an ethic of nonviolent resistance is inherent in the practice of preaching, such nonviolent resistance should itself be considered a "mark" of the church—an essential aspect of what it means to be the church in and for the world. Or, to put it another way, when the church accommodates itself to the world's violence and domination, we are not being the church. The informal little syllogism with which I began might now read something like this:

> Because the practice of preaching constitutes the church as church,
> And because an ethic of nonviolent resistance is inherent in the practice of preaching,
> Therefore nonviolent resistance is a "mark" of the church; it is one of the practices that constitute the church as the community of faith.

Richard Hays, a New Testament scholar, has made a similar claim in his book *The Moral Vision of the New Testament*. Although he does not begin with the practice of preaching, and he does not speak of nonviolence as a mark of the church, Hays nevertheless makes clear the centrality of nonviolence for the community of faith. "The church's embodiment of nonviolence," he writes, "is—according to the Sermon on the Mount—its indispensable witness to the gospel."[39] And Hays concludes that "nonviolence is fundamental to the church's identity and reason for being"; for "only when the church renounces the way of violence will people see what the gospel means, because then they will see the way of Jesus reenacted in the church."[40] I would add that the practice of preaching itself embodies this renunciation of the way of violence and reenacts the nonviolent way of Jesus. Through this practice of preaching, the church is constituted as a community of nonviolent resistance in and for the world.

A CERTAIN AMBIGUITY

I have made some extraordinary claims for preaching as an ethical practice of nonviolent resistance. The reality, however, is complex. In fact, for a white,

---

39. Richard B. Hays, *The Moral Vision of the New Testament: A Contemporary Introduction to New Testament Ethics* (San Francisco: HarperSanFrancisco, 1996), 329.
40. Ibid., 343.

male, middle-class Presbyterian to assert that preaching is an act of nonviolent resistance creates some dangers. People who enjoy power and privilege can easily promote nonviolence to discredit revolutionaries and keep the status quo in place. Moreover, such people can often focus on the nonviolence of individual acts such as preaching or protest while ignoring the enormous violence inherent in oppressive systems that silence and kill people every day. For preaching to be an act of nonviolent resistance with any integrity, we must honestly face and name these realities.

The reality is this: while an ethic of nonviolent resistance is inherent in the practice of preaching, the church's preaching often does not fully live up to that ethic. Even while resisting direct, interpersonal, physical violence, preaching often participates in acts and systems of domination that involve harmful forms of psychological, spiritual, and even physical coercion that must be considered violent. Preachers, for example, have regularly used the pulpit, both implicitly and explicitly, for violent ends. The *what* of Christian preaching has often been anything but a form of nonviolent resistance to the principalities and powers. Christian preachers have, after all, used the pulpit to send believers off to the Crusades and to support wars of all kinds. Christian preaching has also supported slavery, racism, and the oppression of women, gays, and lesbians. And far from resisting the economic violence that comes with capitalism, Christian preaching has been a frequent supporter of the economic status quo.

At a subtler level, preachers have often used language in ways that support and sustain the Domination System. Hierarchical imagery, often with clear biblical support, has not only placed men in a dominant position over women but reinforced the culture's divisions of people into dominant and subordinate. Stories that depict women in subordinate roles or as negative examples simply reinforce the male domination of patriarchy, with the structural violence and personal abuse it brings. Similarly, when images of darkness are always bad and metaphors of light are always good, white racism receives subtle but very real support from the pulpit. And when images of physical disability (e.g., blindness) are used without qualification as metaphors for sin and failure, yet another form of domination and subordination that shapes our culture is reinforced. A former student told me that he preached a sermon one Sunday using blindness as the central, negative metaphor. On that particular Sunday a blind person happened to visit the congregation for the first time. My student was devastated when the blind person walked out of the sanctuary in the middle of the sermon. He learned the hard way how metaphors can reinforce the cultural status quo of domination and subordination.[41]

---

41. One of the best books dealing with this issue is Smith, *Preaching as Weeping, Confession, and Resistance.*

In addition, preachers have frequently used the pulpit as a way of dominating their congregations. The purpose of the sermon becomes that of winning a victory *over* the people in the pews. The preacher places himself or herself *above* the congregation and employs manipulation or threats in order to coerce people toward a certain position. Rather than helping to set people free from captivity to the powers of the Domination System, the preacher simply reinforces that system in the relationship between preacher and parishioner. And while there is no direct physical violence in such preaching, it is nevertheless preaching that occurs within a spirit of violent domination; it can involve psychological and spiritual violence and even verbal abuse.[42] When other persons become simply instruments of the preacher's self-aggrandizement and control, the spirit of violence is at work.[43]

Moreover, by excluding certain voices from the pulpit, Christian preaching often finds itself deeply enmeshed in systems of domination and violence. My own denomination, the Presbyterian Church (U.S.A.), for example, refuses to ordain gay and lesbian people; it refuses to give them voice from the pulpit as ministers of Word and Sacrament. In other denominations the same prohibition still pertains to women—and even in the denominations that ordain women, certain "prestigious" pulpits often remain reserved for men. In these contexts the weekly sermon, delivered by a heterosexual male, cooperates with the powers of death and domination, which welcome some voices and silence others.

At an even broader level, Christian preaching often participates in the larger systemic powers of domination and violence in the society. As Stringfellow argues, the preacher and the pulpit cannot simplistically "step outside" of the violent and deadly work of the powers, for violence is ubiquitous:

> The violence of the Fall is *so* political, so penetrating, and so pervasive that even the victims of violence are not innocent and even those who advocate nonviolence are not absolved. No human being is guiltless of any violence. There are never any innocent bystanders. No creature is exempted or exonerated from corporate and collective responsibility in violence.[44]

More specifically, the church itself—particularly the predominantly white, wealthy, mainline churches—remains very much a part of the Domination

---

42. See Patricia Evans, *The Verbally Abusive Relationship: How to Recognize It and How to Respond*, 2d ed. (Holbrook, Mass.: Adams Media Corporation, 1996).
43. See Jim Douglass, "Civil Disobedience as Prayer," in Wink, ed., *Peace Is the Way*, 149–52; Mary Evelyn Jegen, "The Pacifist Vision," in Wink, ed., *Peace Is the Way*, 51–52.
44. Stringfellow, *Ethic for Christians*, 128.

System, within which its members enjoy enormous privilege and status. As A. J. Muste, like many others, has noted, "The basic fact is that the economic, social, and political order in which we live was built up largely by violence, is now being extended by violence, and is maintained only by violence."[45] To the extent that the church enjoys the privileges of this order, the church, including the pulpit, is complicit in this violence. Thomas Merton has put the issue most pointedly. Writing about the principles of Christian nonviolence, he addresses the troubling ambiguity for Christians in positions of privilege and power:

> Now all these principles are fine and they accord with our Christian faith. But once we view the principles in the light of current *facts*, a practical difficulty confronts us. If the "Gospel is preached to the poor," if the Christian message is essentially a message of hope and redemption for the poor, the oppressed, the underprivileged and those who have no power humanly speaking, how are we to reconcile ourselves to the fact that Christians belong for the most part to the rich and powerful nations of the earth? Seventeen percent of the world's population control eighty percent of the world's wealth, and most of these seventeen percent are supposedly Christian. Admittedly those Christians who are interested in non-violence are not ordinarily the wealthy ones. Nevertheless, like it or not, they share in the power and privilege of the most wealthy and mighty society the world has ever known. Even with the best subjective intentions in the world, how can they avoid a certain ambiguity in preaching non-violence? Is this not a mystification?[46]

And Merton concludes, "We must frankly face the possibility that the non-violence of the European or American preaching Christian meekness may conceivably be adulterated by bourgeois feelings and by an unconscious desire to preserve the status quo against violent upheaval."[47]

In short, while an ethic of nonviolent resistance is inherent in the practice of preaching, preachers cannot avoid a certain ambiguity when they engage in this practice.[48] While preaching clearly enacts an alternative to direct, interpersonal, physical violence, it nevertheless must continually wrestle with its

---

45. A. J. Muste, "Pacifism and Class War," in Wink, ed., *Peace Is the Way*, 5. For an influential radical analysis of systemic violence that rejects the nonviolent option, see James H. Cone, *God of the Oppressed* (New York: Seabury Press, 1975), 217–25.
46. Thomas Merton, *Faith and Violence: Christian Teaching and Christian Practice* (Notre Dame, Ind.: University of Notre Dame Press, 1968), 20.
47. Ibid., 21.
48. Even Jesus resorts at times to rather violent imagery in his preaching. See, for example, Matthew 13:40–42; 25:31–46; Mark 9:42–48; Luke 20:9–16.

implication in the indirect, systemic forms of physical violence, as well as in the forms of psychological and spiritual violence, that bring death in the world. Preaching must continually recognize its complicity with the violence of the Domination System, both within and outside the church. The practice of preaching, as a practice of nonviolent resistance, exists in the eschatological tension of the new age, which has broken into the world but is not yet fulfilled.

Thus, the ethic of nonviolent resistance inherent in the practice of preaching continually challenges the preacher and congregation, calling them all to greater faithfulness. The assertion that preaching is fundamentally a practice of nonviolent resistance is not a cause for moral complacency or comfort but a call to ongoing self-examination, as both preacher and congregation seek to grow into the way of nonviolent resistance to which the practice of preaching calls them. As Henri Nouwen has noted,

> Real resistance requires the humble confession that we are partners in the evil that we seek to resist. This is a very hard and seemingly endless discipline. The more we say no, the more we will discover the all-pervasive presence of death. The more we resist, the more we recognize how much there is to resist. The more we fight, the more we have to face battles yet to be fought. The world—and we are an intimate part of the world—is indeed Satan's territory.[49]

The affirmation that preaching is a practice of nonviolent resistance is thus as much a calling as a present reality. The church's preaching continually challenges both preachers and congregations to grow into the way of nonviolent resistance. Not only the message of the gospel but the practice of preaching itself calls Christians to begin living now in the freedom from violent domination that Jesus has given us through his cross and resurrection.

A CONDITION FOR INTEGRITY: NONVIOLENT *RESISTANCE*

As preachers seek with integrity to engage in preaching as a practice of nonviolent resistance, they will need to remember that *resistance* is the noun, *nonviolent* the adjective. Active resistance to the Domination System is the *sine qua non* of any assertion that preaching is a nonviolent practice. Apart from active resistance to the powers of domination, preaching becomes what Merton fears: an unconscious means of preserving the status quo. As A. J. Muste put it, "In a world built on violence one must be a revolutionary before one can be

---

49. Henri Nouwen, "Saying No to Death," in Wink, ed., *Peace Is the Way*, 143.

a pacifist; in such a world a non-revolutionary pacifist is a contradiction in terms, a monstrosity."[50] A similar word must be spoken to preachers. Amid the tension and ambiguity of preaching as a practice of nonviolent resistance, one must first of all be a revolutionary; otherwise such preaching becomes not only a reinforcement of the Domination System but, in fact, a monstrosity.

For preachers such as myself, who enjoy privilege in this System, such resistance involves placing our voices in solidarity with the victims of violence in the world, including victims of the systemic violence of the social order. In a discussion of the "conditions for relative honesty in the practice of Christian non-violence," Thomas Merton makes precisely this point. Amid the ambiguity of preaching nonviolence, Merton's first two conditions for honesty highlight the centrality of revolutionary solidarity. The first condition states: "Non-violence must be aimed above all at the transformation of the present state of the world, and it must therefore be free from all occult, unconscious connivance with an unjust use of power." The second condition speaks specifically to those who enjoy privilege: the nonviolent resistance of Christians who belong to one of the powerful nations and who are themselves privileged members of world society will have to be clearly not *for themselves* but *for others*—for the poor and underprivileged.[51] Preaching as nonviolent resistance operates under these two conditions.

Jacques Ellul has made a similar point in his treatment of Christian non-violence. Recognizing that violence is to be found "everywhere and at all times, even where people pretend it does not exist,"[52] Ellul recognizes that nonviolence is never a "pure position" but always a voice from within systems of violence. Nevertheless, Ellul affirms that Jesus Christ sets us free to escape the necessity of violence and to struggle against it. Only one line of action is open to Christians who are free in Christ, he writes. They "must struggle against violence precisely *because*, apart from Christ, violence is the form that human relations normally and necessarily take. In other words, the more completely violence seems to be of the order of necessity, the greater is the obligation of believers in Christ's lordship to overcome it by challenging necessity."[53]

For those of us in positions of privilege, this challenge necessarily involves using our voices on behalf of those who are the victims of domination. No one, Ellul writes, can participate in the "discourse of nonviolence" unless that person is "also and simultaneously acting as spokes[person] for the oppressed and

---

50. Muste, "Pacifism and Class War," 6.
51. Merton, *Faith and Violence*, 21.
52. Ellul, *Violence*, 84.
53. Ibid., 128.

attacking the unjust order with every nonviolent weapon."[54] In every situation
of injustice and oppression, Ellul argues, Christians—who cannot deal with it
by violence—must make themselves completely a part of it as *representatives of
the victims*. Christians have spiritual weapons, he concludes. They must state
the case, make it their own, compel the other to see it. They lend their intel-
ligence, their influence, their hands, and their faces to the faceless mass that
has no hands and no influence.[55] For Ellul, too, "resistance" is the noun, "nonviolent" the adjective.

As a practice of nonviolent resistance to the principalities and powers,
preaching lives in the eschatological tension of God's inbreaking reign.
Although preaching lives in the ambiguities of this tension, there are "conditions of honesty" within which the pulpit engages in the practice of nonviolent resistance, conditions that include active resistance to domination and
solidarity with the oppressed. While the Christian pulpit cannot fully dissoci-
ate itself from the systemic violence that shapes our world, but always speaks
from within it, the practice of preaching calls Christians to grow into the freedom given by Christ and to become increasingly a community of nonviolent
resistance in the midst of the Domination System. How preaching may take
up this challenge is the topic of the following chapters, as I turn now from the
that of preaching to its *what*.

---

54. Ibid., 172.
55. Ibid., 152.

5

Vision, Ethics, and Preaching

As a practice of nonviolent resistance to the powers, preaching embodies what Sharon Welch calls an ethic of risk, rather than an ethic of control.[1] An ethic of control defines responsible ethical action as that which can control the future and produce "results." To be responsible means that one can ensure that the aim of one's action will be carried out. Such an ethic inevitably leads to violence as a means that can ensure such "results." An ethic of risk, however, does not define ethical action in terms of control. In an ethic of risk, ethical actions are not primarily those that control outcomes and successfully transform the world. Rather, ethical actions are those acts that *make possible further resistance*.[2]

As an ethical action, preaching has the same purpose; it seeks to make possible

---

1. Sharon D. Welch, *A Feminist Ethic of Risk* (Minneapolis: Fortress Press, 1990).
2. As I am using the term *resistance*, it includes active engagement, not just passive withdrawal. For a helpful discussion of the difference between resistance and transformation, see Christine M. Smith, "Preaching as an Art of Resistance," in *The Arts of Ministry: Feminist-Womanist Approaches*, ed. Christie Cozad Neuger (Louisville, Ky.: Westminster John Knox Press, 1996), 45–46. As Smith writes, "Though a transformed world is the ultimate hope that undergirds such a ministry [of resistance], if preachers listen carefully to the oppressed voices surrounding them, they will discern that the language of struggle, survival, and resistance is what permeates these messages of indictment and hope, not the language of transformation. Transformative language assumes a certain measure of privilege and power that neither accurately describes nor reflects the lived realities of oppressed people" (46). Although Smith focuses on oppressed people, even in privileged congregations the language of resistance takes more seriously the enormity of the principalities and powers than does the language of transformation. In addition, the emphasis on resistance serves as a reminder that the ultimate transformation of the powers is God's work, not ours.

further resistance to the powers. In other words, the *that* of preaching—its fundamental character as an act of nonviolent resistance—shapes its ethical purpose, which is to help create the space and the possibility for a community to engage in further resistance to the powers. Ethical preaching thus involves building up the church as a community of nonviolent resistance in the face of the powers.[3]

As a practice that seeks to create the possibility of further resistance to the powers, preaching is shaped by the life, death, and resurrection of Jesus, who is the center of Christian proclamation. As I noted in chapter 3, Jesus resisted the powers and offered an alternative to them in his ministry; he exposed and overcame the powers in his crucifixion; and he set people free from the fear of the powers of death in his resurrection. In so doing, Jesus created the space and the possibility for a new community to continue his story of resistance to the principalities and powers of the world.[4] The proclamation of the gospel in the church—the proclamation of Jesus' life, death, and resurrection—likewise seeks to create the space and the possibility for further resistance; it seeks to build up the church as a community of resistance.

This overarching ethical purpose informs the *what* of preaching—the specific shape and characteristics that preaching will take. Two general characteristics will shape such preaching. First, preaching will seek to proclaim a *redemptive* word— a word that sets the church free from its captivity to the powers.[5] Preachers will seek to speak a word that enables the people of God to step into the freedom from

---

3. Welch herself is concerned about building up communities of resistance. See Sharon D. Welch, *Communities of Resistance and Solidarity: A Feminist Theology of Liberation* (Maryknoll, N.Y.: Orbis Books, 1985). Similarly, Christine Smith writes, "When preaching is a ministry of resistance, it participates in the shaping and forming of a people. A ministry of resistance informs and helps create whole communities of resistance" (Smith, "Preaching as Art of Resistance," 46).

4. See Nancy J. Duff, "The Significance of Pauline Apocalyptic for Theological Ethics," in *Apocalyptic and the New Testament: Essays in Honor of J. Louis Martyn*, ed. Joel Marcus and Marion Soards, Journal for the Study of the New Testament: Supplement Series 24 (Sheffield: JSOT Press, 1989), 285. For philosophical and sociological accounts of the space of resistance in the midst of the powers, see David Toole, *Waiting for Godot in Sarajevo: Theological Reflections on Nihilism, Tragedy, and Apocalypse* (Boulder, Colo.: Westview Press, 1998), 179–204; and James C. Scott, *Domination and the Arts of Resistance: Hidden Transcripts* (New Haven, Conn.: Yale University Press, 1990).

5. Because I am writing primarily from the context of privileged, mainline, North American churches, I use the language of "redemption from captivity" rather than "liberation from oppression." I believe the language of liberation needs to be reserved for groups who are genuinely oppressed by the powers. I do believe, however, that people in privileged churches are held captive by the powers and need to be redeemed. On preaching as a redemptive activity in the face of evil, see Christine M. Smith, *Preaching as Weeping, Confession, and Resistance: Radical Responses to Radical Evil* (Louisville, Ky.: Westminster/John Knox Press, 1992), 7–9.

the powers given through Jesus' life, death, and resurrection. This redemptive purpose gives general direction to preaching in the midst of the powers.

Amid the powers, the fundamental problem preachers face is not so much evil minds as paralyzed consciences, not so much malevolence as the *de*moralization of people "who have become captive and immobilized as human beings by their habitual obeisance to institutions or other principalities as idols."[6] On most Sunday mornings preachers do not face people who actively seek to do evil but rather people who are complicit with the powers of death that hold them captive. In fact, in many instances these people are deeply frustrated by their complicity because they know that the way they are following is not the way of life.

In this context, sin primarily involves complicity in our own moral death; it is the human inability or refusal to step into the freedom and life made possible in Jesus Christ and enacted in baptism.[7] The problem is as much *weakness* or *powerlessness* as active evil.[8] In the grip of the powers, people, and often the church itself, ironically and tragically live trapped in a tomb whose stone has already been rolled away. In this context redemption takes on its original connotations of release from bondage, and the purpose of preaching becomes empowering the community of faith to step out of that open tomb and begin to live now in the way of the crucified and risen Jesus. Preaching, in Stringfellow's terms, comes to involve "raising the dead in mind and conscience" and empowering the church to live humanly in the face of death.[9]

Within this framework, the focus of ethical critique in preaching changes. Sermons will not be directed against persons, for we are "not contending against enemies of blood and flesh." Instead of making the people in the pews the enemy,

---

6. William Stringfellow, *An Ethic for Christians and Other Aliens in a Strange Land* (Waco, Tex.: Word Books, 1973; 3d paperback ed., 1979), 29–30. On the moral captivity of persons of privilege and influence, see also p. 28.

7. See Romans 6:1–11. Here sin is primarily a power that holds people captive, not simply an internal, individual matter. Nevertheless, human beings remain responsible for their captivity. Being captives does not excuse people from the call to repentance and resistance. On sin as a power that holds people captive, see Duff, "Significance of Pauline Apocalyptic," 282–85.

8. In her recent book on the powers, Marva Dawn has insightfully examined the role of weakness in relation to the powers. Human weakness before the powers always reminds us that we rely on the power of God, not our own strength, in resistance. I emphasize empowerment more than Dawn does, but her reminders about our dependence on God are critical. See Marva Dawn, *Powers, Weakness, and the Tabernacling of God* (Grand Rapids: Wm. B. Eerdmans Publishing Co., 2001). In his earlier, groundbreaking work on the Pauline epistles, Krister Stendahl argued that weakness is more central than sin in Paul's work. See Krister Stendahl, *Paul among Jews and Gentiles, and Other Essays* (Philadelphia: Fortress Press, 1976), 40–52.

9. Stringfellow, *Ethic for Christians*, 143.

the preacher directs the critique at the principalities and powers that hold people captive. The preacher does not stand over against the congregation but rather stands with them as one who also struggles with complicity in the face of the powers; all stand together in need of redemption. The preacher does not "beat up on people" or load them up with guilt but rather seeks to set them free, possibly even tapping into their longing for release. Preaching thus moves beyond simplistically condemning or challenging individuals and moves toward naming and confronting the powers that hold people captive.[10] The "tone" of preaching consequently becomes more empathetic and hopeful than judgmental and angry.

In this kind of preaching, to put it another way, the distinctions between the "pastoral" and the "prophetic" begin to lose some of their sharpness. When prophetic preaching seeks not to condemn individuals but to name the powers that hold people captive and to envision alternatives to the way of death, that preaching is deeply pastoral. Such preaching offers the most profound pastoral care for people who live in captivity to the powers of death. Similarly, in the midst of the powers, pastoral preaching will fundamentally seek to set people free—to offer them redemption—for newness of life, which will require a prophetic exposing and envisioning in relation to the principalities and powers.[11] In this model of ethical preaching, the most profound prophetic work and the deepest pastoral work come together—for both the preacher and the congregation.

Second, within this larger framework of redemption, and inseparable from it, preaching will seek to *build up* the church as a community of resistance. Preaching will seek to form a community that lives into its freedom as a redeemed people in resistance to the powers that would hold them captive. Preaching that takes the powers seriously does not primarily involve "preaching on social issues," as important as that kind of preaching may be from time to time. Such "social issue" preaching, which tends to be the most common understanding of "ethical" preaching, is too limited in a couple ways.[12]

In the first place, social-issue sermons all too often function naively within

---

10. Such preaching does not preclude addressing individuals. There are, after all, individual actions that are evil and abhorrent—and persons need to be held accountable for these. One cannot excuse a spouse abuser, for example, by simplistically asserting that he is a captive to the powers; he remains responsible for his actions. Nevertheless, it is important to remember that spousal abuse remains embedded in a powerfully entrenched system of powers that for millennia has granted men domination over women. Simply to speak of individual abusers apart from these larger principalities and powers fails to address the depths and depravity of spousal abuse. In this sense, the abuser does need to be freed from bondage to the power of death.

11. In the next chapter I explore this exposing and envisioning in detail.

12. Whenever I tell preachers I am working on a book on "preaching and ethics," the immediate response is something like this: "Good! We need some guidance about preaching on social issues."

the world of liberal idealism, which assumes that if we can just get people of goodwill to work together, we can solve all our social problems.[13] Such sermons often remain on the surface, tinkering with issues and trying to discern appropriate choices, without addressing the depths of the powers of death in both their material and spiritual dimensions. Such preaching can too easily beguile Christians into believing that we are the masters of the powers, and if we simply make the right choices we will transform the world. Often these sermons simply negotiate the realistic options within the world of death, rather than setting the church free from bondage to the presuppositions of the powers. This kind of preaching is inadequate as a response to the principalities and powers.

In addition, a social-issues approach to ethical preaching limits the scope of ethics. In the midst of the powers, the ethical dimensions of preaching become much broader than principles of decision-making in the face of particular ethical quandaries.[14] As I noted in the Introduction, the people of Le Chambon, France, did not provide sanctuary to Jewish people during World War II because they sat down and consciously applied ethical principles and norms to a particular quandary. They provided sanctuary because it came "naturally" to them; through their vision of the world and their ongoing communal practices of hospitality, they had become not only a hospitable people but a people of love and hope in the face of the powers of death.

In the face of the powers, what is required are not primarily principles or norms of decision-making but rather a concrete, embodied people. The most important ethical matters involve the daily formation of a community of resistance.[15] In the midst of the powers, any sermon that seeks to redeem people

---

13. Stanley Hauerwas and Jeff Powell, "Creation as Apocalyptic: A Homage to William Stringfellow," in *Radical Christian and Exemplary Lawyer*, ed. Andrew W. McThenia Jr. (Grand Rapids: Wm. B. Eerdmans Publishing Co., 1995), 36.

14. Stringfellow explicitly rejected a decisionist approach to ethics; see William Stringfellow, *Free in Obedience* (New York: Seabury Press, 1964), 127. On the limitations of "quandary" and "decisionist" ethics, see Edmund L. Pincoffs, *Quandaries and Virtues: Against Reductivism in Ethics* (Lawrence, Kans.: University Press of Kansas, 1986); also Charles L. Campbell, "More than Quandaries: Character Ethics and Preaching," *Journal for Preachers* 16 (Pentecost 1993): 31–37. From a different perspective, that of oppressed African American women, Katie Cannon also argues that "decisionist" ethics is inadequate. For people genuinely oppressed by the powers, what is required is an exploration of the virtues that enable them to negotiate life in the midst of their oppression. See Katie G. Cannon, *Black Womanist Ethics*, American Academy of Religion Academy Series, no. 60 (Atlanta: Scholars Press, 1988). While I do not wish to equate suffering people who are oppressed by the powers and privileged people who are held captive by them, in both cases a narrow focus on decisions is inadequate.

15. I am not arguing against social-issue preaching. Undoubtedly, it is necessary at times in confrontation with the powers. In the midst of the powers, however, the ethical dimensions of preaching are much broader than the occasional social-issue sermon.

from captivity and build up the church in the practices and virtues of resistance is fundamentally an ethical sermon. To use traditional ethical categories, the ethical thrust of preaching in this context is not primarily about decisions but about *character*.[16] As Stringfellow put it,

> The Christian, and the whole company which is the Church, need not worry about what is to be done. The task is, rather, to live within the victory of all that has been done by God. For the Christian the issue is not so much about what he [or she] does in this world but about who he [or she] is in this world. There is no serious distinction between who the Christian is and what he [or she] does, between being and doing. These are virtually the same.[17]

The ethical dimensions of preaching are thus much broader and deeper than the typical social-issue sermon. Ethical preaching does not simply direct people to specific decisions or the means to make them, though that will be necessary from time to time. Rather, preaching seeks to free the community of faith to see and live in the world differently—to *be* a different kind of people. The ethical purpose of preaching involves the formation of an "alien" people who see and live in the world in a distinctive way. At the deepest level, every sermon has ethical dimensions, for preaching fundamentally involves the weekly formation of communities of resistance; it involves building up the church as a people who can resist the powers and live free from bondage to death.

THE SERMON ON THE MOUNT

In the Sermon on the Mount, Matthew portrays Jesus as engaged in precisely the kind of ethical preaching I have been suggesting; in the face of the powers of death Jesus seeks to constitute the community of faith as a redeemed, alternative people in the midst of the world.[18] Moreover, in the sermon Jesus suggests the two essential ingredients for this kind of ethical preaching: *vision* and *practice*.[19] The sermon opens with the Beatitudes (5:3–12), which provide a

---

16. The term *character* refers to the qualification of human agency by particular virtues that enable a person to negotiate life in certain ways rather than others. This term is developed much more fully in the chapters that follow.
17. Stringfellow, *Free in Obedience*, 114. Stringfellow does not develop a character ethic, but his work in places points in that direction.
18. For the Sermon on the Mount, see Matthew 5:1–7:27. See also Luke's version, the Sermon on the Plain (Luke 6:17–49).
19. As becomes clear, I am using the word *vision* metaphorically. I am not referring to physical sight but to a way of "inhabiting" the world. Consequently, at times I use

vision of the new creation that is breaking into the world. The Beatitudes are not primarily ethical demands but rather eschatological blessings that provide an alternative vision of the world. In these blessings Jesus simultaneously *exposes* the powers of death that hold people captive and *envisions* an alternative to the powers' construction of reality. For example, when Jesus proclaims, "Blessed are the peacemakers, for they will be called children of God," Jesus unveils a world shaped by domination and violence in which peacemakers are not generally called "blessed"; at the same time he envisions the alternative reality that is breaking into the world in his own life, death, and resurrection, a reality in which peacemakers are indeed children of God. Through this *exposing* and *envisioning* Jesus helps the community of faith to see the world in new ways; he invites them to see the world through a different story—the story that he will enact in his life, death, and resurrection.

In the second section of the sermon (5:13–16) Jesus offers a new vision not of the world but of the community of faith itself: "You *are* the salt of the earth. . . . You *are* the light of the world." Using indicative verbs and two powerful metaphors—salt and light—Jesus begins not with commands (though these will follow) but with a vision. He helps the community "see" itself and its life in the world in a new way. He gives the community a vision to "inhabit," a vision that will shape its life in the world. The Sermon on the Mount, like the letters of Paul, suggests that "in the long run behavior can only be superficially changed unless imaginations are changed, unless angles of vision are renewed."[20]

Having opened his sermon with a new vision of the world and the community, Jesus proceeds in the remainder of the sermon to delineate a set of practices that give shape to that community's life as they seek to live into the vision. Vision and metaphor alone are not sufficient. Once the powers of death have been exposed and the new creation has been envisioned, concrete communal practices are essential for the embodiment and sustenance of the vision in the midst of the world. Living as a redeemed people, who have been set free from captivity to the powers of death, involves both seeing the world differently and engaging in practices that embody and nurture that alternative vision. Like

---

imagination as a synonym for vision. I also avoid using *blindness* as the alternative to vision; the opposite of Christian vision, I suggest, is numbness or lack of imagination or deathly vision.

20. Charles Cousar, "The Theological Task of 1 Corinthians: A Conversation with Gordon D. Fee and Victor Paul Furnish," in *Pauline Theology*, vol. 2, ed. David M. Hay (Minneapolis: Fortress Press, 1993), 97. For further biblical reflections on the importance of vision for the ethical life, see Walter Brueggemann, *Living toward a Vision: Biblical Reflections on Shalom* (Philadelphia: United Church Press, 1976), recently reissued as *Peace* (St. Louis: Chalice Press, 2001).

modern character ethicists, Jesus understood that vision and practices work together to build up the community of faith as a distinctive people.

Like Jesus' sermon, contemporary sermons that seek to build up the church as a community of resistance will include these two dimensions: *vision* and *practice*.[21] In this chapter and in chapters 6 and 7, I examine these two dimensions of ethical preaching in the midst of the powers. Here and in chapter 6, I examine vision, both as it has been appropriated in character ethics and as it functions in preaching that seeks to expose the powers and envision the new creation. In chapter 7, I discuss the role of practices in ethics and preaching.

VISION AND ETHICS

In both moral philosophy and theological ethics, increasing attention has been given in recent years to matters of human character and virtue.[22] In many quarters the focus of ethical reflection has shifted from actions to agents, in line with Aquinas's insight that "the form of an act always follows from a form of the agent."[23] Many moral philosophers and Christian ethicists are coming to realize that there are no abstract, isolated acts apart from the kinds of persons who perform them. And some have given priority to this "background" of action rather than to specific decisions and actions. As Stanley Hauerwas

---

21. Christine Smith also highlights "eschatological vision" and "liberating praxis" as two critical dimensions of Christian ministry and preaching. See Smith, "Preaching as Art of Resistance," 41.

22. The bibliography of contemporary works in the field of character ethics is now substantial. See, for example, Iris Murdoch, *The Sovereignty of Good* (London: Routledge and Kegan Paul, 1970; reprint, London: Ark Paperbacks, 1986); Stanley Hauerwas, *Vision and Virtue: Essays in Christian Ethical Reflection* (Notre Dame, Ind.: Fides Publishers, 1974; reprint, Notre Dame, Ind.: University of Notre Dame Press, 1981) idem; *A Community of Character: Toward a Constructive Christian Social Ethic* (Notre Dame, Ind.: University of Notre Dame Press, 1981); idem, *The Peaceable Kingdom: A Primer in Christian Ethics* (Notre Dame, Ind.: University of Notre Dame Press, 1983); Alasdair MacIntyre, *After Virtue: A Study in Moral Theory*, 2d ed. (Notre Dame, Ind.: University of Notre Dame Press, 1984); Jean Porter, *The Recovery of Virtue: The Relevance of Aquinas for Christian Ethics* (Louisville, Ky.: Westminster/John Knox Press, 1990); Paul J. Wadell, *Friendship and the Christian Life* (Notre Dame, Ind.: University of Notre Dame Press, 1989); and Nancey C. Murphy, Brad J. Kallenberg, and Mark Thiessen Nation, eds., *Virtues and Practices in the Christian Tradition: Christian Ethics after MacIntyre* (Harrisburg, Pa.: Trinity Press International, 1997). In this chapter and the next three, I develop the key dimensions of character ethics—vision, practices, friendship, and virtue—in relation to preaching as a practice of nonviolent resistance to the powers.

23. Thomas Aquinas, *Summa Theologiae* 2, 8.2, a. 24, ad 2.

has written, "Morality is not primarily concerned with quandaries or hard decisions; nor is the moral self simply the collection of such decisions. As persons of character we do not confront situations as mud puddles into which we have to step; rather the kind of 'situations' we confront and how we understand them are a function of the kind of people we are."[24]

The philosopher and novelist Iris Murdoch was one of the first to redirect the attention of contemporary moral philosophers away from isolated acts of the will to what transpires between them. "The moral life," she emphasizes, "is something that goes on continually, not something that is switched on and off between the occurrence of explicit moral choices. What happens between such choices is indeed what is crucial."[25] Murdoch thus places the agent's "continuous fabric of being," rather than overt choices and actions, at the center of moral philosophy.

In taking this approach to ethics, Murdoch explicitly proposes that we think about morality in terms of the metaphor of vision.[26] The approach that regards "moral differences as differences of choice, given a discussible background of facts," Murdoch writes,

> seems less plausible when we attend to the notion of "moral being" as self-reflection or complex attitudes to life which are continuously displayed and elaborated in overt and inward speech but are not separable temporally into situations. Here moral differences look less like differences of choice, given the same facts, and more like differences of vision. In other words, a moral concept seems less like a movable and extensible ring laid down to cover a certain area of fact, and more like a total difference of *Gestalt*. We differ not only because we select different objects out of the same world but because we *see different worlds*.[27]

For Murdoch, vision, as a way of seeing reality and living in the world, takes priority over individual choices; for a person can only choose within the world she can see.[28] Consequently, the most important moral differences are "differences of vision, not of choice."[29] As Murdoch concludes, "By the time the moment of choice has arrived the quality of attention has probably determined the nature of the act."[30]

---

24. Hauerwas, *Community of Character*, 114–15.
25. Murdoch, *Sovereignty of Good*, 37.
26. Ibid., 15.
27. Iris Murdoch, "Vision and Choice in Morality," in *Christian Ethics and Contemporary Philosophy*, ed. Ian T. Ramsey (London: SCM Press, 1966), 203; italics mine.
28. Murdoch, *Sovereignty of Good*, 37.
29. Murdoch, "Vision and Choice," 213.
30. Murdoch, *Sovereignty of Good*, 67; also 37.

Attention thus becomes, for Murdoch, the crucial moral work prior to choice and action. Coming to see the world rightly is a task that requires much effort. We grow, she suggests, "by looking": "The task of attention goes on all the time and at apparently empty and everyday moments we are 'looking,' making those little peering efforts of imagination, which have such important cumulative results."[31] The good life happens only through the disciplined transformation of our vision.[32] For Murdoch, then, vision is the critical category of ethics, and attention is the most crucial moral work that precedes choice and action.

In a remarkable essay, "The Other American Renaissance," Jane Tompkins provides a striking illustration and analysis of what Murdoch means by "vision."[33] In the essay Tompkins cites a nineteenth-century report of a visit made to a dying young woman by a "Visiter" from the New York City Tract Society. The report reads:

> [The young woman] was found by the Visiter supplied with a number of tracts, and kindly directed to the Savior of sinners. Some of her relatives—they cannot be called her friends—attempted to impede the visiter's way to her bedside, and would often present hinderances which she could not remove. God, however showed himself strong in her behalf. . . . For some time clouds hung over her mind, but they were at length dispelled by the sun of righteousness. . . . As she approached the hour which tries men's souls, her strength failed fast; her friends gathered around her; . . . and while they were engaged in a hymn her soul seemed to impart an unnatural energy to her emaciated and dying body. To the astonishment of all, she said to her widowed mother, who bent anxiously over her, "Don't weep for me, I shall soon be in the arms of my Savior." She prayed fervently, and fell asleep in Jesus.[34]

Tompkins then provides an insightful analysis of this report, which clarifies Murdoch's emphasis on the centrality of vision:

> Like all the fiction we label "sentimental," this narrative blocks out the uglier details of life and cuts experience to fit a pattern of pious expec-

---

31. Ibid., 31, 43. For Murdoch, the artist's selfless attention to reality serves as the paradigm of ideal vision. Such loving attention respects the particularity of the "other," draws the agent out of self-centeredness, and frees her from fantasy and illusion (34, 66).
32. Hauerwas, *Vision and Virtue*, 44.
33. Jane P. Tompkins, "The Other American Renaissance," in *Sensational Designs: The Cultural Work of American Fiction, 1790–1860* (New York: Oxford University Press, 1985), 147–85. In this book Tompkins, a feminist literary scholar, explores the cultural work of sentimental fiction in America.
34. Ibid., 151.

tation. The anecdote tells nothing about the personality or background of the young woman, fails to represent even the barest facts of her disease or of her immediate surroundings. For these facts, the report substitutes the panaceas of Christian piety—God's mercy on a miserable sinner, the tears and prayers of a deathbed conversion, falling "asleep in Jesus." Its plot follows a prescribed course from sin to salvation. But what is extraordinary about this anecdote is that it is not a work of fiction, but a factual report. Though its facts do not correspond to what a twentieth-century observer would have recorded, had he or she been at the scene, they faithfully represent what the Tract Society member *saw*. Whereas a modern social worker would have noticed the furniture of the sick room, the kind of house the woman lived in, her neighborhood, would have described her illness, its history and course of treatment, and sketched in her socio-economic background and that of her relatives and friends, the Tract Visiter *sees* only a spiritual predicament: the woman's initial "alarm," the "clouds [that] hung over her mind," God's action on her heart, the turn from sin to righteousness. Whereas the modern observer would have structured the events in a downward spiral, as the woman's condition deteriorated from serious to critical, and ended with her death, the report reverses the progression. Its movement is upward, from "thoughtlessness" to "conviction" to "great tranquility, joy, and triumph."[35]

In Murdoch's words, "We differ not only because we select different objects out of the same world but because we see different worlds." A person can choose only within the world she can see.

In the field of Christian ethics, Stanley Hauerwas, one of the most important contributors to the renewed emphasis on character in contemporary Christian ethics, appropriated Murdoch's emphasis on vision in his early work.[36] As Hauerwas writes,

> Christian ethics . . . is not first of all concerned with "Thou shalt" or "Thou shalt not." Its first task is to help us rightly envision the world. . . . In other words, the enterprise of Christian ethics primarily helps us to see. We can only act within the world we can envision, and we can envision the world rightly only as we are trained to see.[37]

---

35. Ibid., 151–52; italics mine. The Tract Visiter's way of "seeing the world" is in many ways the opposite of what Murdoch would hold up as appropriate attention and ideal vision.
36. Hauerwas notes the influence of Murdoch's work on his: "Her emphasis on vision as the hallmark of the moral life struck me as exactly what was missing from most accounts of the virtues" (*Peaceable Kingdom*, xxiii). Both Murdoch and Hauerwas draw on the work of Ludwig Wittgenstein. On Wittgenstein's ethical emphasis on seeing the world, see James C. Edwards, *Ethics without Philosophy: Wittgenstein and the Moral Life* (Tampa: University Presses of Florida, 1982).
37. Hauerwas, *Peaceable Kingdom*, 29. Hauerwas repeatedly emphasizes that "we can only act in a world we can see." See also Stanley Hauerwas, *Against the Nations: War*

For Hauerwas as for Murdoch, the moral life involves "more than thinking clearly and making rational choices. It is a way of seeing the world."[38]

Similarly, Hauerwas emphasizes the important role that "attending to the world" plays in the moral life. Being a Christian, he writes, "involves more than just making certain decisions; it is a way of attending to the world. It is learning 'to see' the world under the mode of the divine."[39] More than Murdoch, however, Hauerwas emphasizes the role that distinctive communal language plays in training Christian attention to the world: "Our attending cannot be separated from the language or metaphors that form it."[40] For Hauerwas, Christian vision—Christian attending to the world—takes a distinctive shape because it is formed by a particular story and a peculiar speech.[41] Hauerwas's emphasis at this point suggests the important ethical role that preaching may play in helping to train the attention and form the vision of the Christian community.

VISION AND PREACHING

As a practice of nonviolent resistance to the powers, which seeks to open up the space for further resistance, preaching has as one of its fundamental tasks that of helping congregations *attend* to the world. Prior to analyzing particular choices and actions, preaching first and foremost should seek to help people *see* the world through the Christian story. Such new vision is a critical step that helps build up the church as a community of resistance.

In the midst of the powers, such faithful attention to the world and such new vision is particularly important. Through their various strategies—diversion, language and image, secrecy, negative sanctions, and positive reinforcement—the powers keep human beings in ignorance, move them into denial (causing them to ignore, justify, or dismiss what they really see), and lull them

---

and Survival in a Liberal Society (Minneapolis: Winston Press, 1985), 53, 55; idem, *Vision and Virtue*, 2, 33. Hauerwas emphasizes much more strongly than Murdoch the narrative shape of Christian vision, as well as the communal context and practices within which vision is trained. Murdoch works out of a Platonic framework, while Hauerwas draws more on an Aristotelian understanding of the virtues. Along with Hauerwas, I emphasize the role of communal practices in the formation of vision.

38. Hauerwas, *Vision and Virtue*, 36.

39. Ibid., 45–46.

40. Ibid., 46.

41. Hauerwas, *Peaceable Kingdom*, 29–30. Philosophers have also emphasized this connection between language and vision. On the connection between language and ethical vision in Wittgenstein's work, see Edwards, *Ethics without Philosophy*. For a different account, see Janet Martin Soskice, *Metaphor and Religious Language* (Oxford: Oxford University Press, 1985), esp. 57–58.

into numbness. The powers strive to delude people so that the ways of the powers become the "common sense" vision of the world.[42] It is thus not surprising that vision plays such an important role in apocalyptic writing, such as the book of Revelation, through which the author seeks to set people free from their captivity to a world dominated by the material and spiritual realities of the principalities and powers.[43] Creating a "counter-attention" and "counter-vision" helps free people from ignorance, denial, and numbness and is an important step that helps build up the church as a community of resistance.

William Stringfellow understood the importance of Christian attention to the world for living humanly in resistance to the powers. For him, *discernment* was the most basic gift of the Holy Spirit to the church, which enables Christians to expose and rebuke the powers of death while also affirming the living, promising Word of God actively incarnate in the world:

> Discerning signs has to do with comprehending the remarkable in common happenings, with perceiving the saga of salvation within the era of the Fall. It has to do with the ability to interpret ordinary events in both apocalyptic and eschatological connotations, to see portents of death where others find progress or success but, simultaneously, to behold tokens of the reality of the Resurrection or hope where others are consigned to confusion or despair.[44]

This gift of discernment, in the words of Stringfellow scholar Bill Wylie-Kellermann, "enables the people of God to distinguish and recognize, identify and expose, report and rebuke the power of death incarnate in nations and institutions or other creatures, or possessing persons, while they also affirm the Word of God incarnate in all of life, exemplified preeminently in Jesus Christ."[45]

Moreover, Stringfellow understood that such discernment, through the

---

42. On the ways in which the powers shape human vision, see Walter Wink, *Engaging the Powers: Discernment and Resistance in a World of Domination* (Minneapolis: Fortress Press, 1992), 87–104.

43. As some recent commentators have argued, Revelation was written not just for oppressed and persecuted Christians but also for churches that had accommodated to the ways of the powers. See Wes Howard-Brook and Anthony Gwyther, *Unveiling Empire: Reading Revelation Then and Now* (Maryknoll, N.Y.: Orbis Books, 1999).

44. Stringfellow, *Ethic for Christians*, 138–39. J. Louis Martyn speaks of this kind of vision, characteristic of apocalyptic, as "bifocal": "To see bi-focally in Paul's terms is to see *both* the enslaving Old Age and God's invading and liberating new creation" (J. Louis Martyn, *Theological Issues in the Letters of Paul* [Nashville: Abingdon Press, 1997], 284). See also James F. Kay, "The Word of the Cross at the Turn of the Ages," *Interpretation* 53 (January 1999): 44–56; and Duff, "Significance of Pauline Apocalyptic," 286. My emphasis on exposing and envisioning, as becomes clear, involves a similar kind of bifocal vision.

45. Bill Wylie-Kellermann, "Not Vice Versa. Reading the Powers Biblically: Stringfellow, Hermeneutics, and the Principalities," *Anglican Theological Review* 81, 4 (1999): 665.

work of the Spirit, requires an immersion in the "world of the Bible." Indeed, for Stringfellow such immersion in Scripture itself became a "primary, practical, and essential tactic of resistance."[46] Christians learn to discern the work of the crucified and living Jesus in the midst of the powers of death when they come to see the world through the lens of Scripture, rather than interpreting the Bible according to the values and priorities of the world.[47]

Through such an immersion in Scripture, the church develops, as I have argued elsewhere, a "figural imagination."[48] The church comes to see the world through the patterns and figures of the biblical story, and particularly through the story of Jesus, who serves as the central archetype of the biblical story.[49] By means of a figural imagination, the world of the contemporary people of God, including the principalities and powers, can be seen through the patterns of events, people, institutions, and metaphors discerned in the biblical narrative. The biblical story moves forward into the present and future, and the memories of the people of God come to shape the church's vision.

In fact, seeing the contemporary world through the lens of Jesus' resistance to the principalities and powers is itself an act of figural imagination.[50] The church comes to "read" the contemporary world through the figures of Jesus' cross and resurrection, as these expose and overcome the powers of death. Only in this way can the church engage in the kind of discernment that Stringfellow suggests: "comprehending the remarkable in common happenings"; "perceiv-

---

46. Stringfellow, *Ethic for Christians*, 120.
47. Stringfellow was keenly aware of the ways in which the powers seek to co-opt the Bible for their own purposes, and he was adamant that Christians need to understand America biblically rather than interpret the Bible Americanly. See Stringfellow, *Ethic for Christians*, 13. See also Wylie-Kellermann, "Not Vice Versa," 665–82.
48. On figural interpretation and figural imagination, see Charles L. Campbell, *Preaching Jesus: New Directions for Homiletics in Hans Frei's Postliberal Theology* (Grand Rapids: Wm. B. Eerdmans Publishing Co., 1997), 99–100, 184–85, 250–57.
49. I have borrowed the term *archetype* from Justo L. Gonzalez and Catherine Gunsalus Gonzalez, *The Liberating Pulpit* (Nashville: Abingdon Press, 1994), 101. Many other terms have been used, but *archetype* captures most clearly Jesus' pivotal role in defining the pattern of the biblical story. The term should not be confused with the Jungian understanding of archetypes.
50. It is a fascinating and probably significant fact that figural interpretation and the theology of the principalities both fell out of use with the "Constantinian Arrangement" of the fourth century. Called on to legitimate the empire, the church abandoned the social critique that the theology of the powers offered. Similarly, figural interpretation was too particularlistic and radical for the Constantinian age, when interpretation tended to accommodate the Bible to the dominant culture and empire. See Gonzalez and Gonzalez, *Liberating Pulpit*, 103–4; Wylie-Kellermann, "Not Vice Versa," 668–69; J. Denny Weaver, "Atonement for the Nonconstantinian Church," *Modern Theology* 6 (July 1990): 307–33.

ing the saga of salvation within the era of the Fall"; interpreting "ordinary events in both apocalyptic and eschatological connotations"; seeing "portents of death where others find progress or success"; and beholding "tokens of the reality of the Resurrection or hope where others are consigned to confusion or despair." Such discernment is the work of the figural imagination, which is nurtured through an immersion in the world of the Bible.

For Stringfellow, such a thoroughgoing immersion in the Word is essential for any preacher who would dare to resist the principalities and powers. As Stringfellow counseled,

> In the middle of chaos, celebrate the Word. Amidst babel, speak the truth. Confront the noise and verbiage and falsehood of death with the truth and potency and efficacy of the Word of God. Know the Word, teach the Word, nurture the Word, preach the Word, defend the Word, incarnate the Word, do the Word, live the Word. And more than that, in the Word of God expose death and all death's works and wiles, rebuke lies, cast out demons, exorcise, cleanse the possessed, raise those who are dead in mind and conscience.[51]

This Word, Stringfellow recognized, is the great promise and hope for preachers who would resist the powers in their sermons. Although churches and people, including preachers, may be captive to the principalities and powers, the Word of God is not. The Word of God is free and active, continuing to expose the powers and bring the new creation into the world. In the face of the powers, the preacher clings to this promise: the powers cannot take captive the Word of the Lord.

At the center of Christian preaching, then, is this Word—the crucified and risen Jesus. Through his life, death, and resurrection, the principalities and powers have been exposed and overcome, and the new creation (though often hidden to us) has broken into the midst of the fallen world. Preaching begins with the proclamation of Jesus, in whom this new reality has "invaded" and radically changed the world. Out of this event the new perception of the church emerges; the church comes to see the world in new ways.[52] The gift of discernment, shaped by a figural imagination, enables Christians to see the crucified and risen Jesus at work in the world and to attend to the world through this story.[53]

---

51. Stringfellow, *Ethic for Christians*, 143.
52. Duff, "Significance of Pauline Apocalyptic," 281.
53. Exposing and envisioning are not easily separated. Whenever the powers are exposed, some sense of the alternative of the new creation is present. Likewise, when the new creation is envisioned, there is an implicit exposing and critique of the powers of death. The distinction is simply one of emphasis. In addition, as becomes clear in the next chapter, this figural pattern of exposing and envisioning is not limited to Jesus but is already present in the Old Testament.

Ethical preaching, which seeks to renew the church's vision of the world, flows out of the proclamation of Jesus and is inseparable from it. Like the ripples that emerge from a stone thrown in a pond, ethical preaching moves from the new reality inaugurated in Jesus Christ to the new vision of the people of God. From the central proclamation of Jesus, preachers move out into the work of attending to the world and helping people see the world in new ways. Through the use of figural imagination, preachers continue the work of Jesus in the face of the powers.

Just as Jesus *exposed* the powers and *inaugurated* the new creation through his life, death, and resurrection, so preaching seeks to *expose* the powers of death at work in the world and *envision* God's inbreaking new creation. This twofold movement of *exposing* the powers and *envisioning* the new creation provides the crucial dynamic for Christian preaching that moves out from the story of Jesus, attends faithfully to the world, and helps form the church's ethical vision in the midst of the powers. Such preaching announces the Word of redemption, which sets people free and helps create the space for further resistance. Although this kind of preaching often seems to be an "audacious, extemporaneous, fragile, puny, foolish" form of resistance,[54] because the Word of God is involved such preaching is nevertheless full of promise and hope.

Moreover, because of the verbal nature of many of the powers' tactics, preaching, as the counterspeech of the Word of God, can be a particularly important form of resistance. As Walter Wink has put it, linking vision and language in a powerful way, "Evil is not nearly so much a physical phenomenon as a spiritual construct, itself born of words and capable of destruction by the Word of God. Nothing is more revolutionary than a transformation of the fundamental metaphors through which we apprehend the world."[55] With that word of hope, I now turn to the concrete homiletical means of reforming the church's vision.

---

54. Stringfellow, *Ethic for Christians*, 119.
55. Walter Wink, *Naming the Powers: The Language of Power in the New Testament* (Philadelphia: Fortress Press, 1984), 88.

6

Exposing and Envisioning

Vision heals. Mere awareness of the state from which we are fallen is not enough to effect systemic change, but it is its indispensable precondition. Apocalyptic (unveiling) is always a protest against domination. Liberation from negative socialization and internalized oppression is a never-completed task in the discernment of spirits. To exercise this discernment, we need eyes to see the invisible. To break the spell of delusion, we need a vision of God's domination-free order, and a way to implement it.[1]

Redemptive preaching, which seeks to free the church to resist the principalities and powers, engages in a twofold movement: exposing the deadly ways of the powers and envisioning God's new creation. As Walter Wink notes in the preceding quotation, such "unveiling" and envisioning are critical if preachers would help "break the spell of delusion" and enable congregations to see and live in the world in new ways. While exposing and envisioning are often two sides of the same coin—one can rarely envision God's new creation without simultaneously helping people see the powers' ways of death in the present—I examine each move in turn, focusing on some of the concrete ways in which preachers may creatively confront the illusions of the powers and offer an alternative vision for the church.

---

1. Walter Wink, *Engaging the Powers: Discernment and Resistance in a World of Domination* (Minneapolis: Fortress Press, 1992), 103–4.

EXPOSING

In the midst of Babel, redemptive Christian preaching *exposes* the powers of death. The preacher *names* the powers and *unveils* their reality. Like the cross of Jesus, this unveiling of the powers, which uncovers their false claims and deadly lies, marks the beginning of human freedom from the bondage of death. This exposing takes away the "mirrors" by which the powers delude us into thinking they are the divine, life-giving regents of the world. The powers are exposed as emperors without any clothes, a disarming humiliation for those who rely so heavily on their pretensions of dignity and control.[2]

Central to this exposing is Stringfellow's challenge, "Amidst Babel, speak the truth." As I have noted, the powers so shape the world that their ways of death often seem like common sense. Exposing them requires preachers to cut through ignorance, denial, and numbness and speak the truth in creative and powerful ways. Preachers take the place of the child in the "Emperor's New Clothes," who shouts, "He's naked!" demystifying the crowds and setting them free.

After the terrorist attacks on the World Trade Center and the Pentagon, Peter Storey, a South African Christian who teaches ministry at Duke University, wrote an open letter to "Friends in the United States" from his home in South Africa. In the letter Storey highlights the critical and difficult role that preachers play in exposing the powers:

> American preachers have a task more difficult, perhaps, than those faced by us under South Africa's *apartheid*, or Christians under communism. We had obvious evils to engage; you have to unwrap your culture from years of red, white and blue myth. You have to expose, and confront, the great disconnect between the kindness, compassion and caring of most American people, and the ruthless way American power is experienced, directly and indirectly, by the poor of the earth. You have to help good people see how they have let their institutions do their sinning for them. This is not easy among people who really believe that their country does nothing but good, but it is necessary, not only for their future, but for us all.[3]

Exposing the powers of death at work in the world represents a crucial movement in homiletical resistance.

---

2. See Walter Wink, *Naming the Powers: The Language of Power in the New Testament* (Philadelphia: Fortress Press, 1984), 55–60; John Howard Yoder, *The Politics of Jesus: Vicit Agnus Noster* (Grand Rapids: Wm. B. Eerdmans Publishing Co., 1972), 147–50.
3. Peter Storey, "Letter from South Africa," at http://www.divinity.duke.edu/newsbox/WTC/Crisis-Storey.html; accessed on October 15, 2001.

Direct Speech

Preachers can expose the powers in numerous ways. In speaking a redemptive word that addresses ignorance, denial, and numbness, preachers will first of all need to employ clear, direct speech to name the powers and hold up their activities for people to see. Where people are genuinely ignorant, clear naming can be important. Where denial is at work, direct speech may tap into the deep knowledge that is already present and bring it to the surface so it can no longer be denied. Such naming may at times come close to a kind of social-issue preaching, but the goal is actually much broader and deeper. The goal is not to focus on one issue, though that may be the presenting matter, but to expose the powers of death—including their spirituality—in order to empower people to begin to live in new ways.

In exposing the powers, preachers may be helped by secular social analysis, which often serves to unveil the world as governed by the powers in both their material and spiritual dimensions. A few years ago, for example, I was reading Joel Blau's book on homelessness titled *The Visible Poor*. Early in the book Blau examines the sociological "principle of *less eligibility*." This simple principle holds that people on welfare must have a lower standard of living than people who work.[4] Blau describes the way in which the institutional embodiment of this principle has contributed to homelessness in recent decades:

> While this principle has deep roots in U.S. social policy, its most recent implementation has been both consistent with the historical pattern and especially harsh. The current economic transition has witnessed a decline in the working poor's standard of living. Well into the 1960s, a welfare client could receive less than a poorly paid worker and still afford housing. But as the cost of housing began to rise in the 1970s, welfare benefits were reduced to correspond to the working poor's declining income; that is when the risk of homelessness grew—slowly for the working poor, more rapidly for those on welfare. If, in the 1960s, getting less than the working poor meant poor housing, by the 1980s, it often meant the streets.[5]

Although it is presented by Blau as a traditional principle of U.S. social policy rather than a description of the workings of the principalities and powers, a preacher immersed in the New Testament can discern that the principle of less eligibility exposes principalities and powers much larger than individual persons or even specific institutions. The principle unveils the workings of the

---

4. Joel Blau, *The Visible Poor: Homelessness in the United States* (New York: Oxford University Press, 1992), 12.
5. Ibid., 12.

powers in both their institutional and spiritual dimensions. The principle of less eligibility brings into the open the hidden "common sense" presuppositions that form the air people breathe in a competitive, capitalist economy that requires cheap labor. It exposes a cultural spirit shaped more by reward and punishment than by grace, and it unveils a society driven more by hierarchical, economic ranking than by compassion and justice for human need. In addition, it provides a lens for analyzing the concrete ways in which this spirit takes on institutional embodiment in public policy. Finally, it suggests one concrete way in which the powers capture the spirit of privileged people and demoralize them: the spirit and institutions shaped by the principle of less eligibility isolate privileged people in a superior, competitive stance over against suffering people, rather than making possible genuine, life-giving relationships of compassion and solidarity.

In this instance, a clearly stated sociological principle named the powers in a way that helped me see and analyze the world in new ways in relation to the gospel. My point is not that preachers should offer technical sociological terms or detailed sociological analysis in the pulpit, though that could certainly be helpful from time to time. The point is that this single, clearly articulated principle named and exposed a world dominated by the spirituality and institutions of the rebellious powers—a world that undoubtedly shapes the presuppositions of many privileged persons in church pews and contributes to the scapegoating of "welfare recipients" in our society.[6]

When taken into the pulpit, such naming need not involve the detailed presentation of sociological theory or terminology. Exposing the powers in this context will be less technical and more dramatic, often generating further questions and conversation, rather than "analyzing" folks into a stupor. In a recent sermon, for example, Jane Fahey, a former student, engaged in this kind of direct speech, clearly naming the powers in a way that invited the congregation to move beyond ignorance and denial.

Fahey was preaching from Revelation 7:9–17 and was seeking to unveil the "myths of empire" that shape our lives. She began with a specific encounter with a man in a coffee shop and then proceeded directly to expose the powers.

> Ten days ago . . . I was taking a break between classes at a coffee shop when a man sitting across from me interrupted my reading to ask what

---

6. Obviously, many books help with this kind of analysis. The books I have been citing that deal with the powers do significant exposing. Christine Smith's book *Preaching as Weeping, Confession, and Resistance: Radical Responses to Radical Evil* (Louisville, Ky.: Westminster/John Knox Press, 1992) provides a wealth of such analysis. For preaching to privileged congregations, Mary Elizabeth Hobgood's book *Dismantling Privilege: An Ethics of Accountability* (Cleveland: Pilgrim Press, 2000) is invaluable.

I was working on. Early on in the conversation, and for no apparent reason, the man (who had already introduced himself by name) mentioned that he was a Vietnam veteran. After a few minutes of conversation about his own work history and his aspirations, he began to weep. And as I assured him that he needn't apologize, he told me, through tears, about his experience as an eighteen-year-old medic in Vietnam and the horror of being unable to save his two best buddies in the unit. More than once he dried his tears only to begin weeping again as he described how those memories continue to haunt him. For some thirty minutes that afternoon, I listened to a tale of a world so bizarre, so filled with brutality that this man could hardly bring it to speech, and I saw before me a fifty-year-old man who has been fighting his way back to reality ever since.

So I've had reason to think lately about the myths that have shaped our collective national life, the myth that shaped this man's life and the lives of others who served in Vietnam. It was a myth about power and violence, a myth wrapped in political rhetoric telling us that the well-being of the world required the forceful elimination of perceived threats to "western democratic values." As a nation we have become, I think, a bit more critical of this myth as a result of Vietnam. But this myth about the way to a world of well-being still holds powerful sway in some quarters—only now the rhetoric is less about the use of force to prevent the spread of communism and more about its use as a tool of globalization, to ensure the spread of free market capitalism around the world.

Consider, for example, this statement by *New York Times* columnist Thomas Friedman in his book *The Lexus and the Olive Tree*: "The hidden hand of the market will never work without a hidden fist—McDonald's cannot flourish without McDonnell Douglas, the builder of the F-15. And the hidden fist that keeps the world safe for Silicon Valley's technologies is called the United States Army, Air Force, Navy and Marine Corps. . . . Without America on duty, there will be no America Online." Whatever one thinks about the role of the military (and I myself am the daughter and granddaughter of veterans of world wars), we might all pause at the suggestion that the military's chief mission is enhancing the profitability of America's multinational corporations.[7]

In this section of the sermon, Fahey "breaks the silence" that often governs the church by exposing the enormous configuration of economic, military, and political powers that hold us captive through their domination and their "myth of redemptive violence." Moreover, she notes the complex collaboration among these powers in pursuing national economic dominance

---

7. Jane Fahey, "The Liturgy of Our Lives," preached at Central Presbyterian Church, Atlanta, Georgia, May 6, 2001.

and highlights the role of public rhetoric in shaping and reinforcing the powers of death. Her point here, in faithfulness to the book of Revelation, is not to address a specific "social issue" but rather to "unveil empire" and help God's people see the workings of the powers, including their spiritual effect on human lives, with new clarity.[8] Such direct, courageous speech is required amid the deadly "babel" of the world. Too often, however, such speech is missing from the pulpit.

Memory

Directly exposing the powers can also take the form of reenvisioning history, which involves re-forming memory.[9] Human captivity to the powers often results from ignorance and denial about the realities of the past. People in privileged positions, in particular, simply do not know or have managed to deny the history of suffering that the powers have produced. Numbness here takes the form of amnesia, as people seek a way of going on with their lives without being overwhelmed by the history on which their privilege has been built. As Ched Myers has written,

> Those who want to change the relations of power in the present, to break the cycle of violence, must deal with history; those content with the status quo must keep history remote, fragmented, and inaccessible. Thus the "official" historical narratives of the dominant culture in the *locus imperii* are both highly selective and highly mystified. Shameful episodes—the Trail of Tears or the Middle Passage or anti-Chinese immigration laws or the annexation of Hawai'i—have no place in our historical consciousness. What takes their place are heroic tales and high myth: Washington crossing the Delaware; Lincoln weeping at Gettysburg; the boys and the flag at Iwo Jima. Amnesia is the tool of denial.[10]

Amnesia and a "disconnection from history" are important allies of the powers.[11] In exposing the powers, preachers thus need to revisit—and reenvi-

---

8. See Wes Howard-Brook and Anthony Gwyther, *Unveiling Empire: Reading Revelation Then and Now* (Maryknoll, N.Y.: Orbis Books, 1999).
9. Memory and vision are intimately related. Our memories often shape how we see the world. On the importance of such remembering, see Sharon Welch, *Communities of Resistance and Solidarity: A Feminist Theology of Liberation* (Maryknoll, N.Y.: Orbis Books, 1985), 32–54; Ched Myers, *Who Will Roll Away the Stone? Discipleship Queries for First World Christians* (Maryknoll, N.Y.: Orbis Books, 1994), 111–57; and Wink, *Engaging the Powers*, 243–57.
10. Myers, *Who Will Roll the Stone?* 117.
11. Ibid.

sion—history in order to re-form memory and set congregations free from amnesia.

The Bible is clear about the importance of this kind of "dangerous memory." Simply by reading Scripture, the community of faith is forced to remember the suffering and death wreaked by the powers, focused most sharply in the crucifixion of Jesus. And the readers are regularly called to identify not with the powerful "makers of history" but with those who have suffered oppression at the hands of the powers. The Fifth Commandment, as recorded in Deuteronomy 5:12–15, is one poignant instance in which the people of Israel, in the face of the temptations of prosperity and privilege, are called to remember a history of oppression and liberation. The rationale for Sabbath observance in Deuteronomy is not the more familiar one that God rested on the seventh day but is stated as follows:

> Observe the sabbath day and keep it holy, as the LORD your God commanded you. Six days you shall labor and do all your work. But the seventh day is a sabbath to the LORD your God; you shall not do any work—you, or your son or your daughter, or your male or female slave, or your ox or your donkey, or any of your livestock, or the resident alien in your towns, so that your male and female slave may rest as well as you. Remember that you were a slave in the land of Egypt, and the LORD your God brought you out from there with a mighty hand and an outstretched arm; therefore the LORD your God commanded you to keep the sabbath day.

Sabbath observance here is a labor matter; it is inseparably related to the people's ongoing remembrance of their slavery in Egypt and their liberation by the hand of God. By remembering the suffering of slave labor and the joy of liberation, the people of Israel were challenged to a new way of organizing labor in their present context.[12]

As on Israel's Sabbath, such remembering is a critical liturgical and homiletical practice for the church today. Remembering the history of suffering and oppression can still be a powerful way for redemptive preaching to expose the powers and set people free from ignorance and amnesia. In one of my courses I begin by showing the documentary film *Uprising of '34*.[13] The film tells the story of the nationwide textile-mill strike in 1934, which was violently crushed by the "powers that be." It is an extraordinary story, told exclusively in the words of the people who participated in or have been affected by

---

12. The logical trajectory would be to set free all slave laborers, though the text does not yet take that step.
13. *Uprising of '34*, prod. and dir. George Stoney and Judith Helfand, 1995.

the strike. The film provides an enlightening case study of the dynamics of the principalities and powers and of resistance to them.

What is most striking, however, are the responses of my students, many of whom grew up in the Southeast where the heart of the strike and the most violent responses to it occurred. As the students watch the film, they recognize towns and names and places mentioned in it. Often with tears in their eyes, the students make very personal connections to the events. "I grew up right down the road from Honea Path, South Carolina," where the most violent incident of the strike occurred. "The scholarship I received in college came from money given by one of the mills." "I've ridden by Fort MacPherson, where many of the strikers were detained; it's right here in Atlanta, just a few miles from the seminary." "The churches that supported the powers were in my denomination." Then, however, comes the most important and shocking realization: "I've never heard anything about this strike. I didn't even know it had taken place. Why hasn't anyone ever told me about this event so close to where I grew up?"

The powers have managed to silence the realities of the textile-mill strike of 1934. And the students' realization of their ignorance is wrenching and frustrating; anger and tears are common. Nevertheless, through this pain—a kind of grief for the loss of the world as they knew it—they begin to see the world differently. The powers of death have been exposed, and the past has been reenvisioned. The story—the memory—through which the students see and live in the world has been transformed, and their lives begin to change. Such acts of remembering are a critical way in which the powers are exposed. While preachers need to be aware of the deep grief that such remembering can create, they also must heed the poignant words with which the film closes: "The struggle of humanity against power is a struggle of memory against forgetting." Such remembering is one way in which preachers expose the principalities and powers and create the possibility for further resistance.

"Big Pictures"

Another way in which the powers may be exposed is through powerful, dramatic imagery that cuts through the claims of the powers and unveils them for what they are. The preacher provides a counterimagery to that offered by the powers. As the Roman Catholic short-story writer Flannery O'Connor wrote about her bizarre stories and strange characters, "You have to make your vision apparent by shock—to the hard of hearing you shout, and for the almost-blind you draw large and startling pictures."[14] In other words, when we are preach-

---

14. Flannery O'Connor, *Mystery and Manners: Occasional Prose*, ed. Sally Fitzgerald and Robert Fitzgerald (New York: Farrar, Straus & Giroux, 1961), 34.

ing for people whose imaginations have been numbed and bedeviled by the powers, we may have to preach big pictures.

The visionary who penned the book of Revelation engaged in this kind of exposing. In the face of the all-encompassing claims and demands of the empire, the writer of Revelation metaphorically unveiled the empire as a beast that violently destroys people and a whore who seduces people to trust in its deadly ways. It is difficult to imagine a more dramatic unveiling of the divine claims and deadly realities of empire than one finds in the metaphorical visions of Revelation:

> And I saw a beast rising out of the sea, having ten horns and seven heads; and on its horns were ten diadems, and on its heads were blasphemous names. And the beast that I saw was like a leopard, its feet were like a bear's, and its mouth was like a lion's mouth. And the dragon gave it his power and his throne and great authority. One of its heads seemed to have received a deathblow, but its mortal wound had been healed. In amazement the whole earth followed the beast. They worshiped the dragon, for he had given his authority to the beast, and they worshiped the beast, saying, "Who is like the beast, and who can fight against it?" (Rev. 13:1–4)[15]

For people who were suffering oppression at the hands of empire, and for churches who had grown complacent accommodating to the lure of empire, the book of Revelation dramatically and metaphorically sought to expose the powers and free the church from empire's grip.[16]

In a similar way, John Steinbeck seeks to expose the powers of capitalism by naming the bank the "Monster" and by depicting its voracious appetite for profits. Steinbeck similarly exposes the power of technology through the imagery of rape, by means of which he depicts the powers of death at work through a tractor's mechanical penetration of the land:

> Behind the tractor rolled the shining disks, cutting the earth with blades—not plowing but surgery, pushing the cut earth to the right where the second row of disks cut it and pushed it to the left; slicing blades shining, polished by the cut earth. And pulled behind the disks, the harrows combing with iron teeth so that the little clods broke up and the earth lay smooth. Behind the harrows, the long seeders—

---

15. Despite the violent imagery throughout the book of Revelation, it is ultimately the Lamb who was slain (the crucified Jesus) who exposes the beast and reveals him for what he is. The central role of the Lamb serves as a constant countertestimony to the violent imagery through which the defeat of the beast is depicted.
16. The parables also use powerful stories and images to expose the powers and envision the new creation. I discuss them in the next section, on envisioning.

twelve curved iron penes erected in the foundry, orgasms set by gears, raping methodically, raping without passion.[17]

More recently, William Greider, the author of several widely read books on economics, has depicted global capitalism through a similar metaphor:

> Imagine a wondrous new machine, strong and supple, a machine that reaps as it destroys. It is huge and mobile, something like the machines of modern agriculture but vastly more complicated and powerful. Think of this awesome machine running over open terrain and ignoring familiar boundaries. It plows across fields and fencerows with a fierce momentum that is exhilarating to behold and also frightening. As it goes, the machine throws off enormous mows of wealth and bounty while it leaves behind great furrows of wreckage.
>
> Now imagine that there are skillful hands on board, but no one is at the wheel. In fact, this machine has no wheel nor any internal governor to control the speed and direction. It is sustained by its own forward motion, guided mainly by its own appetites. And it is accelerating.[18]

Greider here depicts global capitalism not as a humanly managed or humanely concerned system but as an impersonal machine, driven and devouring by its own "manic logic." The metaphor is both disturbing and eye-opening; it exposes global capitalism as a principality and helps us see the world in a new way. The use of such powerful metaphors and images is yet another way to expose the powers and help build up a people for resistance.

"Radicalizing Moments"

Another way to expose the powers is through sharing what Christine Smith calls "radicalizing moments."[19] Such moments are personal experiences through which the powers have been exposed for the preacher and through which she herself has come to see the world in new ways. Sharing such experiences is important for the preacher, not only because they can help expose the powers but because through them the preacher stands with the congregation, implicated in her own complicity with the powers and vulnerably

---

17. John Steinbeck, *The Grapes of Wrath*, Penguin Great Books of the Twentieth Century (New York: Penguin Books, 1999), 36.

18. William Greider, *One World, Ready or Not: The Manic Logic of Global Capitalism* (New York: Simon & Schuster, 1997), 11. Howard-Brook and Gwyther argue that today global capitalism has characteristics of the beast depicted in the book of Revelation; see their *Unveiling Empire*, 236–77.

19. I have borrowed the phrase "radicalizing moments" from Smith, *Preaching as Weeping, Confession, and Resistance*, 8. Smith shares these moments throughout her book.

recounting those moments when her vision was changed. In addition, sharing such "radicalizing moments" moves the act of "exposing" into everyday life. The powers are unveiled not just through big, dramatic means but through discerning the powers' work in ordinary, everyday events.

Jane Fahey's conversation with the Vietnam veteran in the sermon excerpt cited above is a good example of a radicalizing moment. More recently, I heard another preacher share such a radicalizing moment. In a sermon titled "Dinner with Amos," Ted Wardlaw, pastor of Central Presbyterian Church in Atlanta, sought to expose the human suffering on which economic privilege is based. Toward the end of the sermon he shared this story:

> Before the girls came, and while we were still living in Texas, Kay and I went on a little vacation to the perfectly delightful Spanish colonial city of Oaxaca, in the south of Mexico. Up amid splendid mountains, not far from the ruins of an ancient Indian civilization, amid the glitter of gilded churches and spacious city squares and gorgeous architecture and wonderful pottery and art. We went for a week or so. We lived like royalty—not because we had saved a wad of money for this trip, but because, given the economy, everything could be had for so little. The fancy hotels, the great meals at stunning restaurants—it was just cheap!
>
> One afternoon, after some sightseeing, we were sitting in a little outdoor café right on the main square, having a glass of wine and maybe some sopapillas. And sitting at a table next to us was another American couple about our age. They had been sitting there for some time. From the sense of things, they had had several carafes of wine. They had pretty much exhausted whatever conversation they could have had with one another, and now their attention had turned to the ubiquitous presence in that part of the world of beggars. For amusement, they had beckoned for a little crowd of children to come over to their table. These children had been begging in the square—selling little packages of Chiclets for pocket change—but now this couple had a proposition for them. Run around the square as many times as you can, the man said, and I'll give you x number of pesos for each lap you make. And so now, as we sat there sipping our wine and enjoying our good fortune, these impoverished children were running around the square. Running desperately— like mice on a treadmill trying to get to the food that is just beyond reach—while this couple next to us just laughed. We sat there, and there they would go—round and round the square. "Run faster," he said over and over again. "Don't stop running," he yelled to them, and that couple just laughed. And after a while, as they ran and ran and ran around that square for that handful of pesos, whatever the little feast was in front of us began to smell for all the world like rotten fruit.[20]

---

20. Theodore J. Wardlaw, "Dinner With Amos," preached at Central Presbyterian Church, Atlanta, Georgia, July 22, 2001. The image of rotten fruit, which runs as a refrain throughout the sermon, similarly serves to expose the powers.

I heard this sermon preached, and the story was a painful and unsettling one, moving me toward both grief and confession. I could no longer see the feasts I enjoy in the same way again. The powers that support my privilege had been unveiled. The sharing of such "radicalizing moments" can be a poignant way to expose the powers of death at work in the world and help move congregations through confession toward resistance.[21]

Burlesque

Walter Wink has suggested a final way of exposing the powers, one drawn from Jesus' Sermon on the Mount: *burlesque.* Because the powers stand on their dignity, nothing disempowers them more quickly than burlesque or lampooning.[22] In his interpretation of Matthew 5:40, Wink notes the burlesque character of Jesus' command to "give your inner garment also."[23] The situation is one in which the economic powers have so milked the poor that all they have left to be sued for are their garments. When their outer garment is claimed in court, Wink argues, Jesus counsels them to give the inner one also. That is, the victim of the economic system, who has no other recourse, takes off the inner garment and walks out of the court stark naked. In this way the victim not only retains his or her status as a moral agent but also exposes the system's essential cruelty and "burlesques its pretensions to justice, law, and order."[24] As the person walks out of court naked and people begin to ask what is going on, the economic system itself stands naked and is exposed for what it is—a system that treats the poor as "sponge[s] to be squeezed dry by the rich."[25] By presenting this ethical option in his sermon, Jesus himself actually engages in a homiletical burlesque of the economic system.

Contemporary preachers can likewise engage in this kind of burlesque. One of the best examples I've heard was in a sermon by my colleague Anna Carter Florence, titled "The Woman Who Just Said 'No.'"[26] Her sermon focuses on

---

21. On the movement from confession to resistance, see Smith, *Preaching as Weeping, Confession, and Resistance,* 3–6.

22. Wink, *Engaging the Powers,* 179.

23. Ibid., 177–79. See also Walter Wink, "Neither Passivity nor Violence: Jesus' Third Way," *Forum* 7 (March–June, 1991): 12.

24. Wink, "Jesus' Third Way," 12.

25. Ibid.

26. The sermon is based on Esther 1:1–2:4. Florence's emphasis on the word *no* is important. William Stringfellow argues that the first word of resistance that we speak in the face of the powers is *no.* See William Stringfellow, *An Ethic for Christians and Other Aliens in a Strange Land* (Waco, Tex.: Word Books, 1973; 3d paperback ed., 1979), 155–56. Similarly, as I discussed in chapter 3, Jesus begins his ministry by saying no to the devil in the wilderness.

the story of Vashti in the book of Esther, which, Florence asserts, is a "dangerous memory" for the church, reminding us that the church's own story often has to be remembered or reenvisioned. In the opening section of the sermon, Florence retells the story in a burlesque way:

> Vashti makes her one and only appearance at the beginning of the book of Esther. Right away, we have a clue as to why this is not generally considered to be great Sunday School material: what we are reading about is probably the biggest party ever given in the ancient world. And when I say "party," I don't mean a lovely little fiesta or soiree; I mean a great, big drunken brawl, personally hosted by the king himself. We're talking "Animal House"; we're talking "Tailhook"; we're talking about one hundred and eighty-seven days of straight debauchery.
>
> Here's the story. King Ahasuerus, who ruled lands from Ethiopia to India, decided one day to throw a party for all the officials and governors and soldiers and princes who worked for him in over one hundred and twenty-seven provinces. The purpose of this party was not to *thank* his employees, however. It was to *impress* them. The king wanted to dazzle everyone with the splendor and pomp of his royal palace, and he figured he needed about six months to do it right. So that's what he did: the king invited his workers to leave their posts for about half a year and come party in the capitol of Babylon. There was no agenda except to gorge and drink and be impressed, which they did and were. And after six months of *that*, the king decided this wasn't enough; more people needed to be impressed, and he brought in fresh recruits. The entire capitol was invited to come for a final seven days of royal display, and, as the text says, the whole town drank by the flagons, without restraint, for the king had given orders to all the officials of his palace to do as each one desired.
>
> Heaven only knows how the rest of the kingdom was coping, with the army and government on a six month vacation and no one in charge back home and all the tax dollars going into the entertainment budget. But this is a king whose priority is not to do the *right* thing, but to do the *fun* thing. So it comes as no surprise that on the one hundred and eighty-seventh day of this royal bash, the king decides that he has not yet displayed everything he owns; he has not yet shown the hordes his *wife*. *That* would be a fun thing! Bear in mind that in those days, men and women lived separately. No one—and I mean *no one*—was allowed to look at the king's wives (and yes, there were many of them) except the king and his eunuchs, who were, as you can imagine, no threat at all. But this is a king who likes to flaunt convention, if it will impress his underlings. He orders his servants to bring him the ravishing Queen Vashti, wearing her royal crown, so that everyone can "see her beauty"—which means, basically, that he wants Vashti to come out wearing *only* her crown; nothing else. The king wants all these men who have spent six months eating the king's

food and drinking the king's wine to take a good, long look at the king's wife, as only the king can see her, and to remember that *this* is one thing they can't have.

Here comes the dangerous part of the story. Even though the atmosphere is as charged with testosterone as any you will ever find, Queen Vashti does not do as any obedient subject of the king ought to do, when given a direct order. She does not shuck her clothes, swallow her pride, and pretend that she is Demi Moore trapped in a strip tease joint for the good of her family. Queen Vashti is probably the first woman on record to *just say no*. No, I will not come out and make a display of myself for your benefit. No, I will not lose my integrity so that you can save face in front of your friends. No, I will not do whatever you tell me to do. And I most emphatically will not do it when you have been drunk for one hundred and eighty-seven days.

The king's reaction is predictable. He is enraged and humiliated. Not only that, he is enraged and humiliated in front of all the men of the kingdom. The story spreads. Women in Persia and Media hear of it; women in Ethiopia and India learn of how Queen Vashti *just said no* to the king. They decide to give it a try. Soon, men who may have been snickering at the king in the throne room are no longer snickering. They find that Queen Vashti's example has let loose a tidal wave of rebellion among the women of the empire. Noble ladies everywhere are discovering great potential in *just saying no*. The order of the entire kingdom is disrupted. What to do?

The king, the officials, and the sages put their heads together. They ask: according to the law, what is to be done to Queen Vashti because she has not performed the command of the King? They decide: let her rot. Away with Vashti, and away with any woman who fails to do as her husband commands. Let another queen be chosen to take Vashti's place, and please, God, may her memory die with her.

On one level, the men are successful. Vashti disappears, there is a cattle call for young virgins to come and compete for the queen's title, and eventually, one of them is able to distract the king from the memory of his exiled wife: Esther is crowned queen, and as far as the church is concerned, we can get on to the real story of the book. On one level, the church concurs with the king and all his sages: it has let the memory of Vashti rot.

On another level, however, the story of Vashti cannot be erased. There are echoes of her great *No* reverberating all through the Bible. Vashti may be nothing but a prologue to the book of Esther in the church's eyes, for all that we hear about her, but in the Bible she lives on in the minds of her people, the king, and most importantly, Queen Esther herself.[27]

---

27. Anna Carter Florence, "The Woman Who Just Said 'No,'" *Journal for Preachers* 22 (Advent 1998): 37–39.

Like Jesus, Vashti, through her suffering, exposes the realities of kingship and patriarchy. And by means of burlesque Florence exposes the system of patriarchy, disarms it, and creates a space for resistance. In addition, by simply retelling the story, Florence suggests that the *text itself* engages in precisely this kind of burlesque.

Such a comic and burlesque style can be a powerful way to expose the powers. Through the use of risky humor, preaching may unfold the logical consequences of the ways of the powers and thereby unmask them for what they are, burst their pretentious bubbles, and free worshipers from their tyranny. Instead of somber, self-important sermons dealing with such matters as capitalism or individualism, preachers from time to time may offer startlingly comic or burlesque depictions of the powers, lampooning the absurdity of their claims. Then a space may be created for the redemptive power of the Word, not just for the hearers but for the powers themselves.[28]

Whether through direct speech or through other, more creative approaches, preachers confronting the powers will find ways to expose them. At times such resistance will indeed seem fragile, puny, and foolish. Often the preacher will meet with opposition or create conflict. At other times, the preacher will need to become a pastor dealing with the tears of grief and lament over worlds that have to die before the new can be born. At all times, such preaching will require imagination, compassion, and courage. Nevertheless, the preacher is called to speak the truth and expose the powers. In the midst of "babel," such truthtelling is essential for the vision and life of the church, as well as for the redemption of the world.

ENVISIONING

Simply exposing the principalities and powers and unveiling their ways of death in the world is not sufficient for preachers. If preachers stopped with exposing, they would deny the good news of the gospel that the new creation has, in fact, broken into the world in Jesus' life, death, and resurrection and will be brought to completion in the fullness of time. If all preachers do is expose the principalities and powers, congregations might be left in despair, overwhelmed by the enormity of the powers' work, without the hope that is

---

28. Because the powers are not destroyed or violently overthrown, the possibility is opened for their redemption, their return to the good purposes for which they were created. See Wink, "Jesus' Third Way," 12; idem, *Engaging the Powers*, 73–85. William Stringfellow also hopes for the redemption of the powers; see, for example, his *Free in Obedience* (New York: Seabury Press, 1964), 73.

essential to sustain the life of resistance. Such a result would play right into the hands of the powers, which, as I noted in chapter 2, seek to overwhelm people and paralyze them by making them feel that all resistance is fruitless.

Consequently, the other movement in preaching amid the powers involves "envisioning" the new creation by helping the congregation discern "tokens of the resurrection" in the midst of a world of death and by enabling God's people to imagine alternatives to a world governed by the powers. Just as, in the Beatitudes, Jesus simultaneously exposes the ways of death in the world and envisions the new creation, so, in preaching, exposing and envisioning go hand in hand; exposing the powers' ways of death is necessarily accompanied by envisioning the new creation that is breaking into the world and coming in fullness. Such envisioning seeks to set people free from the fear of death and to generate hope that empowers new life in and for the world.

The Example of the Parables

Jesus' parables provide a critical example of homiletical resistance to the powers by reconstruing the world and envisioning alternatives to the ways of death. In narrative form, the parables do what Walter Brueggemann has argued the poet/preacher does: "The poet/prophet is a voice that shatters settled reality and evokes new possibility in the listening assembly. Preaching continues that dangerous, indispensable habit of speech. The poetic speech of text and of sermon is a prophetic construal of a world beyond the one taken for granted."[29] Although often domesticated in contemporary homiletics, the parables are subversive acts of resistance, which invite the hearers to see the world in radically new ways.[30]

Gilbert Meilaender begins an essay on preaching and ethics with a discussion of the parable of the Good Samaritan. His conclusion highlights the way in which the parable invites people to envision and live into a new world: "The most characteristic aspect of the Samaritan's behavior is that it is not of this world. . . . Hearing that message we really are taken out of this world. Or, per-

---

29. Walter Brueggemann, *Finally Comes the Poet: Daring Speech for Proclamation* (Philadelphia: Fortress Press, 1989), 4. See also Walter Brueggemann, "Preaching as Reimagination," *Theology Today* 52 (October 1995): 313–29.
30. On the domestication of the parables in contemporary homiletics, see Susan Bond, "Taming the Parable: The Problem of Parable as Substitute Myth," in *Papers of the Annual Meeting of the Academy of Homiletics* (1999), 167–77. On the parables as tactics of resistance, see David Toole, *Waiting for Godot in Sarajevo: Theological Reflections on Nihilism, Tragedy, and Apocalypse* (Boulder, Colo.: Westview Press, 1998), 235–41. On the subversive character of the parables, see William R. Herzog II, *Parables as Subversive Speech: Jesus as Pedagogue of the Oppressed* (Louisville, Ky.: Westminster John Knox Press, 1994).

haps better, we are put to death with this world in order to be raised in the new one of God's making."[31] In this parable, as Meilaender suggests, Jesus holds before his hearers a new reality, a vision of the world in light of God's present and coming reign, which he himself embodies.

Similarly, Leander Keck has captured this link between the parables and a new way of seeing the world. According to Keck, the reign of God "restructures everyone's present," and the parables present a vision of God's reign which facilitates that restructuring.[32] The parables "lean toward something that is not self-evident but which, nonetheless, can be seen if one looks through the parable and with the parable; appropriately, that to which they point becomes visible only through the parables."[33] The hearer looks through the parable and sees the world in a new way. Often disruptive, hyperbolic, and bizarre, "the parable is a metaphor that presents an imaged action to the hearer in a way sufficiently arresting to require him [or her] to rethink the whole in a new way."[34] The parables ultimately challenge the hearers' vision of reality. They construe a new and different world—an alternative to the powers' world of death—in which the community of faith may live.

Moreover, the parables cannot be isolated from the life, death, and resurrection of Jesus. Ultimately the story of Jesus itself is the "master parable" that reconstrues the world, and within which the spoken parables must be understood.[35] As Keck writes, "Since the whole Jesus was permeated by the Kingdom of God, and since that Kingdom is the effectuation of God's reign, it is Jesus as a whole who points to the Kingdom in a new way. . . . [Jesus invited people] to look through him into the Kingdom, with the result that his hearers could not respond to the Kingdom without responding to him."[36]

---

31. Gilbert Meilaender, "The Place of Ethics in the Theological Task," *Currents in Theology and Mission* 6 (1979): 197–98. Despite his insight into the workings of the parable, Meilaender argues that the parable is not really about ethics. As I have argued earlier, however, in helping people see the world in a new way, the parable is precisely about that more fundamental level of ethics—attention and vision—that underlies decisions and actions.

32. Leander E. Keck, *A Future for the Historical Jesus: The Place of Jesus in Preaching and Theology* (Philadelphia: Fortress Press, 1981), 225, 247.

33. Ibid., 244.

34. Ibid., 245, 247.

35. On the inseparability of the parables from the story of Jesus, see Charles L. Campbell, *Preaching Jesus: New Directions for Homiletics in Hans Frei's Postliberal Theology* (Grand Rapids: Wm. B. Eerdmans Publishing Co., 1997), 177–80.

36. Keck, *Future for the Historical Jesus*, 245. In Mark 4:11, Jesus tells his disciples, "To you has been given the secret of the kingdom of God." Jesus himself is, of course, that secret. See Paul J. Achtemeier, *Invitation to Mark* (Garden City, N.Y.: Image Books, 1978), 70. Distinctions between "preaching Jesus" and "preaching the kingdom" are inappropriate.

The reign of God—the new creation—that is breaking into the world is inseparable from Jesus, in whose life, death, and resurrection the new creation is both present and coming. Jesus himself confronts his hearers with a new reality, which challenges their ways of seeing the world. At the heart of the New Testament, as Keck suggests, is a new vision of reality embodied in the life, death, and resurrection of Jesus Christ and brought to speech, in part, in the parables. In this sense the parables serve a function similar to the Beatitudes in the Sermon on the Mount.

More recently, Ched Myers has clarified the ways in which parables function as acts of resistance and envision a concrete political alternative to the powers that be. The parable of the Sower in Mark 4:3–8, for example, which can be read as a parable about the proclamation of the gospel, is also, according to Myers, a subversive challenge to the economic powers that oppressed poor indentured farmers in first-century Palestine. The closing words of the parable—"Other seed fell into good soil and brought forth grain, growing up and increasing and yielding thirty and sixty and a hundredfold"—represent an "agrarian eschatology," in which blessing takes the form of an astounding harvest. Such a blessing stands in stark contrast to the economic realities of first-century Palestine, where "wealthy landlords always extracted enough of the harvest to ensure that the farmer remained indentured to the land, strangling any prospects . . . of economic security."[37]

Against this background, the promise of an astounding harvest, made to the *sower* and *not* the landlords, envisions a new reality that subverts the principalities and powers of the world. As Myers writes, this promise "symbolically represents a dramatic shattering of the vassal relationship between peasant and landlord. With such surplus the farmer could not only eat and pay his rent, tithes, and debts, but indeed even purchase the land, and thus end his servitude forever. 'The kingdom is like *this*,' says Jesus: it *envisions* the abolition of the oppressive relationships of production that determined the horizons of the Palestinian farmer's social world."[38]

What Meilaender and Keck suggest in a general way, Myers makes concrete in the midst of the harsh political and economic realities of a world governed by the powers of death: The parables subvert the principalities and powers and "reimagine" the world for their hearers. The purpose of the parables is not simply to help individuals experience the gospel and make their own decisions. Rather, like the story of Jesus as a whole, of which they are a part, the parables

---

37. Ched Myers, *Binding the Strong Man: A Political Reading of Mark's Story of Jesus* (Maryknoll, N.Y.: Orbis Books, 1988), 176.
38. Ibid., 176; italics mine. See also the broader discussion in Toole, *Godot in Sarajevo*, 236–41.

subvert the world of the powers. They provide a lens through which people may see the new creation breaking into the world, and they seek to empower people to live into that newly envisioned reality in resistance to the powers of death.

"Tokens of the Resurrection"

Like the Beatitudes, the parables invite preachers to engage in similar kinds of envisioning in their sermons. Such envisioning will take a couple of different forms. One form involves, in Stringfellow's words, discerning "tokens of the reality of the Resurrection or hope where others are consigned to confusion or despair."[39] In the midst of the powers of death, the preacher directs the congregation's attention to glimpses of God's Shalom that is *already* breaking into the world. There is no technique to enable such discernment. Rather, it involves an ongoing attention to the world through the Christian story, just as Jesus invited his hearers to attend to the world through his preaching and parables and, more fully, through his own life, death, and resurrection. In fact, such "tokens of the resurrection" often come in surprising ways and surprising places—places where death and resurrection often are in tension.

In my own life, these glimpses of God's Shalom have often come on the streets of Atlanta among homeless people. Several months ago, for example, I was leading worship in the front yard of the Open Door Community, a Christian community that ministers with homeless people.[40] A group of us were standing in a circle, holding hands, praising God amid the noise of rush-hour traffic on Ponce de Leon Avenue, one of the busiest streets in Atlanta. It was an odd group—a few volunteers such as myself but mostly homeless men and women. We had a call to worship, a prayer, and a song. Then, as I looked around the circle, I noticed one homeless man waving to me and pointing to himself, indicating he wanted to do something. I was surprised when I saw him, for the man can neither hear nor speak, and normally he is very reserved. But there he was, urgently waving to me, requesting to provide leadership for the worship.

I nodded to him, and he stepped into the middle of the circle. Then, after bowing his head for a few moments in silence, he began to sign a hymn for us. It was remarkable, beautiful, like a dance. And while the rest of us didn't

---

39. Stringfellow, *Ethic for Christians*, 139.
40. For more information about the Open Door Community and homelessness in Atlanta, see Stanley P. Saunders and Charles L. Campbell, *The Word on the Street: Performing the Scriptures in the Urban Context* (Grand Rapids: Wm. B. Eerdmans Publishing Co., 2000). The book also contains other examples of "tokens of the resurrection."

understand all of the signs, some of them were unmistakable, like the sign for Jesus on the cross. And we all knew the Word the man proclaimed through his dance.

In the face of the power of death called homelessness, we all glimpsed a token of the resurrection; we glimpsed, for a moment, God's domination-free order in which the old categories that divide people come crumbling down. A person whom our society views as "unclean" and whom many of our wealthy churches do not welcome into their sanctuary became the inspired leader of the community's worship.

Moreover, in that moment all of our notions of "abled" and "disabled" were turned upside down. We discovered that this particular homeless man, whom the world views as disabled, actually had been given the most important gift of all that morning. In the midst of the noise of the street, the rest of us had been shouting to be heard; and despite all our efforts, the traffic often drowned us out. But the noise was no problem for our friend who could neither speak nor hear. The noise did not interrupt his signing. And we had no trouble "hearing" the Word he offered. A homeless man who could neither hear nor speak became the light in the middle of the circle, shining the gospel on all of us, drawing us together, even if just for a moment, into a more profound community. Our worship became a token of the resurrection in the midst of the powers of death, a glimpse of God's beloved community.

The experience was not unlike what James Cone sees happening each Sunday morning in African American worship. Such worship, Cone argues, becomes a sign of the inbreaking reign of God, a glimpse—and for the worshipers, an experience—of the resurrection in the face of the powers of death. As Cone writes,

> Black people who have been humiliated and oppressed by the structures of white society six days of the week, gather together each Sunday morning in order to experience a new definition of their humanity. The transition from Saturday to Sunday is not just a chronological change from the seventh to the first day of the week. It is rather a rupture in time, a kairos-event which produces a radical transformation in the people's identity. The janitor becomes the chairperson of the Deacon Board; the maid becomes the president of the Stewardess Board. . . . Everybody becomes Mr. and Mrs., or Brother and Sister. The last becomes first, making a radical change in the perception of self and one's calling in the society. Every person becomes somebody.[41]

---

41. James Cone, "Sanctification, Liberation, and Black Worship," *Theology Today* 35 (1978–79): 140.

Discerning and sharing such tokens of the resurrection, preachers envision God's domination-free order in their preaching and help congregations attend to the world in new ways. Moreover, as Cone suggests, *being* such a token of the resurrection is one way in which the church can live in resistance to the Domination System shaped by the principalities and powers.

"Hyperbolic Imagination"

The second way in which preachers envision God's redeemed creation is through what has been called "disjunctive vision."[42] This kind of envisioning involves not discerning tokens of the resurrection *already* in the world but audaciously holding before the congregation a vision of the new creation that is coming, even when there is no evidence for it in the present.[43] Such envisioning calls for a "hyperbolic imagination" that provides bold counter-metaphors to those of the powers, "opens our myopic vision," and stirs the imagination from numbness.[44] This kind of speech invites a "rhetoric of excess"—the poetics of the impossible rather than the prose of the probable.[45] Such disjunctive, hyperbolic envisioning is an act of resistance to the powers; it interrupts business as usual and subverts the status quo, calling us to "withstand all that goes without saying, all that we would like to take for granted."[46] Such a hyperbolic imagination, "informed by the (il)logic of the parables and the narrative of Jesus' triumph through suffering, sees the world as it really is, but, in addition, sees it as it most certainly is not—that is, as what it can become and, therefore, was meant to be."[47]

The Bible is full of this kind of hyperbolic, disjunctive envisioning. The parable of the Sower, which I examined earlier, concludes with such hyperbole—an astonishing, disjunctive vision of a harvest "yielding thirty and sixty and a hundredfold" for impoverished indentured farmers. One also finds such visions of God's Shalom in the words of the prophets:

---

42. The idea of "disjunctive vision" comes from James F. Kay, "Preaching in Advent," *Journal for Preachers* 13 (Advent 1989): 11–16.

43. Ibid., 14.

44. On "hyperbolic imagination" see Stephen H. Webb, "A Hyperbolic Imagination: Theology and the Rhetoric of Excess," *Theology Today* 50 (April 1993): 56–67. Flannery O'Connor's comment about "big pictures" applies here too. The final vision in O'Connor's well-known short story "Revelation" is an extraordinary example of this kind of envisioning. See Flannery O'Connor, "Revelation," in *Everything That Rises Must Converge* (New York: Farrar, Straus & Giroux, 1965), 191–218.

45. Webb, "Hyperbolic Imagination," 67.

46. Ibid., 62.

47. Ibid., 64.

The wolf shall live with the lamb,
> the leopard shall lie down with the kid,
the calf and the lion and the fatling together,
> and a little child shall lead them.
The cow and the bear shall graze,
> their young shall lie down together;
> and the lion shall eat straw like the ox.
The nursing child shall play over the hole of the asp,
> and the weaned child shall put its hand on the adder's den.
They will not hurt or destroy
> on all my holy mountain;
For the earth will be full of the knowledge of the LORD
> as the waters cover the sea.

(Isa. 11:6–9)

Not surprisingly, the book of Revelation concludes the Bible with one of the grandest hyperbolic visions. In the face of both the suffering born of persecution by the empire and the numbness born of accommodation to the empire, the visionary who wrote the book of Revelation declares:

> Then I saw a new heaven and a new earth; for the first heaven and the first earth had passed away, and the sea was no more. And I saw the holy city, the new Jerusalem, coming down out of heaven from God, prepared as a bride adorned for her husband. And I heard a loud voice from the throne saying,
>
> > "See, the home of God is among mortals.
> > [God] will dwell with them;
> > they will be [God's] peoples,
> > and God . . . will be with them;
> > [God] will wipe every tear from their eyes.
> > Death will be no more;
> > mourning and crying and pain will be no more,
> > for the first things have passed away."

(Rev. 21:1–4)[48]

Such disjunctive visions have been echoed in our own time by Martin Luther King Jr. in his famous "I Have a Dream" speech. Standing in the face of the powers that be in Washington, D.C., and speaking from the midst of the realities of racism, King created a space for further resistance with his concluding vision:

---

48. It is important to note how many of these visions draw on the community's memories, just as Revelation does in its use of the language of covenant—"they will be [God's] peoples." The hyperbolic visions, such as the exilic visions of a new exodus (see Isa. 40:3–5), are often informed by a "figural imagination" shaped by the stories of the people.

I have a dream that one day on the red hills of Georgia, sons of former slaves and sons of former slave-owners will be able to sit down together at the table of brotherhood.

I have a dream that one day, even the state of Mississippi, a state sweltering with the heat of injustice, sweltering with the heat of oppression, will be transformed into an oasis of freedom and justice.

I have a dream my four little children will one day live in a nation where they will not be judged by the color of their skin but by the content of their character. I have a dream today!

I have a dream that one day, down in Alabama, with its vicious racists, with its governor having his lips dripping with the words of interposition and nullification, that one day, right there in Alabama, little black boys and black girls will be able to join hands with little white boys and white girls as sisters and brothers. I have a dream today!

I have a dream that one day every valley shall be exalted, every hill and mountain shall be made low, the rough places shall be made plain, and the crooked places shall be made straight and the glory of the Lord will be revealed and all flesh shall see it together.[49]

In this extraordinary section of the speech, King both concretely *exposes* the power of white racism and offers a disjunctive *vision* of the future. He concludes the section by framing his vision through the figure of the "new exodus," taken from Isaiah 40:3–5 and Luke 3:5–6. Possibly nowhere else in recent years has the potential of such envisioning to set people free for resistance to the powers been more evident.

In a wide variety of ways, then, preachers seek to resist the principalities and powers, exposing their deadly ways and envisioning God's redeemed creation. Through these various tactics of exposing and envisioning, preachers help create the space for the church's further resistance to the powers of death. Such exposing and envisioning, however, are not sufficient by themselves. In addition, the preacher must attend to the communal practices that both nurture the vision and enable the church to live into it. To the role of such practices in preaching I now turn.

---

49. Martin Luther King Jr., *A Testament of Hope: The Essential Writings and Speeches of Martin Luther King, Jr.*, ed. James Melvin Washington (San Francisco: HarperSanFrancisco, 1986; 1st HarperCollins paperback ed., 1991), 219. As numerous African American leaders have pointed out, this portion of King's speech has itself been co-opted by the powers who would like to divert attention from King's radical critique of the "American dream," which became increasingly pronounced in his later years. The prophetic vision of this speech should not be divorced from the prophetic rage that shaped many of King's speeches in his later life. For another powerful example of this kind of vision, see the "Statement of Faith from South Africa," in *The Iona Community Worship Book* (Glasgow: Wild Goose Publications, 1997), 72.

7

Preaching What We Practice

Recent Christian scholarship has emphasized the crucial role that practices play in the life of the community of faith.[1] Increasingly, theologians and ethicists are coming to recognize that the Christian faith is not simply a matter of abstract ideas or individual experiences but rather must be embodied in concrete communal practices that shape the lives of believers.[2] The church, these writers suggest, is best understood not as an institution or a group of individuals but as a set of communal practices that form the character of God's people.

---

1. Nancey C. Murphy, Brad J. Kallenberg, and Mark Thiessen Nation, eds., *Virtues and Practices in the Christian Tradition: Christian Ethics after MacIntyre* (Harrisburg, Pa.: Trinity Press International, 1997); Dorothy C. Bass, ed., *Practicing Our Faith: A Way of Life for a Searching People* (San Francisco: Jossey-Bass, 1997); Philip D. Kenneson, *Life on the Vine: Cultivating the Fruit of the Spirit in Christian Community* (Downers Grove, Ill.: InterVarsity Press, 1999); Miroslav Volf and Dorothy C. Bass, eds., *Practicing Theology: Beliefs and Practices in Christian Life* (Grand Rapids: Wm. B. Eerdmans Publishing Co., 2001). While I examine some of the church's practices in what follows, it is not my intention to provide an extensive account of the practices essential to the life of the church as a community of nonviolent resistance. Such an undertaking would require another book. Rather, I examine the ways in which preaching may nurture practices. The particular practices that sermons address will depend on both the texts that are used for the sermon and the particular context in which the congregation finds itself. Within this context, preachers and congregations will seek to discern and develop practices that embody alternatives to the powers of domination, violence, and death.

2. This turn is similar to the cultural-linguistic turn in Christian theology. See George Lindbeck, *The Nature of Doctrine: Religion and Theology in a Postliberal Age* (Philadelphia: Westminster Press, 1984); Charles L. Campbell, *Preaching Jesus: New Directions for Homiletics in Hans Frei's Postliberal Theology* (Grand Rapids: Wm. B. Eerdmans Publishing Co., 1997).

In the field of Christian ethics, in particular, ethicists focusing on character rather than decisions have increasingly emphasized the importance of practices in the moral formation of believers.[3] Whereas Iris Murdoch early on influenced the redevelopment of character ethics through the metaphor of vision, in recent years Alasdair MacIntyre, through his enormously influential book *After Virtue*, has turned the attention of Christian ethicists to the role of communal practices in shaping the moral life.[4] "Practice" has joined "vision" as a critical category in Christian ethics.

In the work of Stanley Hauerwas, who has been influenced by both Murdoch and MacIntyre, the connection between vision and practice becomes explicit. While he stresses that we can act only in a world we can see, Hauerwas also emphasizes the role that practices—both linguistic and corporal—play in shaping Christian vision or imagination. Seeing the world faithfully does not just happen but requires training in the disciplined skills or practices that shape our vision. Drawing on the image of the artist, Hauerwas not only emphasizes the aesthetic dimension of ethics through the metaphor of vision (or imagination) but likewise emphasizes the necessary training and practices that go into the development of the artist's vision and craft.[5] The jazz saxophonist John Coltrane, for example, had an extraordinary vision of the world that he sought to express through his art. But that vision, as well as his expression of it, was inseparable from the countless hours during which he practiced his scales and chords.[6]

In a similar way, Hauerwas argues, vision and practice are inseparable in the life of discipleship. "To become a disciple is not a matter of a new or changed self-understanding, but rather to become part of a different community with a different set of practices."[7] Taking up the practices of discipleship, Christians

---

3. For example, see Murphy, Kallenberg, and Nation, *Virtues and Practices*; and James William McClendon, *Systematic Theology: Ethics* (Nashville: Abingdon Press, 1986). See also the work of Stanley Hauerwas, which was discussed in chapter 5 and is discussed further below.

4. Alasdair MacIntyre, *After Virtue: A Study in Moral Theory*, 2d ed. (Notre Dame, Ind.: University of Notre Dame Press, 1984). Murdoch would certainly have recognized the importance of practices. Indeed, for her, attending properly to the world is a kind of practice, which must be "trained."

5. Stanley Hauerwas, "On Keeping Theological Ethics Imaginative," in *Against the Nations: War and Survival in a Liberal Society* (Minneapolis: Winston Press, 1985), 51–60.

6. For an excellent account of Coltrane's life and work, see Eric Nisenson, *Ascension: John Coltrane and His Quest* (New York: St. Martin's Press, 1993).

7. Stanley Hauerwas, "The Politics of the Church: How We Lay Bricks and Make Disciples," in *After Christendom? How the Church Is to Behave if Freedom, Justice, and a Christian Nation Are Bad Ideas* (Nashville: Abingdon Press, 1991), 107.

are formed in a particular storied tradition with a peculiar language and distinctive skills and virtues; Christians are formed, that is, in a peculiar vision of the world. Through the practices of the Christian community, imaginations take shape; believers come to attend to the world and negotiate life in distinctive ways.

> For the imagination is not simply a container of images or ideas that we now entertain in preference to other images and ideas. Rather imagination is a set of habits and relations that can only be carried by a group of people in distinction from the world's habits. For example, nothing is more important for the church's imagination than the meal we share together in the presence of our crucified and resurrected Lord. For it is in that meal, that set of habits and relations, that the world is offered alternatives to the habits of disunity which war breeds.[8]

We can act only in a world we can see or imagine. But our vision is formed in critical ways through the practices that shape our character. Ethical preaching, Hauerwas suggests, not only needs to expose the powers of death and envision the new creation but also must nurture communities in the practices that shape how Christians see and live in the world.

In other fields of Christian scholarship, this connection between vision and practice has likewise received fresh attention. The New Testament scholar Marianne Sawicki, in her book *Seeing the Lord: Resurrection and Early Christian Practices*, has traced this essential relationship between vision and practices back to the New Testament itself. According to Sawicki, the early church understood that seeing the risen Christ in the world (or, in Stringfellow's terms, "discerning tokens of the resurrection") necessitated a set of practices that made such vision possible. Indeed, she argues that the Gospels themselves were written precisely to move Christian communities into the specific practices that would enable believers to come into the presence of the living Lord. The Gospels wrestle with a question not unlike one many church members ask today: How do I come into the presence of Jesus now that he has been raised? In response, the Gospels not only delineate the identity of Jesus but serve as a kind of communal catechesis for the development of the practices necessary to discern him and encounter him in the world.

Writing about the Gospels of Matthew and Luke, Sawicki highlights this essential connection between vision and practice:

---

8. Stanley Hauerwas, "Should War Be Eliminated?" in *Against the Nations*, 197. In the paragraph following this quotation, Hauerwas speaks of the Eucharist as a "practice" that encompasses habits and relations. For more on practices, see Hauerwas's recent book *In Good Company: The Church as Polis* (Notre Dame, Ind.: University of Notre Dame Press, 1995).

These texts specify the means of access to resurrection experience as the originating communities understood it: the possibility of identifying Jesus and Risen Lord in such a way that one's own destiny also becomes clear. The texts are, quite self-consciously, words. Yet curiously, the New Testament words assert that words are not sufficient for the possibility of resurrection. The insufficiency of text must be grasped in order to grasp the necessity of the other conditions.

What are those other conditions, besides words? *According to Luke-Acts*, what makes it possible to grasp resurrection is participation in a community whose members can be hungry, recognize hungry persons, and respond to their needs. *According to Matthew*, what is required is to put certain ethical teachings into practice. Both Gospels expressly link these conditions to recognition of the identity and significance of Jesus, while at the same time they discount the efficacy of merely verbal identifications—a highly ironic assertion to find in a literary text.[9]

The words of the New Testament canon, Sawicki argues, intend "to inspire and partner with certain kinds of action."[10] They seek to achieve their meaning only through certain practices that accompany their hearing. Mere talk about Jesus' resurrection has no meaning apart from such practices, because the very "meaning" of resurrection for the Christian community involves the practices that bring believers into the presence of the living Lord.[11]

Although this brief overview does not do justice to Sawicki's profound study, it should make clear the startling challenge that Sawicki presents to preachers, who have too often neglected the critical role of practices in relation to preaching: Homiletical metaphor, vision, and imagination cannot be isolated from the concrete practices of Christian communities. As Sawicki puts it, the "power for truth" of pulpit talk about the resurrection *depends* on the congregation's "explicit and deliberate" engagement in particular kinds of practices.[12] If preaching is to be faithful to Scripture, sermons will seek to nurture congregations in the practices that enable them to "see the Lord" in the world. In the terms I have been using, redemption from the powers of death for life in the presence of the living Christ calls for preaching that, like the Sermon on the Mount, holds together both vision and practices.

Michael Warren has similarly highlighted the integral relationship between the life practices of Christians and the vision of the world offered in the liturgy. Warren emphasizes that the relationship between vision and practice is not simply one way. Naive assumptions about worship (including preaching)

---

9. Marianne Sawicki, *Seeing the Lord: Resurrection and Early Christian Practices* (Minneapolis: Fortress Press, 1994), 83.
10. Ibid., 93.
11. Ibid.
12. Ibid. Sawicki highlights particularly caring for the poor and sharing their grief.

shaping Christian vision, he argues, must be balanced with a recognition of the ways in which our life practices—our everyday practices in the world—may distort worship's vision:

> If we accept that worship is no "pure" realm of activity independent of the lived vision of the worshipers and if we further accept that the actual vision of life brought to worship is influenced by the pattern of commitment worked out in one's life practice, then the everyday life practices of both individuals and of the local church itself need examination.[13]

Warren traces this connection between vision and practices back to the catechesis of the early church, in which life practices took priority over understanding in the early stages of Christian initiation:

> A vision of life is not verified so much by its truth claims as in the life practice it fosters or produces, which is why a key feature of the early procedure of preparing neophytes for full membership in the church was the correction of life practice. Understanding was not sufficient; correct practice of that understanding was an indispensable precondition.[14]

Congregations, he argues, should be engaged in a "process of struggle" whereby they seek "to embrace specific patterns of practice by which a gospel perspective can be lived out in [their] concrete circumstances."[15] It follows, then, that only a coherent confluence of vision and practice enables the Christian community to become a people whose life together "contests" the powers of death at work in the world.[16]

Hauerwas, Sawicki, and Warren suggest that preaching needs to augment homiletical vision and imagination with an emphasis on the communal practices through which the church embodies resistance to the powers of death in the world.[17] While exposing the powers and envisioning the new creation

---

13. Michael Warren, *At This Time, in This Place: The Spirit Embodied in the Local Assembly* (Harrisburg, Pa.: Trinity Press International, 1999), 13.

14. Ibid., 12. Warren also cites Origen: "The profound and secret mysteries must not be given, at first, to disciples, but they must be first instructed in the correction of their life style" (12).

15. Ibid., 56.

16. Warren argues that the church should become a "zone of cultural contestation." See ibid., 7–23; also Michael Warren, "The Worshiping Assembly: Possible Zone of Cultural Contestation," *Worship* 163, 1 (1989): 2–16.

17. Marva Dawn, in her recent book on the powers, has also linked vision and practice; see her *Powers, Weakness, and the Tabernacling of God* (Grand Rapids: Wm. B. Eerdmans Publishing Co., 2001). Homiletically, Susan Bond has noted the connection between the church's practices and the vision of the *basileia*. See L. Susan Bond, *Trouble with Jesus: Women, Christology, and Preaching* (St. Louis: Chalice Press, 1999), esp. 151–82.

are essential for redemptive preaching in the midst of the powers, these approaches must be accompanied by a move to the communal practices that shape the church's life. Not only are such practices necessary to enact and nurture the church's vision, but through such practices the church itself becomes a concrete, communal embodiment of resistance to the principalities and powers.

The church's resistance to the powers, in fact, begins with its own communal practices. Such resistance does not primarily involve a set of ethical norms or moral pronouncements or decision-making processes but rather a specific people who practice a concrete alternative to the ways of death in the world. When the new creation broke into the world with the rush of the Spirit on Pentecost, the result was a community embodied in a set of concrete, everyday practices that offered an alternative to the powers that be (Acts 2:41–47).[18] Likewise today, an essential dimension of the church's resistance to the powers is its embodiment of its peculiar vision in a set of practices that contest the powers' ways of death. As Nancy Duff has put it, in the midst of a society that lives according to the Old Age, "the Church provides 'pockets' of new life. . . . The Church fights the powers and principalities by refusing to live according to their ways."[19] In the midst of the powers, as Stanley Hauerwas asserts, the church doesn't simply *have* an ethic; the church seeks to practice—to *be*—an ethic.[20] The church seeks, in Stringfellow's terms, to embody the new Jerusalem in the midst of Babylon.[21] In the metaphors of the Sermon on the Mount, the church, through its specific practices, is to be salt and light in and for the world.[22]

---

18. These practices include teaching, fellowship, the breaking of the bread, prayers, signs and wonders, economic redistribution, and worship. See Marva Dawn's detailed discussion of these practices in *Powers, Weakness*, 78–117. For another helpful account of the discipleship of New Testament communities, see Gerhard Lohfink, *Jesus and Community: The Social Dimension of Christian Faith*, trans. John P. Galvin (Philadelphia: Fortress Press, 1984), 75–147.

19. Nancy J. Duff, "The Significance of Pauline Apocalyptic for Theological Ethics," in *Apocalyptic and the New Testament: Essays in Honor of J. Louis Martyn*, ed. Joel Marcus and Marion L. Soards, Journal for the Study of the New Testament: Supplement Series 24 (Sheffield: JSOT Press, 1989), 287.

20. Stanley Hauerwas, *The Peaceable Kingdom: A Primer in Christian Ethics* (Notre Dame, Ind.: University of Notre Dame Press, 1983), 99–102.

21. William Stringfellow, *An Ethic for Christians and Other Aliens in a Strange Land* (Waco, Tex.: Word Books, 1973; 3d paperback ed., 1979), 57–64; Wes Howard-Brook and Anthony Gwyther, *Unveiling Empire: Reading Revelation Then and Now* (Maryknoll, N.Y.: Orbis Books, 1999), 260–77.

22. As becomes clear in what follows, the church's practices necessarily move the community out into the world. Indeed, the church's "internal" practices build up a people capable of resisting the powers in the public arena.

No one has stated this calling more clearly than Hendrik Berkhof:

> All resistance and every attack against the gods of this age will be unfruitful, unless the church herself *is* resistance and attack, unless she demonstrates in her life and fellowship how [people] can live freed from the Powers. We can only preach the manifold wisdom of God to Mammon if our life displays that we are joyfully freed from its clutches. To reject nationalism we must begin by no longer recognizing in our own bosoms any difference between peoples. We shall only resist social injustice and the disintegration of community if justice and mercy prevail in our own life and social differences have lost their power to divide. Clairvoyant and warning words and deeds aimed at state or nation are meaningful only in so far as they spring from a church whose inner life is itself her proclamation of God's manifold wisdom to the "Powers in the air."[23]

As Berkhof notes, the church preaches to the powers (Eph. 3:10), not simply through words but also through the practices that the church embodies in the world, practices that offer an alternative to the ways of domination and death. Sermons preached in the church not only bear witness to Jesus Christ in the face of the powers but also serve this larger, embodied proclamation to the powers by helping to build up the church as a community of resistance.[24] Essential to such preaching is an attention to the church's practices.

PRACTICES

Michael Warren identifies three levels of practice that can help preachers discern the various kinds of practices to which they need to attend in sermons.[25]

---

23. Hendrik Berkhof, *Christ and the Powers*, trans. John H. Yoder (Scottdale, Pa.: Herald Press, 1962), 51.

24. Pablo Richard emphasizes that Christian resistance to the powers includes both practices and testimony; see his *Apocalypse: A People's Commentary on the Book of Revelation*, trans. Phillip Berryman (Maryknoll, N.Y.: Orbis Books, 1995), 32–33.

25. Warren also mentions a fourth understanding of practice—"praxis"—which is "practice as used in Marxist analysis to name a self-creating and world-creating activity tied to theoretical considerations" (*At This Time*, 128). Warren himself does not directly use this term, though much of what he writes moves in the direction of this kind of practice. Like Warren, I am not employing the term *praxis*, though it could describe the direction of some of the church's practices that I examine. Because "praxis" carries distinctive connotations within liberation theology, being associated with the praxis of the oppressed, I have decided not to use it for the practices of mainline congregations, just as I chose to speak of such congregations as "captive" to the powers rather than oppressed by them.

1. *Routine practices of the church.* The first and simplest level involves the "range of activities used by local churches as a way of being church."[26] These practices are the activities the church does regularly and ordinarily. They are relatively unintentional and are done so routinely as to receive little reflection. Activities such as Sunday school, potluck suppers, worship, and committee meetings are practices at this level. While critical for the life of the church, these practices often become routine; they are rarely "brought through the gate of religious intention" to discern if they actually do what we want them to do.[27]

2. *Unconscious, culturally shaped practices.* The second level of practice refers to the range of social activities that function at the edge of human awareness but have a profound impact on the shape—indeed, the spirit—of human life. These practices are produced by and function within the larger framework of a "habitus," which refers to the socially shaped patterns of behavior that function as unquestioned, even unconscious, "givens" in life—a kind of "second nature."[28] In Warren's words, a habitus is "a matrix of perceptions, appreciations, and actions functioning as a kind of law written into each person's life from early upbringing."[29] As Warren translates the concept for a consumer culture: "You can take the boy or girl out of the mall, but it is not so easy to take the mall out of the boy or girl."[30] A habitus thus configures a whole set of practices—from ways of speaking and dressing to patterns of relating and acting—into a totality. It gives people a "feel for the game" of the culture, enabling them to "play that game" fully and unreflectively.

   In this sense, a habitus and the practices it produces are closely related to the workings of the powers that I have described in the previous chapters. A habitus, in fact, provides a way of describing the total configuration of the powers' work, which becomes the "air we breathe," unconsciously shaping our patterns of acting—our practices—according to its rules.[31] Practices shaped by a habitus thus exercise a powerful, if

---

26. Warren, *At This Time*, 128.
27. Ibid.
28. This understanding of practice is taken from the work of Pierre Bourdieu, the French social thinker. See Pierre Bourdieu, *Outline of a Theory of Practice*, trans. Richard Nice (Cambridge: Cambridge University Press, 1977), esp. 72–95. I am drawing primarily on Michael Warren's helpful account of Bourdieu's work in *At This Time*, 106–11.
29. Warren, *At This Time*, 107.
30. Ibid.
31. Warren's description of the functioning of the habitus actually sounds like a description of the workings of the powers: "The social orchestration of attitude and action is 'conductorless.' Since the functioning of the social and economic order is the agent at work, there is no conspiracy on any individual's part to instill these attitudes. It is human to dance, but the choreography of this particular dance is determined socially. Habitus is not a matter of individual influences" (Warren, *At This Time*, 110). See also Bourdieu, *Outline*, 72. A necessary and complementary concept in Bourdieu's work is

unconscious, influence on human lives; in fact, a habitus and the practices it produces are so pervasive that it is difficult, though not impossible, to bring them to awareness.[32] Because these socially taken-for-granted practices often corrupt distinctive Christian practices, they require the serious attention of preachers.

3. *Intentional and disciplined practices.* The third level of practice highlighted by Warren involves practices that are highly intentional and disciplined. According to this understanding, developed by Alasdair MacIntyre in his book *After Virtue*, a practice is a socially established, cooperative activity in which the participants pursue specific standards of excellence appropriate to the activity and enjoy goods internal to the activity.[33] Because of the importance of this understanding of practice for the remainder of this book, I examine it in some detail.

MacIntyre identifies five characteristics of this level of practice:[34]

1. These practices are socially established and cooperative human activities. They cannot be undertaken alone but require the participation of others with similar purposes. In addition, these activities are complex enough to be challenging and coherent enough to aim at some goal in a unified fashion. In this sense, jazz is a practice but listening to the radio is not. Similarly, preaching is a practice but shaking hands after worship is not.

2. These practices have goods that are internal to the activity. MacIntyre makes a sharp and important distinction between goods internal to prac-

---

"doxa," which describes the "matrix of culturally induced but unspoken assumptions that become embodied in practices" in the habitus. "What keeps a habitus in place are assumptions or doxa, which are actually opinions whose power is maintained by being widely assumed" (Warren, *At This Time*, 108, 111). Together, habitus and doxa may thus be understood to describe the material and spiritual dimensions of the powers' work as it becomes embodied in unconscious practices. On doxa, see Bourdieu, *Outline*, 159–71.

32. In my discussion of "exposing the powers" in the previous chapter, I was in part discussing how preachers may bring the habitus to awareness. I examine this more fully in terms of practices below.

33. MacIntyre's own definition is rather tortuous. He defines a practice as "any coherent and complex form of socially established cooperative human activity through which goods internal to that form of activity are realized in the course of trying to achieve those standards of excellence which are appropriate to, and partially definitive of, that form of activity, with the result that human powers to achieve excellence and human conceptions of the ends and goods involved are systematically extended" (*After Virtue*, 187).

34. I am indebted to Brad J. Kallenberg, who has helpfully highlighted four of these characteristics of MacIntyre's understanding of practice. See Brad J. Kallenberg, "The Master Argument of MacIntyre's *After Virtue*," in Murphy, Kallenberg, and Nation, eds., *Virtues and Practices*, 21–22. For MacIntyre's treatment of practice, see *After Virtue*, esp. 181–203.

tices and goods external to them. Internal goods are those rewards that are directly related to the excellence of the practice and can be recognized and appreciated only by participants. External goods are by-products of the practice, which are not inherent in the practice itself.[35] Where external goods become the focus, the practice is actually harmed, rather than enriched; they become the means by which the powers can take practices captive and distort them.[36]

The practice of preaching, for example, often brings external goods, beginning with a preacher's seminary education. In many seminaries, including my own, grades are given in preaching classes, and these grades are often connected to financial aid. Grades and financial aid, however, are goods external to the practice of preaching.[37] They do not initiate the preacher into the larger community of preachers through the ages, nor do they enable the student to come to appreciate the joy and challenge of faithful preaching. And such external goods certainly do not encourage the student to engage in preaching as a practice of nonviolent resistance to the powers. Nevertheless, grades and financial aid often become the driving concerns of students learning to preach. When this happens, preaching becomes a competitive enterprise, through which students seek external goods, rather than a cooperative practice, within which students together strive for excellence. Not surprisingly, having been formed to compete for grades and financial aid in seminary, students often become pastors for whom preaching becomes a means to a high salary and a "tall steeple." In this way, the requirements of the seminary as an academic institution contribute to the corruption of the practice of preaching. And the church as an institution, functioning within a competitive, career model, perpetuates this corruption. In short, to be faithfully undertaken, practices require a focus on internal rather than external goods—a fact that has serious implications for the ways in which seminaries train preachers.

3. These practices have standards of excellence, determined by the historical community of practitioners, without which internal goods cannot be achieved.[38] Indeed, the quest for excellence lies at the heart of practices in this sense; achieving the standards of excellence is the most significant

35. MacIntyre, *After Virtue*, 188–91.
36. Ibid., 194–95. MacIntyre distinguishes practices from institutions, which are necessarily concerned with external goods. Although practices are necessarily sustained by institutions (i.e., powers), institutions tend to corrupt practices.
37. Grades and financial aid contain several key characteristics of external goods as MacIntyre understands them. When they are achieved, they are always someone's property or possession; they are in limited supply, and the more someone has of them, the less there is for other people. Consequently, such external goods are objects of competition in which there are winners and losers. Internal goods can be the outcome of a competition to excel, but "their achievement is a good for the whole community who participate in the practice," not just an individual (MacIntyre, *After Virtue*, 190–91).
38. Ibid.

internal good the practice can offer. When a jazz musician, for example, offers up a rich improvisation, meeting the standards of excellence developed in the jazz community, he or she enjoys the internal goods of the practice of jazz—doing it *well*. Faithful preachers likewise sense when they have preached well and moved toward the standards of excellence in that practice; they experience the internal goods of the practice of preaching.[39]

4. The practices are systematically extended. As the participants in the practice have pursued excellence through the years, the standards of the practice, including the practitioners' abilities to achieve these standards, have slowly developed in new directions.[40] Although dependent on the larger community of practitioners, certain people come along who extend the practice in new and faithful ways. The story of jazz, for example, is a story of those practitioners who extended the practice in radically new directions, which nevertheless grew out of the larger history of the practice. Names such as Jelly Roll Morton, Louis Armstrong, Duke Ellington, Billie Holiday, Charlie Parker, and John Coltrane immediately come to mind. Similarly, the story of Christian discipleship might focus on the lives of the saints who have pointed the way to new levels of excellence in that practice.[41] Or, if the fundamental Christian practice involves community formation, then one might seek out various Christian communities who have extended the excellence of that practice in new and faithful ways.[42] Practices, then, are grounded in traditions but regularly extend those traditions in new directions.

5. The practices provide the immediate context for the development and exercise of virtues. *Virtue* in this context is a functional term, which refers to a particular quality needed to achieve some good.[43] For example, a clock should possess the virtue of telling time accurately. Similarly, human virtues are those qualifications of human agency that enable a person to engage in a practice and achieve the goods internal to the practice, including both the excellence of performing the practice and the excellence of a way of life inherent in the practice.[44] The nature of the particular practice

---

39. MacIntyre notes two kinds of excellence in a practice: the excellence of the "product" (e.g., the sermon), where one is produced, and the excellence of a way of life that is inherent in the practice (ibid., 189–90).

40. Kallenberg, "Master Argument," 21.

41. Michael Warren speaks of discipleship as a practice in this sense, though it might also be viewed as constituted by a number of related practices. See Warren, *At This Time*, 131.

42. Kallenberg argues that the fundamental Christian practice is community formation, with subpractices (e.g., witness, worship, works of mercy, discernment, and discipleship) contributing to this larger practice. See Kallenberg, "Master Argument," 22.

43. MacIntyre, *After Virtue*, 148–49.

44. Ibid., 191–203. As MacIntyre writes, "A virtue is an acquired human quality the possession and exercise of which tends to enable us to achieve those goods which are internal to practices and the lack of which effectively prevents us from achieving any such

will shape the nature of the virtues required for it. Practices thus provide a critical framework for understanding the virtues that shape the moral life.[45]

As these five characteristics make clear, the third level of practice is neither routine nor unconscious. Unlike the routine practices of the church and the unconscious practices shaped by the culture, this level of practice requires both intentionality and discipline. Warren helpfully compares these different levels of practice to the difference between a man sauntering down the street and a woman walking across a tightrope. The skill of the tightrope walker is a disciplined practice, similar to what MacIntyre describes, while the man sauntering down the street enacts the first two kinds of practice, whether as routine church activities or unconscious social practices shaped by a habitus.[46] All three levels of practice need to be addressed by preaching that seeks to build up churches as communities of resistance.

PREACHING AND PRACTICES

Any examination of the role of preaching in forming the church's practices must begin with a caveat: the movement between preaching and practices is not simply one way. The church's ongoing practices shape how congregations read Scripture, participate in worship, and hear sermons, as much as or more than sermons build up the church in particular practices. In fact, the limitations of preaching at this point are significant and call for more homiletical modesty than one often finds in books about preaching. While preaching can help build up the congregation in its distinctive speech, talking about practices often has a limited effect; practices, by their very nature, must be *done* habitually to take hold.[47]

---

goods" (191). MacIntyre's larger understanding of virtue includes three elements: practice, narrative, and tradition. The virtues are (*a*) qualities necessary for the achievement of goods internal to a practice; (*b*) qualities contributing to the good of a whole life (understood narratively); and (*c*) qualities directed toward a good for human beings that is possessed and elaborated within an ongoing tradition. See ibid., 191–225.

45. The virtues that are emphasized will depend on the way in which particular stories and traditions shape a community's understanding of the purpose of life—what it means to live well. Christian virtues, shaped by the story of Jesus, for example, differ significantly from the virtues Aristotle emphasized for living well in the Greek *polis*. For an ingenious development of MacIntyre's understanding of a practice in relation to Christian discipleship, see Hauerwas, "Politics of the Church," 93–111. For another helpful account, see Paul J. Wadell, *Friendship and the Moral Life* (Notre Dame, Ind.: University of Notre Dame Press, 1989). Friendship, which plays a critical role in the development of virtue, is discussed in the next chapter.

46. Warren, *At This Time*, 109.

47. For a fuller discussion of these matters, see Campbell, *Preaching Jesus*, 231–50.

Even Aristotle, despite his profound sense of the linguistic character of human life and his appreciation for the power of rhetoric, understood the limitations of words in shaping a virtuous people:

> Now if words alone would suffice to make us good, they would rightly "harvest many rewards and great." . . . But as it is, while words evidently do have the power to encourage and stimulate young men of generous mind, and while they can cause a character well-born and truly enamoured of what is noble to be possessed by virtue, they do not have the power to turn the common run of people to goodness and nobility. . . . To change by argument what has long been ingrained in character is impossible, or, at least not easy.[48]

According to Aristotle, words are not nearly as powerful in forming character as the ongoing communal practices that shape human lives. In fact, those practices themselves, when corrupt, can corrupt the practice of rhetoric. While Aristotle affirms that rhetoric can shape the ethos and practices of the *polis* in positive ways, it is clear that rhetoric simultaneously relies on an incorrupt "body politic" for its effectiveness.[49]

Michael Warren has also highlighted the ways in which life practices can belie the words and actions of the liturgy on Sunday morning. In a chilling example, he notes that in the 1970s and early 1980s, as thousands of young people were "disappeared"—murdered—in Argentina, the nation's generals gathered each year with Roman Catholic bishops to celebrate what was called the Military Mass.[50] Warren rightly wonders if in this context the Eucharist doesn't become a "ritual lie": "When what the community does outside the ritual space is a countersign of the gospel, the sign value of what it does within the ritual space has little effect. Worse, the Eucharist could be a ritual lie."[51] Warren uses this illustration to remind the church that while ritual has the self-implicating power to move people into discipleship, life practices also

---

48. Aristotle, *Nichomachean Ethics*, trans. Martin Ostwald, Library of the Liberal Arts (New York: Macmillan, 1986), 1179b4–19.

49. Ibid., 1099b30–32, 1179b32–1180a17, 1354a17–1354b16. See also Larry Arnhart, *Aristotle on Political Reasoning: A Commentary on the Rhetoric* (Dekalb, Ill.: Northern Illinois University Press, 1981), 6. Although I am emphasizing Aristotle's sense that practices are more important than rhetoric and can even corrupt rhetoric, Aristotle argues also that rhetoric can contribute to the formation of people by helping to shape the ethos of the *polis*, rather than by addressing individuals. Rhetoric helps form a virtuous people through its contribution to the ethos of the political realm. See Eugene Ryan, "Aristotle's *Rhetoric* and *Ethics* and the Ethos of Society, " *Greek, Roman, and Byzantine Studies* 13 (1972), 291–308.

50. Warren, *At This Time*, 8.

51. Ibid., 9.

have the power to corrupt liturgy.[52] In the terms I have been using through-out this book, the powers of death that shape our life practices in significant ways exercise a profound influence in our worship. As Warren concludes, "The quality of the community's worship is determined more by the quality of the community's life structure, that is, actual patterns of living, than by the quality of the words spoken or the rituals enacted during worship. Put more simply: the sacramentality of worship and the sacramentality of life practice cannot be divorced."[53]

While not wanting to deny the power of the Holy Spirit at work in the liturgy, Warren nevertheless sets preachers on notice about the dangers of making overly extravagant claims for the influence of liturgical speech, includ-ing preaching. He reminds pastors that attention to the practices of the com-munity of faith must be an ongoing part of the church's life and not just a focus of the Sunday sermon. Indeed, attention to the practices of the church *between* sermons is critical for sermons to be faithfully preached and heard at all.

Despite this caveat, however, I believe sermons can make several important contributions to build up congregations in practices that embody resistance to the powers of death. Sermons can address each of the three levels of practice discussed earlier and, in a modest way, contribute to the formation of congre-gations in a deeper practice of discipleship. First, preaching can help make the routine practices of the church more intentional by redescribing them as prac-tices of resistance to the powers. Second, preaching can bring the larger, unconscious social practices to speech and expose the ways in which the church's practices have accommodated to the powers of death, causing the church itself to act as a fallen power.[54] Third, preaching can seek to cultivate in the church those intentional practices of discipleship and community for-mation that embody the way of resistance to the powers of death in and for the world. I briefly examine each of these approaches.

Redescribing the Routine

Many routine church practices are in fact practices of resistance to the powers of death in the world. Because these practices have become routine, however, congregations are often not aware of their radical character as practices of

---

52. Liturgical speech, according to Warren, is self-implicating; it "deliberately impli-cates oneself in the work of Jesus, no matter what the consequences" (ibid., 9–10). To the extent that liturgical speech fails to be self-implicating, it is not liturgical speech.
53. Ibid., 13–14. For another example, see Warren's discussion of the differences between the "worship of the rich" and the "worship of the poor" (19).
54. Marva Dawn discusses numerous ways in which churches come to be and act as fallen powers. See Dawn, *Powers, Weakness*, 73–122.

resistance. One of the important roles that preaching can play in building up the church as a community of resistance involves redescribing these practices and highlighting their significance in the face of the powers so they can be practiced with more intentionality not only within the community of faith but in the church's mission to the world. To borrow Warren's image, preaching seeks to transform routine congregational "sauntering" into something more like tightrope walking.

Worship

In the context of the principalities and powers, Christian worship is fundamentally an act of resistance. As I have noted, what the powers desire most from human beings is our worship; they claim to be the divine regents of the world and to offer us life if we will only serve them. In this context, it is not surprising that the fundamental practice of the redeemed community in the book of Revelation is worship. There is no more subversive act where the powers are concerned than praising the God of Jesus Christ, who has exposed and overcome them. Indeed, in Revelation such worship is offered up, not coincidentally, by the martyrs, highlighting the connection between worship and resistance.

As might be expected, one of the first practices the powers try to undermine in their quest for domination is worship. Sometimes worship will literally be forbidden, as often happens in tyrannical regimes. At other times, as in the case of American liberal society, the powers will affirm "freedom of worship" but relegate it to the private realm in order to dispel any of its radical public implications. Liberalism can co-opt worship and drain it of its power as effectively as tyranny.[55] In fact, one of the reasons the subversive character of worship has been lost in many churches today is that the powers have so effectively trained Americans to perceive it as a private and individual matter with no significant implications for the public arena. When Christian worship becomes so relegated to the private realm, the nation itself easily comes to claim believers' public worship and service, particularly in times of crisis or war.[56]

---

55. Stanley Hauerwas, "The Politics of Freedom: Why Freedom of Religion Is a Subtle Temptation," in *After Christendom*, 69–92.

56. When worship does "go public," it tends to be co-opted for the purposes of the powers. The worship in the National Cathedral following the September 11, 2001, terrorist attack is a good case in point. Replete with U.S. flags, uniformed military personnel, and a "sermon" by the president, the worship, which took place immediately after Congress gave approval for the war effort, was little more than a means of supporting and blessing future military action by the United States. As Peter Storey wrote in his letter to friends in the United States, "It was sad to see the Church (and other religious traditions) laid so supinely at the disposal of Caesar and his chaplains. It is one thing for

By its very nature, however, Christian worship, even when distorted, involves some level of resistance to the claims of the principalities and powers. In gathering for worship, even contemporary mainline, privileged Christians join this tradition of resistance. Believers not only resist the countless diversions the powers offer up to keep us away from worship on Sunday morning—the comfort of a warm bed, free time for exercise, soccer games—but they also publicly embody their loyalty to the living God, rather than to the lesser powers that seek to become idols. While the motives for participating in this practice are varied, and while participating in worship is often routine for many people, preachers can redescribe this practice and remind the church of the life of resistance in which worship implicates them. Such redescription may not only be redemptive and empowering for the worshipers, giving them a sense of the extraordinary adventure they undertake in the liturgy. It may also invite the congregation into deeper intentionality and reflection about the internal goods of worship and what counts as excellence in worship. In addition, such worship may prepare believers for more radical acts of liturgical resistance—and even public exorcisms—that expose the powers of death in the "public square."[57] Finally, such redescribed worship becomes the context for nurturing the virtue of hope, which enables the church to resist the powers beyond the liturgy through its life in and for the world.

Stewardship

Another practice that deserves redescription in relation to the powers is stewardship. In American consumer culture, no greater power holds spirits captive than Mammon. Consequently, whenever churches are dealing with money, they are dealing with the critical matters of captivity, redemption, and resistance. In

---

the Church to invite the leaders of the land to come like any others, to pray, to seek God's healing and the guidance of God's word. It is theologically an entirely different matter to provide a pulpit to the head of state, enabling him to use a house of worship to rally the nation for war, exactly contradicting some of the Scriptures that were read. When uniforms and flags crowd God's house, it is hard for God's word to be heard. A British TV reporter said afterward: 'This morning, in quick succession, President Bush got approval for his war, first from Congress, then from the religious leaders.' Did it occur to anyone just how much this action resembled the use made of mosque pulpits by the political leaders of some extreme Muslim fundamentalist states?" (Peter Storey, "Letter from South Africa," at http:///www.divinity.duke.edu/newsbox/WTC/Crisis-Storey.html; accessed on October 15, 2001).

57. On liturgical acts of resistance and public exorcisms, see Bill Wylie-Kellermann, *Seasons of Faith and Conscience: Kairos, Confession, Liturgy* (Maryknoll, N.Y.: Orbis Books, 1991); also Walter Wink, *Unmasking the Powers: The Invisible Forces That Determine Human Existence* (Philadelphia: Fortress Press, 1986), 64–68; and Stringfellow, *Ethic for Christians*, 150–51.

this context it is not enough to talk about giving out of gratitude to God, though that is important. Nor is it appropriate to turn giving into a moralistic demand, as a narrow emphasis on the tithe often does. Rather, in American culture, where spirits are shaped by accumulation and security is promised by Mammon, giving money away is fundamentally an act of resistance. It is a concrete means of living into the redemption accomplished in Jesus' life, death, and resurrection.

Jacques Ellul has highlighted this connection between giving and resistance:

> How overcome the spiritual "power" of money? Not by accumulating more money, not by using money for good purposes, not by being just and fair in our dealings. The *law of money* is the law of accumulation, of buying and selling. That is why the only way to overcome the spiritual "power" of money is to give our money away, thus desacrilizing it and freeing ourselves from its control. And these benefits accrue not only to us but to all [people]. To give away money is to win a victory over the spiritual power that oppresses us. There is an example of what the fight of faith means.[58]

When Christians resist the power of Mammon by giving away money, as Ellul notes elsewhere, money becomes a sign of grace ("giving") rather than domination.[59]

Redescribing stewardship in this way invites the church to transform Christian giving from a routine matter of filling out pledge cards and writing checks into a disciplined practice of resistance to the principalities and powers—one that extends beyond the walls of the church into the life practice of believers.[60] As with a redescription of worship, this transformation invites believers into a much more daring and dramatic adventure than they find in traditional approaches to the stewardship campaign. In fact, such redescription of the church's routine practices has the potential to transform not only individual members of the congregation but the church's mission to the world as well, which may be dangerous to the church as an institution. If members of the

---

58. Jacques Ellul, *Violence: Reflections from a Christian Perspective*, trans. Cecelia Gaul Kings (New York: Seabury Press, 1969), 166.

59. Jacques Ellul, *The Subversion of Christianity*, trans. Geoffrey W. Bromiley (Grand Rapids: Wm. B. Eerdmans Publishing Co., 1986), 180.

60. As Christians begin giving away money in resistance to the powers, their lifestyles inevitably have to become simpler because they have less money to use for the accumulation of goods. In shaping simpler lifestyles, stewardship-as-resistance indirectly moves believers into lifestyles that are themselves acts of resistance to the powers in a consumer culture.

congregation catch on to the significance of giving as an act of resistance to the powers, they will probably begin to ask questions about the church's own use of its money and particularly about its accumulation of endowments. The monetary act of resistance will spill over from the individual member's own stewardship to the stewardship of the church, including the church's own captivity to Mammon.[61]

Exposing Accommodation

Preaching also seeks to expose those practices in the church's life that have been taken captive by the spirit of the powers; it seeks to unveil the taken-for-granted cultural practices in which the church itself accommodates its life to the priorities of the Domination System and acts as a "fallen power."[62] While practices associated with a habitus (like the "air we breathe") run far deeper than language, preaching may nevertheless play an important role in exposing them. In fact, preaching is one place in the life of the church where speech can make explicit and disrupt practices that are simply taken for granted; it is one place where the activity of the powers within the church itself may be contested and changed.[63]

While numerous examples might be given, two will suffice—one extreme and the other subtler. As an extreme example of how the powers' influence creeps into and shapes the practices of the church, one can note the growing presence of security guards at many churches today, particularly at urban churches. In many congregations, believers enter the church under the watchful eye of uniformed and, often, armed security guards. When discussions arise about the presence of such guards at the church, responses almost inevitably sound something like this: "We had no choice. We had to hire the guards to provide a safe space for our members and to continue our ministry in this place."[64] Admittedly, at some of these churches the threat of violence is real, and concerns about security are not unfounded. Indeed, the churches themselves are to be commended

---

61. Obviously, there are many other practices in the church that can be redescribed. Baptism, for example, is an act of resistance to the culture's manifold hierarchical arrangements of domination (Gal. 3:28); the Eucharist is, among other things, an act of resistance to the economic inequalities and oppression in the society (1 Cor. 11:17–34). Preachers should examine all of the church's traditional practices to discern the ways in which they are meant to be practices of resistance to the powers.
62. Warren, *At This Time*, 57, 59.
63. According to Warren, who draws on the work of Bourdieu, speech is required to bring such practices into consciousness and change them (ibid., 110).
64. I have encountered security guards at more than one church in Atlanta, and I have participated in discussions about these guards with church members.

for resisting the temptation to move out to a safer and more comfortable environment, which itself must be affirmed as a form of resistance to the principalities and powers.

Nevertheless, this practice of guarding churches belies the message of the gospel and accommodates the church to the powers of death in the world in three ways. First and most obvious, the myth of redemptive violence that lies at the heart of the Domination System comes to be embodied in a practice of the church, in contradiction to the nonviolent witness to which the church is called in the face of the powers. One is faced with the grotesque irony of the body of the crucified Christ being defended by the violent means of the powers. Second, the turn to security guards often represents the spirit of efficiency (a key characteristic of the powers shaped by the spirit of violence, capitalism, and technology) at work in the church. Seduced by the promises inherent in the myth of redemptive violence, the church chooses the most efficient way of responding to the threat of violence, rather than the most faithful way. Finally, security guards actually represent a perversion of the central Christian practice of hospitality. While providing a safe, hospitable place for church members, and posing no threat to respectable-looking, well-dressed folks, such guards offer not a welcome but rather a threat to poor, homeless people. The very people to whom the church is called to extend hospitality are turned away by the presence of security guards.

The practice of hiring security guards, in short, represents an accommodation of the church to the powers of death in the world. Indeed, the very sense that such guards are a "necessity" reveals the captivity of the church to the Domination System.[65] Vision and practice alike become captive to the habitus of the powers, and the church cannot even imagine alternatives to the myth of redemptive violence. In such a context, preachers have the responsibility not only to bring such distorted practices to speech but to help the congregation envision alternatives and put them into practice.

The second example, highlighted by Marva Dawn, is subtler but equally formative of many churches' lives. This is the seemingly innocuous (because so taken for granted) practice of "majority rule." Although affirming high "democratic" principles, "majority rule" actually undercuts the practice of fellowship that is central to the church's life.[66] In the first place, as with security guards, majority rule represents for most churches an accommodation to the

---

65. As Ellul argues throughout his work, the powers create a realm of "necessity," which is opposed to Christian freedom in the gospel.
66. See Dawn's discussion of the practice of fellowship and the counterpractice of majority rule in *Powers, Weakness,* 94–97.

spirit of efficiency. Operating efficiently becomes more important than taking the time to move toward genuine corporate discernment and consensus. In addition, such an approach to decision-making actually embodies the fundamental metaphor of "winners" and "losers" that shapes the spirit of the Domination System. The reality brought to speech by that metaphor is inherent in the practice of majority rule—as the very phrase, "majority *rule*," suggests. On the contrary, the practice of making decisions by consensus serves as an act of resistance to the spirit of the Domination System. As with the practice of employing security guards, this practice may be exposed by bringing it to speech in preaching. In the process, the church may be moved toward more faithful forms of decision-making.

The preacher is thus called to attend to the church's practices in order to discern which practices are shaped more by the powers of domination and death than by the way of Jesus. In exposing the church's corrupt practices—bringing them into the open through speech—the preacher does not simply criticize the church or "beat up" on individual members. Rather, by bringing taken-for-granted practices into active Christian reflection, the preacher speaks a redemptive word, enabling the church to see more clearly its captivity to the powers, to imagine alternatives to the ways of domination, and to take concrete steps into the freedom given through the life, death, and resurrection of Jesus Christ. Through such discernment and exposing the wind of the Spirit may blow, just as she did in Acts 2, and move the church toward new practices that resist the powers of death at work in the world.

Nurturing Faithful Practices

As I have suggested, once the preacher begins redescribing routine practices and exposing corrupt practices, he or she is already beginning to envision alternative practices and to move the congregation toward embodying them. In redescribing worship and stewardship as acts of resistance to the principalities, the preacher begins to direct the congregation toward renewed engagement in those practices. Similarly, in exposing security guards and majority rule as practices that embody an accommodation to the ways of the fallen powers, preachers necessarily generate reflection and conversation about new and different practices that will provide alternatives to those of the Domination System. Redescribing and exposing current practices can serve as a redemptive word that creates the space for resistance to the powers through new and renewed practices in the life of the church.

Preachers also need to take the next step, however. They need to call churches to engage in new and renewed practices of resistance to the powers of death in the world. And they need to issue this call in concrete ways, moving in sermons from a vision of the new creation to the specific practices that such a vision invites.[67]

Such a move has not been popular in contemporary homiletical theory. Recent approaches to preaching have advised preachers to leave sermons open so individuals can experience the gospel for themselves and draw their own conclusions for their lives. The indicative has reigned supreme, and "telling people what to do" has been virtually anathema. Preachers are to engage in an open-ended conversation rather than make any claims or demands on the congregation.

There are, to be sure, good reasons for these current emphases. Moralistic preaching, which places human rules and works before the work of God in Jesus Christ, is counter to the gospel, transforming the gospel of God's gracious initiative into the burden of human efforts. Similarly, contemporary homileticians are rightly wary of preachers imposing their own agenda on a congregation—something that certainly happens all too frequently in the church. A preacher who seeks to dominate the congregation with his or her demands turns preaching itself into a practice shaped by the Domination System. A healthy dose of suspicion at this point is essential to avoid moralistic, authoritarian, and often manipulative directives from the pulpit.

Such a healthy suspicion, however, should not deter preachers from exploring ways in which concrete practices may be nurtured from the pulpit. Jesus, after all, did not avoid this move to practices, as I have noted several times in relation to the Sermon on the Mount. Likewise, Paul regularly makes a similar turn as he moves from theological vision to ecclesial practices in the course of his letters. Such a homiletical move was critical for the Gospels and for Paul, for they understood that concrete practices form and sustain the church's vision. In Marianne Sawicki's terms, if preachers share with people a vision of the risen Christ without directing them to the practices concomitant with this vision, preachers not only shortchange the congregation; they in fact fail to preach the gospel itself, which seeks to move people toward the practices that enable them to "see the Lord."

In addition, such practices should not simplistically be placed in opposition to God's grace, as is often suggested in positions emphasizing the dichotomy between grace and works. Practices can lead one into grace just as often as grace empowers practices. Engagement in the concrete practices of the Christian community may, in fact, become not a means of works righteousness but

---

67. I do not mean to suggest that every sermon should move from vision to practice but rather that in the course of a congregation's preaching ministry both dimensions will be present and work together.

a means to coming into a fuller sense of God's grace. In the Gospels, for example, Jesus first invites the Twelve to "follow me"; only on the journey of discipleship do the disciples come to sense the reality of their own sin and the power of God's grace.[68] Similarly, it is only when the disciples on the road to Emmaus engage in the practice of hospitality to the stranger that they ultimately come to "see" the risen Lord and return to Jerusalem (the place of death) in the power of the new creation. Dietrich Bonhoeffer was right: grace is inseparable from the practices of discipleship; the relationship between the two is reciprocal rather than one-directional.[69]

In seeking to nurture the congregation in new and renewed practices, then, preachers should not shy away from naming concrete practices that seem to emerge from the gospel. At the same time, however, they should go about this calling in a particular way. Most generally, preachers will remember that preaching amid the powers seeks to be a *redemptive* activity. In building up a community of resistance, the preacher seeks to set people free from captivity to the powers. In preaching about practices, preachers will keep this redemptive purpose in mind. Such preaching will not be based on guilt, which tends to cripple people rather than free them for action. Nor will such preaching seek to motivate people through fear. Fear of being punished if one does not engage in the correct practices turns the gospel into a burden.[70] Neither guilt nor fear serves the purposes of redemptive proclamation.

Such preaching also avoids moralizing, "in which one person seeks to prescribe behavior for another but from outside the horizon of that other person."[71] While the preacher may clearly name and clarify the importance of particular practices, these practices cannot be imposed on people from the outside but must grow from within the life of the community. Nurturing faithful practices through preaching is thus necessarily part of a larger process of discernment within a community of ethical discourse, in which a congregation struggles together "to embrace specific patterns of practice by which a gospel perspective can be lived out in its concrete circumstances."[72] Preachers may

---

68. This is true not only in the Synoptic Gospels but in the Gospel of John. Jesus tells potential disciples, "Come and see" (John 1:39) The order of the words in Jesus' invitation is important. First the disciples are to follow ("come"), and only then will they begin to "see" who Jesus is.

69. See Dietrich Bonhoeffer, *The Cost of Discipleship*, rev. ed., trans. R. H. Fuller (New York: Macmillan, 1959). In book 4 of his *Institutes*, John Calvin discusses the church's practices as "means of grace."

70. Duff, "Significance of Pauline Apocalyptic," 290–91. As Duff notes, while confession of guilt is essential for true repentance, it is not a helpful motivation to action.

71. Warren, *At This Time*, 69.

72. Ibid., 56.

"sow seeds," but their growth depends on the work of the Spirit, the larger life and conversation of the community, and other ecclesial practices. In this larger context, preaching should be understood as one particular practice—albeit an important one—within the community's entire life, understood as a "school of practice."[73]

In this context, however, preachers should not hesitate in sermons to name and nurture particular communal practices within the congregation. They can do this redemptively in numerous ways, five of which I briefly note.

1. First of all, and most broadly, preachers can present these practices as a grateful response to God's gracious acts of redemption. God takes the initiative to redeem the world, and the church's practices represent the thankful response of God's people for all that God has done. Examples of this kind of turn to practices abound in Scripture. For example, in Romans 12:1, Paul writes: "I appeal to you therefore, brothers and sisters, by the mercies of God, to present your bodies as a living sacrifice, holy and acceptable to God, which is your spiritual worship." Paul then proceeds in the remainder of the letter to delineate various practices that flesh out the community's response to God's mercies. This move is also typical in the Old Testament. The Ten Commandments themselves are presented in Exodus 20 as a response to God's redemptive activity on behalf of the people of Israel. The list of commandments opens with the reminder of God's work: "I am the Lord your God, who brought you out of the land of Egypt, out of the house of slavery." Only then is the community given the set of practices for living into the redemption that God has accomplished for them.[74] Such a move to practices, based on the gracious initiative of God, will keep preachers from moralizing and from depending on guilt and fear as motivations for the community's practices of discipleship.

2. Within an apocalyptic framework, such practices may be presented as means of participating in the new creation that has broken into the world in Jesus Christ. A "new space" of freedom and life has been opened up in the midst of the powers through Jesus' life, death, and resurrection, and particular practices offer the means for living into that new reality. While recognizing the continuation of the Old Age and the suffering it brings, the preacher nevertheless invites the church to begin living now in the new creation in order to embody before the world a new possibility in the midst of the old.

The apostle Paul, for example, takes this approach in Galatians 3:28 when he announces the new space opened up by Jesus—"there is no longer Jew or Greek, there is no longer slave or free, there is no longer

---

73. Ibid., 22.
74. On the Ten Commandments as a set of communal practices, see James William McClendon Jr., *Systematic Theology: Ethics* (Nashville: Abingdon Press, 1986), 177–84.

male and female"—and calls the community of baptized Christians to live into that new reality. As Nancy Duff writes,

> Paul is not . . . proposing an "interim ethic" showing us how to live in the Old Age before the New Age arrives. Although we must be alert to the dangers of enthusiasm, we nevertheless live *now* in that new space created by the powerful invasion of Christ. Living within that new space we can no longer tolerate the Old Age distinctions in the social and political order which oppress and destroy. We refuse to allow the political order which has foundations in the Old Age to operate under the slogan "business as usual," because we do not recognize its legitimacy in God's world. It is in that new space created in Christ that the church is called into being and action.[75]

After helping the congregation see the new creation that has broken into the world, the preacher may turn to particular practices as the means for living into this new reality. In this way the turn to practices is not burdensome but redemptive—and possibly even exciting!

3. Within a more future-oriented eschatology, practices may be offered to the congregation as means for "living toward the vision" of God's new creation.[76] Unlike in apocalyptic, the vision remains in the future but nevertheless impinges on the present as the people of God seek to live toward it. The radical practices of resistance of Philip Berrigan and the Plowshares Group, who hammer and pour blood on weapons of destruction, represent a means of living toward Isaiah's vision of Shalom by enacting it now in the midst of the powers of death: "They shall beat their swords into plowshares, and their spears into pruning hooks; nation shall not lift up sword against nation, neither shall they learn war any more" (Isa. 2:4). Less dramatic practices of Shalom may also be understood in this way. When churches practice hospitality to the stranger or offer sanctuary to the refugee, they are similarly living toward the vision of Shalom and beginning to make it a reality here and now. Indeed, even such "trivial" acts as taking the time to listen to others may be seen as practices through which the people of God live toward this vision. Whether radical or trivial, such communal practices offer a means for

---

75. Duff, "Significance of Pauline Apocalyptic," 286–87. While she doesn't speak of the powers in this particular quotation, Duff refers to the powers throughout her essay. The "space" Jesus creates is a space of freedom from captivity to the powers (282–85). Duff notes that apocalyptic involves both the new reality that invades the world in Jesus Christ and a new way of seeing the world. In Jesus Christ, both the world and our way of perceiving it have changed (281).

76. I have borrowed this phrase from Walter Brueggemann, *Living toward a Vision: Biblical Reflections on Shalom* (Philadelphia: United Church Press, 1976). As becomes clear, this future-oriented eschatology is not completely or easily distinguished from the apocalyptic orientation just discussed. The difference is a matter of emphasis.

Christian churches to live now toward the vision of God's coming new creation.

4. As Marianne Sawicki suggests, such practices may also be offered as means for meeting the risen Lord. Within this framework, which Sawicki argues is typical of the Gospels, practices are presented in the context of the promise of the resurrection. Jesus has been raised from the dead, setting us free from the powers of death and the fear of death. And particular Christian practices—for example, feeding the hungry or showing hospitality to the stranger—provide the means for meeting the risen Jesus in the midst of everyday life. Such practices are not shaped by the burden of guilt or the fear of punishment but are encouraged by the promise of "seeing" the risen Lord, in whose presence we live free from the powers of death.

This approach is important because it reminds the church that vision does not always precede practice; practice also shapes vision, enabling the church to see the world in new and more faithful ways. The promise of "seeing" the risen Lord through engagement in particular practices thus includes a promise to begin seeing the world itself in new ways. When churches share meals with homeless people and meet the risen Christ at that table, for example, the powers of death are exposed; the structures that create homelessness begin to come into view, and homeless people themselves begin to be seen not as lazy "bums" or "winos" but as those in whom Christ comes to us.

5. A final way of approaching practices redemptively is through praise—praise for those "saints" who have embodied excellence in a particular practice. Even Aristotle recognized the close connection between praise and "advice": "Praise and counsels have a common aspect; for what you might suggest in counseling becomes encomium by a change in the phrase. . . . Accordingly, if you desire to praise, look what you would suggest; if you desire to suggest, look what you would praise."[77]

David DeSilva has highlighted this approach in the book of Hebrews. By providing a host of exemplars of the virtues of trust and firmness in 10:32–12:3, the author of Hebrews "sets out to praise those who have embodied the course he is advising. The effect of this encomium should be the arousal of the emotion of emulation: the hearers are encouraged and even made ambitious to embody the same virtue as these figures who have attained a praiseworthy resemblance."[78] Just as any practice has a history of practitioners who have achieved excellence in the practice and set new standards for it, so the practices of Christian discipleship have such "virtuoso performers," whom we call saints. Recognizing the importance of such practitioners, the preacher of Hebrews holds before the

---

77. Aristotle, *Rhetoric* 1.9.35–36. Quoted in David A. DeSilva, *Perseverance in Gratitude: A Socio-Rhetorical Commentary on the Epistle "to the Hebrews"* (Grand Rapids: Wm. B. Eerdmans Publishing Co., 2000), 355.
78. DeSilva, *Perseverance in Gratitude,* 355.

congregation the lives and practices of these saints in order to inspire believers to similar faithfulness.[79]

Like the preacher of Hebrews, contemporary preachers may tell the stories of virtuoso practitioners from the history of the Christian tradition. In addition, preachers may wish to highlight contemporary saints, particularly those "everyday" saints in the congregation who embody particular practices in exemplary ways. Finally, preachers may wish to tell the stories of particular Christian *communities,* past or present, whose life together embodies the excellence of particular practices.[80] By sharing these lives and stories, the preacher seeks not to make people feel guilty but to hold forth the possibility of life set free from the principalities and powers. Such stories, as DeSilva argues, do not need to become a burden but can rather be an inspiration grounded in the power and grace of God.

A Biblical Example: The Practice of Dislocation

Preachers may thus hold particular practices before the congregation in various ways that are empowering and redemptive, rather than guilt-inducing or burdensome. A rich example of this kind of preaching, which focuses on a practice that is critical for many privileged congregations today, can be found in Hebrews 13:7–16. The practice is suggested in verses 12–13: "Therefore Jesus also suffered outside the city gate in order to sanctify the people by his own blood. Let us then go to him outside the camp and bear the abuse he endured." The preacher of Hebrews here invites the church to engage in what might be called the practice of dislocation.[81] The church is called intentionally and habitually to move out of the places of security and comfort into those "unclean" places where Jesus suffers "outside the gate of our sacred compounds," whether those compounds are shaped by religion or class or race or culture.[82]

This practice of dislocation is critical for many congregations today. The

---

79. Many commentators refer to Hebrews as a "sermon" and the writer as a "preacher." See, for example, DeSilva, *Perseverance in Gratitude;* and Thomas G. Long, *Hebrews* (Louisville, Ky.: Westminster John Knox Press, 1997).

80. Telling the stories of "everyday" saints and communities is important. Such stories provide examples of faithful practices that seem attainable to the congregation. If the saints that are praised are too "distant" from the congregation, they may at times lead to frustration and paralysis. Nevertheless, such examples of virtuoso practitioners are important to keep the vision of faithful practices alive. For a helpful book that explores the practices of intentional Christian communities and their implications for more traditional congregations, see Luther E. Smith Jr., *Intimacy and Mission: Intentional Community as a Crucible for Radical Discipleship* (Scottdale, Pa.: Herald Press, 1994).

81. I am borrowing the term *dislocation* from Warren, *At This Time,* 68, 71–72.

82. Orlando E. Costas, *Christ Outside the Gate: Mission beyond Christendom* (Maryknoll, N.Y.: Orbis Books, 1982), 192. Warren, in speaking of dislocation, refers to our need to step out of "sacralizing social class" (*At This Time,* 68).

powers seek to isolate comfortable, privileged people from the suffering of those on the margins. Gated communities and churches—both figuratively and literally—keep many Christians separate from the "unclean" places of poverty and oppression where Jesus continues to "bear abuse" at the hands of the powers today. One of the most important practices for such churches is to move outside their comfortable compounds to be with people in those places "outside the gate." Through such dislocation, privileged Christians cross the boundaries that keep the privileged and oppressed apart and take a first step toward solidarity with the poor, which, in a consumer culture, is one way of radically contesting the Domination System.[83]

Moreover, such dislocation is critical to the process of discerning the work of the powers in the world. By stepping out of their own social context and spending time with people who are the most visible victims of the Domination System, privileged Christians not only begin to see the deadly work of the powers among the marginalized in new ways; they also begin to discern more clearly the ways in which they themselves are captive to the powers. Through dislocation from their comfortable, taken-for-granted life structure, privileged Christians may examine that structure in new ways. Everything looks different when viewed from the "periphery."[84] To borrow an old cliché, by becoming "fish *out* of water," privileged Christians may be able to scrutinize anew the "water" in which they normally live and move and have their being. As Warren argues, churches may begin to develop a "hermeneutics of dislocation," which is critical for the discernment of the powers' work:

> Here the norms of fidelity are not found via self-interest but by crossing over to the needs of those trapped in situations of economic misery and other forms of oppression. Stances of dislocation point to the strangers, to those who first appear to be nonneighbors but come to be seen as the human face of God. Bonds with such neighbors are forged through actions of solidarity. Such actions dislocate the comfortable from their life structure, allowing it to be scrutinized.[85]

---

83. I focus on dislocation rather than solidarity because I think it is too grandiose to speak of most privileged, mainline congregations as being in "solidarity" with the poor. The first step is dislocation, in which Christians take themselves to the places of oppression and begin learning from the most visible victims of the powers.

84. Warren, *At This Time*, 68; Costas, *Christ Outside the Gate*, 192.

85. Warren, *At This Time*, 68. For an extended experiential account of the importance of dislocation for discerning the work of the powers, see Stanley P. Saunders and Charles L. Campbell, *The Word on the Street: Performing the Scriptures in the Urban Context* (Grand Rapids: Wm. B. Eerdmans Publishing Co., 2000). I discuss the practice of dislocation and the virtues it nurtures more fully in the next chapter.

In calling Christians "outside the gate" to the places where Christ suffers, the preacher of Hebrews invites Christians to this critical practice of dislocation.[86]

Just as important as Hebrews's call to the practice of dislocation is the way in which the preacher frames the exhortation to engage in this practice. To begin with, the preacher first praises the "leaders" (13:7) who have faithfully engaged in this practice. As in so many other places in the book of Hebrews, the "saints" are held up to inspire the church to faithful living. In this text, moreover, the saints are not simply those great figures from the tradition but the local leaders whom the people know. "Remember your leaders," the preacher proclaims, "those who spoke the word of God to you; consider the outcome of their way of life, and imitate their faith."

Similar virtuoso performers of the practice of dislocation may be held up for contemporary congregations. DeSilva, for example, notes St. Francis of Assisi as one who inhabited the "fringes and interstices of the social structure of his time," practicing dislocation with an excellence matched by few in the Christian tradition.[87] Contemporary saints and communities, such as Dorothy Day and the Catholic Worker, come to mind as well. And in countless cities and towns around the world, similar intentional communities practice dislocation. Even in mainline congregations such saints exist, spending time with homeless people, serving in housing projects, visiting prisoners, and going on mission trips.[88] Such practices of dislocation provide faithful examples to praise and imitate.[89]

In addition to praising the saints, the preacher of Hebrews employs two other methods I noted above in calling the church to the practice of dislocation. First of all, the call contains the implicit promise that believers will indeed meet Jesus outside the gate. Christians do not possess Jesus inside their "sacred compounds" and take Jesus outside to others. Rather, Jesus is already

---

86. DeSilva argues that Hebrews calls Christians to a constant state of liminality (*Perseverance in Gratitude*, 503).

87. Ibid. Francis was also genuinely engaged in the more radical practice of solidarity.

88. For a discussion of the critical difference between a genuine practice of dislocation and mere "tourism," which often characterizes congregational mission trips, see Saunders and Campbell, *Word on the Street*, 132–34.

89. Such practices of dislocation ideally progress not only to more genuine solidarity but to activity that publicly addresses the systemic injustice that perpetuates poverty and oppression. The downtown congregation I attend, for example, has for years worked with homeless people through a shelter, a medical clinic, and an outreach center. These practices, which involved "dislocation" for many privileged members of the congregation, have now led to plans for an advocacy office in the church, which will move the congregation toward addressing matters of public policy that contribute to systemic injustice. The move from the practice of "dislocation" to the work for justice is taking place in this particular congregation.

"outside the gate," and believers go outside to meet him there. In fact, the "sacred space" where we come into God's presence is radically transformed in the Hebrews text; that space is now "outside the camp" rather than in the temple. Drawing near to God and going outside the camp to follow Jesus are *one and the same move;* we actually enter holy space as we leave behind our space in the camp, in human society.[90] The practice of dislocation, in Sawicki's terms, brings with it a promise of meeting the crucified and risen Lord on the periphery.[91] As Orlando Costas writes, "The risen Lord is to be located in the battles and heat of history, among the non-persons of society."[92] The call to the practice of dislocation is placed in the context of the promise to meet Jesus "outside the gate."

Finally, the call to the practice of dislocation is motivated by a vision of the city that is to come. In moving "outside the gate," the church is living toward a vision of that city in which there are no more gates and God is all in all: "Let us then go to him outside the camp and bear the abuse he endured. For here we have no lasting city, but we are looking for the city that is to come" (Heb. 13:13–14). The church's mission outside the gate takes place on the way to the new Jerusalem—the new creation—the "definitive transformation of the world by the power of God."[93] That vision, and the hope it brings with it, impinges on the present and empowers the church to go to Jesus outside the gate without fear or intimidation.[94]

At the conclusion of this passage from Hebrews, then, we return to the integral connection between vision and practice, both of which come together as preachers seek to build up the church as a community of resistance to the principalities and powers. By exposing the powers and envisioning the new creation, preachers help the people of God see the world in new ways. By redescribing routine practices, exposing corrupt practices, and nurturing faithful practices, preachers give concrete shape to the vision of life in the new creation and help Christian congregations to begin living into the redemption that God has accomplished through the life, death, and resurrection of Jesus Christ. When vision and practice come together in sermons, informing and supporting each other, preaching can become one means by which the people of God are built up into a community of resistance that embodies an alternative to the powers of death in and for the world.

---

90. DeSilva, *Perseverance in Gratitude*, 501–2.
91. This promise is not unlike the promise in Matthew 25:31–46, where Jesus informs us that we meet him (even when we do not recognize him) in the "least of these."
92. Costas, *Christ Outside the Gate*, 7.
93. Ibid., 193.
94. Ibid.

8

Practicing What We Preach

In chapters 6 and 7, I provided concrete homiletical suggestions for resisting the principalities and powers and building up a community of resistance through preaching. While such specific homiletical techniques are important, however, they are not the entire story, or even the most important part. When preaching is understood as a practice of nonviolent resistance to the powers, the character of the preacher comes to play an important role. Such preaching cannot be limited to homiletical or hermeneutical techniques but requires certain practices, virtues, and disciplines of the preacher at a more personal level. Because the spirit of the Domination System so deeply influences the spirits of those who live within it, preachers, who are as susceptible to captivity to the powers as anyone else, must develop particular virtues that resist that system; they must nurture a spirituality of nonviolent resistance that will shape their character as preachers. The Sunday-morning sermon will then be grounded in daily Christian practices that resist the powers; it will be part of a larger spiritual discipline that forms the preacher's heart, mind, and body in the ways of nonviolent resistance.[1]

A comment John Coltrane made about his music applies to this relationship between life practices and preaching:

> My goal is to live the truly religious life, and express it through my music. If you live it, when you play there's no problem because the

---

1. Barbara Patterson, "Preaching as Nonviolent Resistance," in *Telling the Truth: Preaching about Sexual and Domestic Violence*, ed. John S. McClure and Nancy J. Ramsey (Cleveland: United Church Press, 1998), 100. This is an excellent article on the crucial role of practices in the life of the preacher.

music is part of the whole thing. To be a musician is really something. It goes very, very deep. My music is the spiritual expression of what I am, my faith, my knowledge, my being.[2]

Paraphrasing Coltrane's comment, one may capture the importance of the preacher's life for the practice of preaching:

My goal is to live the truly Christian life, and express it through my preaching. If you live it, when you preach there's no problem because the sermon is part of the whole thing. To be a preacher is really something. It goes very, very deep. My preaching is the spiritual expression of what I am, my faith, my knowledge, my being.

Preaching in the face of the powers requires pastors to live their lives engaged in the practices of nonviolent resistance. Without that commitment, preachers will not be able to discern the workings of the powers in the world or to resist them nonviolently in the pulpit.

William Stringfellow has likewise emphasized the importance of the life of the preacher who would resist the powers with the Word of God. He locates the preaching of the Word among a host of other "practices of the Word": "Know the Word, teach the Word, nurture the Word, *preach the Word*, defend the Word, incarnate the Word, do the Word, live the Word."[3] Preachers are fundamentally called to be "keepers of the Word," both in the pulpit and in their lives; preaching and life are inseparable.[4] In a time when homileticians often focus on matters of technique, Stringfellow reminds us that preaching, as a practice of nonviolent resistance to the powers, is necessarily part of a larger fabric of personal and communal practices.

If these practices and virtues do not form the preacher, then preaching all too easily becomes captive to the threats and seductions of the powers, and it forfeits either its character as resistance or its character as nonviolence. Without spiritual formation in the virtues of nonviolent resistance, the preacher first of all may simply become complacent in his or her privilege. Enjoying the benefits of conformity to the ways of the powers, the preacher speaks no word of resistance from the pulpit. Preaching becomes simply a means of "success" according to the values of the Domination System. Second, the preacher may become demoralized, despairing over the possibility of any change whatsoever

---

2. Quoted in Eric Nisenson, *Ascension: John Coltrane and His Quest* (New York: St. Martin's Press, 1993), 42.

3. William Stringfellow, *An Ethic for Christians and Other Aliens in a Strange Land* (Waco, Tex.: Word Books, 1973; 3d paperback ed., 1979), 143; italics mine.

4. In his eulogy for Stringfellow, Daniel Berrigan referred to him as a "keeper of the Word."

and losing the will to resist. In this case, preaching becomes either a frustrating burden that brings with it a load of guilt or a cynical activity in which the preacher just goes through the motions. Third, in the face of the powers the preacher who continues to resist may simply grow frustrated, ranting and raving against everyone and everything. As a result, preaching becomes not a practice of nonviolent resistance to the powers but a form of violent manipulation and even verbal abuse that is thoroughly shaped by the spirit of the Domination System. In short, the concrete suggestions given in chapters 6 and 7 depend in a profound way on the practices and virtues of the one who preaches.

In this chapter I turn to some of the practices and virtues that shape the lives of those who would engage in preaching as a practice of nonviolent resistance to the powers. First, I examine the practice of friendship within the church, including the critical homiletical virtue of love that it nurtures. As a model for the church, friendship provides not only the context for preaching as a practice of nonviolent resistance but also the context in which the virtues are formed and the life of resistance is lived out. After this discussion of friendship, I examine four other virtues that are necessary for the preacher who engages in preaching as a practice of nonviolent resistance: truthfulness, anger, patience, and hope.[5]

A COMMUNITY OF FRIENDS

In John 15:12–17, Jesus speaks the following words to the community of disciples:

> This is my commandment, that you love one another as I have loved you. No one has greater love than this, to lay down one's life for one's friends. You are my friends if you do what I command you. I do not call you servants any longer, because the servant does not know what the master is doing; but I have called you friends, because I have made known to you everything I have heard from my Father. You did not choose me but I chose you. And I appointed you to go and bear fruit, fruit that will last, so that the Father will give you whatever you ask

---

5. My discussion of friendship and the virtues is necessarily suggestive rather than exhaustive. Instead of providing a "laundry list" of general homiletical practices and virtues, I highlight some distinctive practices and virtues related to preaching as a practice of nonviolent resistance, though I do not claim that these are the only ones. For some other accounts of the character of the preacher, see Richard Eslinger, "The Homiletic Virtues: Explorations into the Character of the Preacher," *Worship Arts* 43 (July–August 1998): 8–11; and André Resner, *Preacher and Cross: Person and Message in Theology and Rhetoric* (Grand Rapids: Wm. B. Eerdmans Publishing Co., 1999).

him in my name. I am giving you these commands so that you may
love one another.

In this remarkable passage, Jesus not only calls the disciples friends rather
than servants, but he establishes the church itself as a community of friends.[6]
Jesus tells the disciples that they will live as his friends if they love one another
as he has loved them—as friends who give their lives for each other. Jesus thus
states that friendship, understood as mutual love in which believers give themselves for each other's good, shapes the life of the church. Such friendship,
Jesus affirms, is both a gracious gift to the church ("You did not choose me but
I chose you") and a responsibility that can be commanded (vv. 12, 14, 17).

Although not emphasizing the language of friendship, Gerhard Lohfink
has similarly highlighted the mutuality and equality of relationships in the
Christian community by focusing on the reciprocal pronoun "one another"
(*allēlōn*). He argues that this pronoun, which shapes Jesus' words to the disciples in John 15:12–17, is a critical aspect of Christian ecclesiology in the
epistles. The texts using this pronoun provide a distinctively Christian understanding of the mutual love that characterizes the community of friends growing together in the life of discipleship:

> Outdo one another in showing honor. (Rom. 12:10)
> Live in harmony with one another. (Rom. 12:16)
> Welcome one another. (Rom. 15:7)
> Admonish one another. (Rom. 15:14)
> Greet one another with a holy kiss. (Rom 16:16)
> Wait for one another. (1 Cor. 11:33)
> Have the same care for one another. (1 Cor. 12:25)
> Be servants of one another. (Gal. 5:13)
> Bear one another's burdens. (Gal. 6:2)
> Comfort one another. (1 Thess. 5:11)
> Build one another up. (1 Thess. 5:11)
> Be at peace with one another. (1 Thess. 5:13)
> Do good to one another. (1 Thess. 5:15)
> Bear with one another lovingly. (Eph. 4:2)
> Be kind and compassionate to one another. (Eph. 4:32)
> Be subject to one another. (Eph. 5:21)
> Forgive one another. (Col. 3:13)
> Confess your sins to one another. (James 5:16)

---

6. For another discussion of the church as a community of friends, see Celia Allison
Hahn, *Sexual Paradox: Creative Tensions in Our Lives and in Our Congregations* (New
York: Pilgrim Press, 1991), 159–74. See also Stanley Hauerwas, "Companions on the
Way: The Necessity of Friendship," *Asbury Theological Journal* 45, 1 (Spring 1990):
35–48.

Pray for one another. (James 5:16)
Love one another from the heart. (1 Peter 1:22)
Be hospitable to one another. (1 Peter 4:9)
Meet one another with humility. (1 Peter 5:5)
Have fellowship with one another. (1 John 1:7)[7]

As a community of friends, believers give themselves in love for each other by engaging in these kinds of mutual encouragement, support, and correction.

Such a community of friends provides the context for the kind of preaching I have suggested throughout this book. Mutual, self-giving love for others in the community is a primary virtue of the preacher. As the preacher shares in the community of friends and understands herself to be preaching among friends, her preaching may become a bold and faithful practice of nonviolent resistance to the powers.

Preaching among Friends

Preaching as nonviolent resistance faces specific challenges. As is clear by now, such preaching will often call for strong words. Preachers will make claims, share convictions, and even seek to persuade. As a practice of nonviolent resistance to the powers, preaching often does not employ an open-ended inductive or conversational style that simply seeks to create the space for people to draw their own conclusions and make their own decisions.[8] Nevertheless, the concerns that led to the development of inductive and conversational preaching are important for sermons that seek to be acts of nonviolent resistance to the powers. Because the authority of the Word is the authority of the one who "laid down his life for his friends," the office of the preacher, as Lohfink writes, "must not reflect the world's structure of power and domination."[9] As inductive and conversational homileticians have rightly argued, preachers cannot proclaim this Word by means of domination or coercion.

The great challenge for preaching as a practice of nonviolent resistance is that it make claims—and even speak with authority—without becoming another form of domination. On the one hand, preaching inevitably involves power and always

---

7. Gerhard Lohfink, *Jesus and Community: The Social Dimension of Christian Faith*, trans. John P. Galvin (Philadelphia: Fortress Press, 1984), 99–100. On the egalitarian character of the Christian community, see also 115–22.
8. On inductive preaching, see Fred B. Craddock, *As One without Authority*, 4th ed. (St. Louis: Chalice Press, 2001). On conversational preaching, see Lucy Atkinson Rose, *Sharing the Word: Preaching in the Roundtable Church* (Louisville, Ky.: Westminster John Knox Press, 1997).
9. Lohfink, *Jesus and Community*, 121.

runs the risk of becoming the voice that silences all other voices; one person speaks, telling others what to think and do, while everyone else remains silent and passive.[10] If that happens, the preacher and the sermon have become part of the Domination System. On the other hand, preaching that dares to make no claims—that avoids exposing the powers, envisioning God's alternative, and nurturing the church in practices of resistance—can hardly be adequate in the face of the powers. In the face of the powers, speech must be bold and daring.

To walk this fine line, the preacher must take up the stance of the friend in a community of friends. This stance enables the preacher to speak with conviction and even authority without silencing all other voices and turning preaching itself into an act of domination. Such an approach shifts the attention away from the twenty minutes of the sermon to the communal relationships within which the sermon occurs. In the community of friends, the preacher does not seek to control or dominate the congregation through her sermons but rather seeks the good of the community out of love for her friends. The critical issue is not that the sermon itself be formally "open-ended" and "conversational" but that the sermon be spoken out of love and offered as part of the larger discourse in the community of friends.

When understood in this way, preaching can be bold and even carry authority without becoming a form of domination. When a friend speaks to us, we are willing to listen. We know we share a common purpose with the friend, and we know the friend cares for us and seeks our good. Within this relationship, we are even willing to listen to strong words from a friend—words of critique and challenge as well as words of comfort and support. Friends can and do "admonish one another" (Rom. 15:14). Indeed, some of the most challenging words I have ever heard were words from a trusted and respected friend, who spoke a difficult truth to me. Although I didn't like what I heard, I was willing to listen because of our friendship. Moreover, because of our relationship, my friend's words carried authority—without being authoritarian. I listened to them carefully, and I took them seriously. They made a claim on me; I knew I had to respond in some way, not because I was coerced but because of our relationship. Friends can indeed "be subject to one another" (Eph. 5:21) without that relationship being one of domination.[11]

In the context of the Christian community, preaching likewise functions as an encounter among friends. A preacher whose stance is one of friendship,

---

10. Michael Warren, *At This Time, in This Place: The Spirit Embodied in the Local Assembly* (Harrisburg, Pa.: Trinity Press International, 1999), 79–83, 96.

11. The distinctiveness of friendship can be seen by contrasting it to other traditional, hierarchical relationships, such as wives and husbands or slaves and masters, in which unqualified calls to "be subject" are problematic.

who lovingly seeks the good of her friends, may at times proclaim challenging words, even words of judgment, in order to build up the community. Indeed, such words would be expected on occasion among friends; and friends would be willing to listen, even if they disagreed with the message. Moreover, in this context the preacher may speak with authority without becoming authoritarian. The preacher speaks with the authority of the friend, an authority that is located not simplistically in the person of the preacher but rather in the community that participates in the friendship. Authority is given to the preacher as friend rather than claimed by the preacher as power. Among friends, challenging and authoritative words may be spoken without the sermon becoming an act of domination.

At the same time, in the community of friends the preacher does not become the one voice that silences all other voices. Because the character of friendship involves mutuality and equality, the preacher is open and vulnerable to the congregation. The members of the congregation are full, active participants in the friendship, at times challenging and admonishing as well as supporting and comforting the preacher as they struggle together with the character of discipleship in their context. In the community of friends, every voice may carry authority—the authority of the friend that comes not with ordination but in the relationship. The preacher will necessarily learn from the saints of the church who have been richly nurtured in the practices and virtues of resistance. These saints will often remind the preacher of his own captivity to the powers and invite him to a new vision of the world and new practices of resistance.

Indeed, in the community of friends the pulpit itself does not ultimately "belong" to any one person but remains open to various voices in the congregation. Among friends, practices and power are shared, and the pulpit is no exception. While the pastor has particular responsibility for this ministry, no one can be excluded; everyone in the congregation is invited to speak in the community of friends. Other believers than the preacher may need to be the ones to expose certain powers, envision alternatives, and nurture the congregation in the practices of resistance. In fact, those people traditionally excluded from the pulpit may have uniquely experienced the work of the powers in both the church and the world and may have a particularly important word to proclaim.[12] In opening up the pulpit in this way, the preacher most fully embodies an "ethic of risk" rather than an "ethic of control" in her

---

12. John McClure has suggested one way of including various voices in both the process of sermon preparation and in the sermon itself. See John S. McClure, *The Roundtable Pulpit: Where Leadership and Preaching Meet* (Nashville: Abingdon Press, 1995). In McClure's work, the pastor still remains the one who actually speaks from the pulpit.

preaching. In a profound sense, she gives her life for the good of her friends. In the process the practice of preaching becomes an embodiment of the mutual love Christians have for one another; it becomes a practice of resistance to the principalities and powers, avoiding captivity to the ways of the Domination System.

Friendship and Character Ethics

As a model for the church, friendship provides not only the context for preaching but also a helpful way for viewing the moral life of the community, including its life of resistance to the powers. In the field of character ethics, friendship plays an important role. Because of the relational character of human beings, we become the persons we are through our relationships with others. What is true about our lives in general is true about the development of the specific virtues necessary to negotiate life in resistance to the principalities and powers. The virtues cannot be developed in isolation but require a community in which they are nurtured. In relationship with others who share the same vision, seek the same good, and engage in common practices, people develop the virtues necessary for resistance. Indeed, because isolation is one of the strategies the powers use to get their way in the world, the gathering of a community that nurtures the virtues of resistance is itself a critical dimension of resistance to the powers.

In the tradition of character ethics, friendship has been a primary way of describing the central relationships through which the virtues are formed. Because the focus of ethics was not primarily on problems and decisions but on persons, friendship became a central concern for ethics. Instead of trying to develop rational rules and principles according to which isolated individuals could make ethical decisions (a modern approach), ethics focused on those relationships in which a person's character was formed. In his *Nichomachean Ethics*, for example, Aristotle devotes two of his ten chapters to friendship.[13] And in strands of the Christian tradition that have valued character ethics, friendship has played an important role.[14] Paul Wadell, a Christian ethicist, has captured the essential role of friendship in the moral life:

---

13. Aristotle, *Nichomachean Ethics*, trans. Martin Ostwald, Library of Liberal Arts (New York: Macmillan, 1986), books 8–9.
14. See, for example, Paul J. Wadell, *Friendship and the Moral Life* (Notre Dame, Ind.: University of Notre Dame Press, 1989); and Elizabeth Stuart, *Just Good Friends: Towards a Lesbian and Gay Theology of Relationships* (London: Mowbray, 1996), 29–32. The Roman Catholic tradition has tended more than the Protestant tradition to focus on character ethics, though as I noted earlier Protestant theologians such as Stanley Hauerwas have recently contributed to the revival of character ethics in contemporary Christian ethics.

Thus, friendship is not just a good for the moral life, it is indispensable; there simply is no other way to come in touch with the goods that make us whole than through relationships with those who share them. That is why we can say friendship is the crucible of moral development, the center of moral formation. One reason we have friends is that there is a good we share with them, but the reason friendships grow and become such a delight is that we cannot be good without them, indeed, we cannot be at all.[15]

Within the framework of character ethics, then, friendship should not be understood in any "sentimental" way; it is not romantic or shallow or unthoughtful.[16] Rather, friends are those who share a vision of the world and a common purpose in life.[17] Friendship provides a "school of virtue," a community in which people are formed in the virtues necessary for living out their common vision and purpose.[18] Friends journey toward a common good; they are "fellow pilgrims . . . travelers on the same quest."[19] Along the way, they nurture and sustain the virtues necessary for that journey. Friendship is thus not simply a relationship but a moral enterprise.[20]

The church, as a community of friends, is just such a pilgrim people journeying together toward the good of God's Shalom. In the context of the powers, that journey takes the form of resistance as the church seeks to embody an alternative to the powers' ways of domination, violence, and death. Members of the church share a vision of God's new order and seek to nurture the practices and virtues that enable the community to sustain and live out that vision. The members of the community mutually critique, encourage, support, and challenge one another, enabling the community to grow together in the virtues and practices that shape the journey toward God's Shalom. As a community of friends, believers grow together in the moral life of resistance.

Moreover, when Christian friendship is shaped by the story of Jesus and seeks God's Shalom, the community does not become closed in on itself but always opens up toward the world, including the stranger and the enemy. Faithful Christian friendship leads to a broadening, not a narrowing, of Christian love. In the Christian community the "preferential love" of friendship is

---

15. Wadell, *Friendship and the Moral Life*, 5–6.
16. Stuart, *Just Good Friends*, 38.
17. C. S. Lewis, *The Four Loves* (New York: Harcourt, Brace & Co., 1960; reprint, San Diego: Harvest Books, 1988), 65–67, 71; Stuart, *Just Good Friends*, 48; Wadell, *Friendship and the Moral Life*, 3–4.
18. On friendship as a "school of virtue," see Lewis, *Four Loves*, 57; and Wadell, *Friendship and the Moral Life*, 79.
19. Lewis, *Four Loves*, 67.
20. Wadell, *Friendship and the Moral Life*, 62.

not opposed to the "universal love" of *agape*.[21] Rather, the church as a community of friends actually nurtures believers in *agape*, which extends to the world the love shared within the church. As Wadell writes, the distinction between *agape* and friendship (*philia*) is an artificial one:

> Any friendship bonded by a love that seeks first the Kingdom of God explodes into a friendship for a humanity for whom the Kingdom of God rightly is home. . . . If a community of faith is bonded together by a common endeavor to prefer the ways of God, then this preference does not impede, but actually becomes the means by which they learn to love the world. True, there is a special love among them because they see burning in another what they have come to cherish in themselves, a hunger and thirst for God, a deep desire to love God with whole heart and soul. True, they love one another in a way they do not love someone else because like Aristotle's friends, they agree on what they think important. But because their friendship is founded on this desire that is shared among them, it is also the relationship by which they learn to love the ones God has loved, the lowly, the downcast, the misbegotten, the overlooked, and even the enemy.[22]

From a very different theological perspective, the feminist theologian Mary E. Hunt has come to a similar conclusion. For Hunt, genuine friendship does not close in upon itself but involves the "mutual search for justice."[23] In this sense, the Christian community of friends necessarily nurtures and sustains such practices as dislocation and hospitality, which move Christians beyond their privilege and comfort into the spaces and lives of the most visible victims of the powers. In this way, the church, as a community of friends, nurtures believers in the love of the "other" that is essential for resistance to the ways of domination.

---

21. One of the traditional criticisms of friendship as a model for the Christian community has been that friendship (*philia*) is "preferential love," as opposed to the "universal love" of Christian *agape*. Friendship, it has been argued, is too limited and "comfortable" a form of love to be genuinely Christian. Biblical texts emphasizing love of the enemy, the stranger, and the marginalized seem to support this viewpoint. For a helpful discussion of the Christian suspicions about friendship, as well as a compelling counterargument, see Wadell, *Friendship and the Moral Life*, 70–119.

22. Ibid., 74, 95–96. John 15:12–17 similarly blurs this artificial distinction between *philia* and *agape*. *Agape* is used to describe the mutual love the disciples are to have for one another, which Jesus describes as friendship.

23. Mary E. Hunt, *Fierce Tenderness: A Feminist Theology of Friendship* (New York: Crossroad, 1991), 18. Hunt defines friendship as "those voluntary human relationships that are entered into by people who intend one another's well-being and who intend that their love relationship is part of a justice-seeking community" (29). Here Hunt captures both the love that seeks the good of the friend and the love that moves outward toward the world.

Friendship and Resistance

Because it is characterized by mutuality and equality, friendship itself can be a practice of resistance to the powers of the Domination System. Not surprisingly, in the face of hierarchical and exclusive understandings of "family" that often leave them "outside the gate," gay and lesbian people not only have turned to friendship as a primary form of relationship but also have emphasized the character of friendship as resistance.[24] Because friendship by its very nature requires mutuality and equality, it represents a way of relating that counters hierarchical models of relationship, including at times the family.[25] From this perspective, friendship itself potentially becomes a radical form of resistance.

The character of friendship as resistance has been highlighted by even such a traditional writer as C. S. Lewis. Because friends share a distinct vision and purpose, Lewis argues, friendships necessarily counter the "outside world" and sustain and embolden friends to be different. "Every real friendship," he notes, "is a sort of secession, even a rebellion . . . a pocket of potential resistance." Consequently, "Authority" often frowns on friendship.[26] Indeed, Lewis even relates this character of friendship as resistance to the early church: "The little pockets of early Christians survived because they cared exclusively for the love of 'the brethren' and stopped their ears to the opinion of the Pagan society all around them."[27] While such friendship can become dangerously prideful and exclusive, Christian friendship, which is a gift of God and is shaped by the story of Jesus, seeks to move beyond this danger.[28]

Contemporary feminist, gay, and lesbian writers have emphasized other ways in which friendship embodies a practice of resistance. By its very nature friendship provides an alternative to relationships shaped by the Domination System, moving people from relationships of domination and submission to those of mutuality and equality.[29] Indeed, consistent with the church's call to nonviolence, Elizabeth Stuart has even noted that "violence and friendship are incompatible."[30] According to these authors, certain kinds of friendship become radical practices of resistance. In the midst of a Domination System

---

24. For important explorations of friendships among gay and lesbian people, see Hunt, *Fierce Tenderness;* Stuart, *Just Good Friends;* and Peter M. Nardi, *Gay Men's Friendships: Invincible Communities, Worlds of Desire* (Chicago: University of Chicago Press, 1999).
25. Indeed, the family itself can act as a principality. See Bill Wylie-Kellermann, "Family: Icon and Principality," *The Witness* 77 (December 1994): 17–23.
26. Lewis, *Four Loves*, 80.
27. Ibid., 79.
28. Ibid., 80–90. Some people, including Lewis himself, have argued that genuine friendship always remains open to others being included.
29. Stuart, *Just Good Friends*, xiv.
30. Ibid., xv.

that oppresses women, for example, friendships between women become a form of resistance. Such friendships provide spaces that affirm and nurture women's identity and growth outside a patriarchal system. They represent a radical form of resistance to the idea that women are fully human only in relation to men. In addition, such friendships often provide the relationships within which political resistance to patriarchy is nurtured.[31] Indeed, such practices of friendship actually subvert some traditional understandings of friendship, including Aristotle's, that have considered friendship to be a relationship solely for elite males and have thereby considered women incapable of being true friends.

Similarly, gay and lesbian friendships often take on the character of resistance. For gay and lesbian people, friends often replace the family in providing the communities of support necessary for life in an oppressive culture. Friendships provide identity-affirming relationships of mutuality and equality in the midst of powers, including the church, that teach gay and lesbian people to despise themselves and that deprive them of a sense of self. Friendships among gay and lesbian people thus become subversive by allowing them to "be themselves" in the midst of a cultural context that does not approve of that self.[32] Such friendships also take on political dimensions. As Peter Nardi, who has written extensively on gay men's friendships, has argued, "Friendships formed by a shared marginal identity take on powerful political dimensions as they organise around a stigmatized status to confront the dominant culture in solidarity."[33]

Finally, friendship becomes a practice of resistance when friendships are formed "across the boundaries" of traditional relationships shaped by domination and submission. For example, when men and women genuinely become friends, they counter the system of patriarchy and offer an alternative to its ways. Indeed, in the early church friendships between men and women played precisely this subversive role of "breaking boundaries" and creating alternative communities.[34] Similarly, when gay men and heterosexual men become friends, they form a bond of mutuality and equality in a relationship that is often characterized by domination and even physical violence. Similar affirmations could be made about friendships that cross racial and class boundaries. Such friendships embody subversive relationships that create a kind of counterculture.[35] As Elizabeth Stuart writes,

---

31. Ibid., 36–43. Hunt also makes this point throughout her book *Fierce Tenderness*.
32. Stuart, *Just Good Friends*, 44. See also Nardi, *Gay Men's Friendships*, 154–88.
33. Quoted in Stuart, *Just Good Friends*, 36. See also Nardi, *Gay Men's Friendships*, 189–206.
34. See Rosemary Rader, *Breaking Boundaries: Male/Female Friendship in Early Christian Communities* (New York: Paulist Press, 1983).
35. This was recognized as early as Plato. See Stuart, *Just Good Friends*, 29.

> Friendships between unlikely people do occur and . . . it is often these
> friendships that motivate the struggle against social inequality. People
> who are locked into structural inequality sometimes do manage to
> struggle toward equality in personal terms whilst never losing sight of
> the structural differences which need to be fought. This is the sub-
> versive power of friendship. . . . Friendship can break rank, and when
> this happens we are given a tantalizing foretaste of what life could be
> like . . . we are recovering creation as God created it to be, we are redis-
> covering our equality.[36]

Friendship is thus no innocuous, innocent activity but a relationship that is
charged with the potential for resistance to the powers.

In these various ways, the practice of friendship actually challenges Christians
to resist the powers by living into their baptisms, in which there is "neither Jew
nor Greek, slave nor free, male and female." By becoming a diverse community
of friends, the church offers an alternative to the Domination System and embodies an intimation of what God's reign promises to be—the "utter unity of humanity in God."[37] As a genuine community of friends, the church offers the world a
glimpse of the new Jerusalem in the midst of empire. In such a community the
virtues necessary for nonviolent resistance to the powers may be nurtured.

VIRTUES OF THE PREACHER

In addition to the love that is oriented to the "other" and lays down its life for
the community of friends, four virtues characterize preachers who engage in
preaching as a practice of nonviolent resistance to the powers: truthfulness,
anger, patience, and hope. The first two of these—truthfulness and anger—are
virtues primarily necessary for resistance, while the latter two—patience and
hope—focus more on the nonviolent character of this resistance. While these
virtues and the practices associated with them are important for preachers, they
do not simply contribute to the task of preaching but are themselves inherently
means of resisting the powers nonviolently in daily life. In this sense they are
virtues not simply for the preacher but for the entire community of friends,
whose life together embodies a way of resistance in the face of the powers.

Truthfulness

Because the principalities and powers rely so heavily on illusion and deception
to order the world in their image, the preacher is called to speak the truth,

---

36. Ibid., 43–44.
37. Wadell, *Friendship and the Moral Life*, 103.

exposing the deadly work of the powers and offering the alternative of God's way. For the preacher as for the Christian community itself, Shalom involves not the avoidance of conflict but the truthful confrontation of the powers of death with the Word of life. As Stanley Hauerwas has written, "The Christian commitment to living peaceably cannot be that of Stoic acceptance, since the peace that has come challenges those orders, both personal and social, which promise security at the price of truth."[38] In the midst of the Babel created by the powers, preachers are called to speak the truth.

Such truthtelling in the pulpit will be most faithful and profound when it is grounded in a life of truthfulness. The preacher will not speak the truth in a compelling way on Sunday morning if she hasn't nurtured the virtue of truthfulness throughout her life. Two dimensions of such truthfulness are critical for preaching as nonviolent resistance to the powers. First, the preacher will nurture truthfulness in relation to the principalities and powers themselves. Second, the preacher will become truthful with regard to his or her own complicity with the powers of death.

Truthfulness about the Powers

While there may be many practices through which preachers may develop the virtue of truthfulness in relation to the powers, the practice of dislocation, which I mentioned in chapter 7, is particularly important. Because the spirit of the Domination System can become the "air we breathe" in our own familiar contexts, preachers often need to "dislocate" themselves into new and unfamiliar spaces in order to discern the powers at work. A willingness to be dislocated and to be open to truth from the "other" is essential for the virtue of truthfulness.[39] For privileged preachers, such dislocation will involve spending time in the spaces of marginalized and oppressed people, who are the most visible victims of the powers.

With regard to this practice and its nurture of truthfulness in relation to the powers, Christian preachers actually have a "saint" to emulate: William Stringfellow.[40] After graduating from Harvard Law School, Stringfellow moved to East Harlem, where he lived and practiced street law for seven years. While "dislocated" in Harlem, Stringfellow spent time with and listened to

---

38. Stanley Hauerwas, *The Peaceable Kingdom: A Primer in Christian Ethics* (Notre Dame, Ind.: University of Notre Dame Press, 1983), 145.
39. On the ethical significance of the "other" for preaching, see John S. McClure, *Other-Wise Preaching: A Postmodern Ethic for Homiletics* (St. Louis: Chalice Press, 2001).
40. In his book *Free in Obedience* (New York: Seabury Press, 1964), 40–42, William Stringfellow directly challenges church leaders to go "outside the gate" to learn about the powers.

the poor people who lived in his neighborhood, and he immersed himself in the study of the Bible.[41] Engaging in these activities enabled Stringfellow to discern the principalities at work in Harlem and moved him to develop his theology of the powers. In Harlem,

> the people on the street first clued him in on the biblical import of the principalities. He would hear folks speak of the gas company, the slum real estate lords, the social bureaucracies, the city administration, the Mafia, and police agencies as though they were predatory beasts, arrayed against the neighborhood and human beings, eating them alive. His writings have since become notorious, among other things, for explicating a biblical doctrine of the powers as precisely that: fallen and predatory creatures, acting with an independent life of their own.[42]

Dislocated from his familiar, privileged social context, Stringfellow discerned the powers at work in the world. His bold and truthful words about the powers were nurtured as he immersed himself in the lives of poor people and the texts of the Bible.

As Stringfellow's experience suggests, genuine dislocation involves much more than simply going to an unusual space; it involves preachers having their own *lives* "dislocated" by learning from the "other" and by allowing crucial homiletical practices—for example, biblical interpretation—to be shaped by a new space and different voices. Such a practice of dislocation provides a critical means for nurturing the virtue of truthfulness. As privileged preachers step out of their familiar, taken-for-granted worlds, they may discern the workings of the powers more clearly; the illusions and deceptions that inhibit truthfulness are stripped away. As "dislocated" preachers open themselves to the lives of oppressed people and simultaneously immerse themselves in Scripture, where the powers are named and exposed, they nurture the virtue of truthfulness in relation to the powers.[43]

---

41. Stringfellow wrote about his years in East Harlem in *My People Is the Enemy: An Autobiographical Polemic* (New York: Holt, Rinehart & Winston, 1964).
42. Bill Wylie-Kellermann, "Bill, the Bible, and the Seminary Underground," in *Radical Christian and Exemplary Lawyer*, ed. Andrew W. McThenia Jr. (Grand Rapids: Wm. B. Eerdmans Publishing Co., 1995), 68.
43. The physical space in which we read Scripture significantly shapes our interpretation. For a more detailed account of the importance of "dislocating" Bible study, see Stanley P. Saunders and Charles L. Campbell, *The Word on the Street: Performing the Scriptures in the Urban Context* (Grand Rapids: Wm. B. Eerdmans Publishing Co., 2000), 86–94. See also Patterson, "Preaching as Nonviolent Resistance," 105. Patterson emphasizes the need to spend time listening to abused women in order to develop a nonviolent preaching practice in resistance to the violence of abuse.

For many preachers today, such a practice of dislocation itself embodies an act of resistance to the powers. Although few mainline preachers will actually move to a place like East Harlem, even small attempts to be with and listen to poor people entail active resistance to the powers in the context of contemporary ministry. Indeed, the effort to spend significant time among marginalized people immediately confronts the preacher with the realities of the powers, including the institutional church, which actively work to keep privileged pastors and poor people apart. If these two groups were to spend much time together, the fallout for the powers might be enormous—and threatening.

Preachers, like the members of their congregations, stay busy with many important activities. There are sermons to prepare, people to visit, meetings to attend, classes to lead; on and on it goes. Being the pastor of a church is, after all, a full-time job. The thought of spending significant time among marginalized people and reading Scripture in their "space" may be almost unimaginable for many pastors. As I noted earlier, however, such "busyness" is one way in which the powers divert people—including pastors—from discerning their work in the world (not to mention one of the ways in which the powers "kill" pastors by burning them out). The busyness created by the institutional church can be an effective means of diverting pastors from the work of the powers, stifling discernment, and keeping the pulpit silent about the ways of death in the world. Busyness, in short, can inhibit truthfulness, not only about the principalities and powers but about the church's own captivity to them.

The institutional church, after all, may not desire truthfulness. As an institution, the church, like all the powers, can become obsessed with its own survival and prefer "safe" preachers who will not threaten its comfortable existence. Whether subtly or directly, the institutional church may press preachers to accommodate themselves to the status quo. Despite their best intentions and ideals, preachers easily become frenetic servants of the institution, driven by its demands and aspiring to the external goods the church offers as standards of success. Salary, buildings, membership, titles, perks, popularity, and influence become the focus—not unlike the standards of success in other institutions. Slowly, almost imperceptibly, the powers wear preachers down and make them numb; the sharp edges of the gospel are worn away, and truthfulness suffers.

Amid these temptations, one of the most important acts of resistance in which preachers can engage involves taking the time to become apprentices to marginalized people—the poor, the prisoner, the abused. This practice of dislocation not only announces a clear "No!" to the powers who would kill our moral conscience but also models resistance for the community of friends. Such a practice embodies an essential spiritual discipline that nurtures the virtue of truthfulness and enables the preacher to resist the principalities and powers, including at times the church itself, in the pulpit.

Truthfulness about Oneself

In addition to being truthful about the powers, preachers need to be truthful about themselves. The spirit of the powers, as I have regularly noted, does not simply exist "out there" but dwells deep within human beings. Domination and violence not only shape the enormous works of the principalities and powers, but also corrupt everyday life and relationships. Consequently, genuine truthfulness cannot create a simplistic us-against-them spirit but involves the preacher's own honesty about the ways in which he or she lives in captivity to the powers' spirit of domination and violence. Indeed, even nonviolent resistance can become captive to the spirit and illusions of the powers and seek to dominate others; it can involve a "demonic underside, power turned upside down, which wishes to gain the upper hand."[44] When we define evil as simply external to us and we ignore its reality in our own lives, we can unwittingly end up cooperating with that evil, allowing it to harden its presence within us.[45] Truthfulness about our own cooperation with the powers of death is a critical virtue for resistance to the principalities and powers.

The practice of dislocation can move privileged preachers to deeper truthfulness about themselves, particularly about their own complicity with the powers. Listening to the stories of marginalized and oppressed people confronts one at a personal level with the privileges one often complacently enjoys. In these encounters, abstract truths known in the mind can become deep truthfulness in the heart. For example, I grew up in Little Rock, Arkansas, and regularly heard stories about the desegregation of Central High School in the late 1950s. All my life I have known about the reality of racism. However, when I began to spend time with homeless people on the streets of Atlanta and young boys in the housing projects of the city, almost all of them African American, I had to confront at a deeply personal level both the power of white racism and the privileges I enjoy as a white man in our society. On the streets and in the housing projects, I had to become truthful about my privilege and my complicity—indeed, my own captivity—in a Domination System shaped by the powers of racism.[46]

---

44. Jim Douglass, "Civil Disobedience as Prayer," in *Peace Is the Way: Writings on Nonviolence from the Fellowship of Reconciliation*, ed. Walter Wink (Maryknoll, N.Y.: Orbis Books, 2000), 149.
45. Ibid., 151.
46. See Saunders and Campbell, *Word on the Street*, 48–50.

Such truthfulness about our complicity with the powers also requires an exploration of the violence in our own lives.[47] Truthfulness about this violence dispels the illusions in which many of us live, as Stanley Hauerwas has noted:

> Our greatest illusion and deception . . . is that we are a peaceable people, nonviolent to the core. We are peaceable so long as no one disturbs our illusions. We are nonviolent so long as no one challenges our turf. . . . So violence becomes needlessly woven into our lives. . . . The order of our lives is built upon our potential for violence.[48]

Preachers have to be truthful: we live in a system whose order, which often guarantees our privilege, is maintained by violence; and the spirit of violence often shapes our life in the world. The violence that enables the powers to do their work lies in each of our spirits.[49] Nurturing the virtue of truthfulness thus involves, as Barbara Patterson writes, coming "to terms with the violence within us, the gap between our own lives and the incarnation of Christ. We recognize our own capacities for sending Christ to Golgotha."[50]

Truthfulness about the violence within us does not focus solely on flagrantly violent acts, such as murder or physical abuse, which might enable many preachers to excuse themselves. Rather, truthfulness about the violence in our lives often begins with "trivial" actions that reveal our propensity to dominate other people and our complicity with the powers of death.[51] Indeed, such trivial activities often underlie the larger workings of the powers. As an Indian philosopher has written, "War is a result of our so-called peace, which is a series of everyday brutalities, exploitation, narrowness and so on. Without changing our daily life we can't have peace, and war is a spectacular expression of our daily conduct."[52]

Over the past few years, for example, I have had to become truthful about my bad habit of interrupting people. At one level, such an activity might be dismissed as simply impolite. In some instances it might even be an excusable sign of passionate engagement in a conversation. It would hardly seem to qualify as "violence." However, taking away the voice of another person—

---

47. For Wink's discussion of the importance of monitoring our inner violence, see Walter Wink, *Engaging the Powers: Discernment and Resistance in a World of Domination* (Minneapolis: Fortress Press, 1992), 279–95.
48. Hauerwas, *Peaceable Kingdom*, 144.
49. Ibid., 150.
50. Patterson, "Preaching as Nonviolent Resistance," 103.
51. Stanley Hauerwas, "Taking Time for Peace: The Ethical Significance of the Trivial," in *Christian Existence Today: Essays on Church, World, and Living in Between* (Durham, N.C.: Labyrinth Press, 1988), 263. As Hauerwas notes, "trivial" does not simply mean trifling but rather activities that can be met anywhere.
52. Jiddu Krishnamurti, quoted in Nisenson, *Ascension*, 168.

silencing another person—undoubtedly contains an element of violence. Moreover, when a professor repeatedly interrupts students, such an action may reflect a world of assumptions about power and control—assumptions that breed violence. When a white man interrupts other people, particularly women or people of color, he may be enacting in a "trivial" way the presuppositions of the Domination System, which violently maintains the privileges of white men. And when a preacher continually interrupts others, he may be enacting assumptions about the power of the preacher, assumptions that may lead to manipulation and domination in the pulpit itself. When understood in these terms, the habit of interrupting others does not appear as innocent as I might have originally wanted to think.

As I have examined this habit and the undercurrent of domination that forms it, I have come to realize my need to be more intentional about listening to others and avoiding interruptions. I have had to confess to others when I have cut them off, and I have had to ask friends and colleagues to hold me accountable for my actions. In short, I have had to become truthful about the propensities to violence within myself and about the assumptions of domination, control, and privilege behind them. And I have had to begin taking steps to change my habit—though, as those who know me will undoubtedly attest, I still have a long way to go.

Truthfulness begins with the preacher's own life, and such truthfulness about oneself can be painful; it is often accompanied by weeping and confession.[53] The preacher not only weeps because of the suffering people endure at the hands of the powers but because of his or her own complicity in that suffering. And the preacher's confession of this complicity becomes one of the most profound expressions of truthfulness. For privileged preachers, the truthfulness that moves toward resistance often passes through weeping and confession.

Such truthfulness becomes possible only in the assurance of God's redemption and forgiveness, which is the ultimate truth about our lives. Only when we know the possibility of forgiveness can we dare engage in truthful confession. Otherwise, truthfulness is too threatening. Consequently, most "calls to confession" in the liturgy include a promise of forgiveness: "If we say that we have no sin, we deceive ourselves, and the truth is not in us. If we confess our sins, the one who is faithful and just will forgive us our sins and cleanse us from all unrighteousness."[54] The good news of the gospel announces that God in Jesus Christ redeems us from our captivity to the powers and forgives us for

---

53. See Christine Smith's compelling account in *Preaching as Weeping, Confession, and Resistance: Radical Responses to Radical Evil* (Louisville, Ky.: Westminster/John Knox Press, 1992), esp. 3–6. See also Saunders and Campbell, *Word on the Street*, 48–50.
54. This widely used Call to Confession is based on 1 John 1:8–9.

our complicity with their work. This assurance enables preachers to be truthful in the face of the powers and truthful about themselves.[55]

The illusions and deceptions of the powers thus shape not only the world in which we live but our personal lives as well. In the midst of these illusions, truthfulness is not simply a means to the end of faithful preaching but a disposition that shapes a life of resistance to the powers. Nevertheless, the virtue of truthfulness also grounds the practice of preaching. Truthfulness about the powers frees preachers to expose and resist their deadly ways in sermons. Truthfulness about themselves enables preachers to resist the powers of death in their own lives, including in their preaching. Truthful preachers will thus speak a word of resistance to the powers. Just as important, these preachers will do so standing *within* the community of friends as redeemed and forgiven sinners, rather than standing over against the congregation as self-righteous judges of the people in the pews.

Anger

As preachers become truthful about the activities of the principalities and powers, they may begin to nurture another critical virtue essential for preaching as nonviolent resistance: *anger*. Anger is rarely considered a virtue for the preacher—indeed, it is more often listed among the deadly sins. And there are good reasons why the Christian tradition has looked with suspicion on anger. Anger can and often does lead to social violence, which, as I have argued throughout this book, does not represent the way of Jesus. Similarly, anger can be turned against other individuals in violent and destructive ways; it can become a means of intimidation and control. At its most deadly, anger can become hatred, which is "anger turned rigid, fixated, deadened."[56] When the pulpit becomes the outlet for such anger, preachers may end up verbally abusing congregations rather than speaking a redemptive word. Moreover, anger can be self-destructive; when it has no outlet and becomes turned in upon the self, it can create debilitating guilt or self-hatred. In short, one needs to be careful when discussing anger as a virtue for the preacher.

Nevertheless, anger is often appropriately stirred up as privileged people "dislocate" themselves and see the oppression wreaked by the powers of death. When we spend time on the streets with homeless people and listen to their

---

55. Stanley Hauerwas, "Peacemaking: The Virtue of the Church," in *Christian Existence Today*, 93.
56. Beverly Wildung Harrison, "The Power of Anger in the Work of Love: Christian Ethics for Women and Other Strangers," in *Feminist Theology: A Reader*, ed. Ann Loades (Louisville, Ky.: Westminster/John Knox Press, 1990), 207.

stories, for example, anger—indeed, moral outrage—at the principalities and powers is an appropriate response. When we share the pain of an abused woman and discern the system of patriarchy that contributes to that abuse, anger at that system is a virtuous response.[57] Once we begin to discern the predatory work of the powers that crush human lives, anger *should* be stirred up; it is a virtue in the face of the powers of death. Although God is "slow to anger," God regularly becomes angry over the injustices in the world.[58]

The kind of anger I have in mind has two distinctive characteristics. In the first place, this anger is intimately related to love. Beverly Wildung Harrison has emphasized this relationship:

> It is my thesis that we Christians have come very close to killing love precisely because we have understood anger to be a deadly sin. Anger is not the opposite of love. It is better understood as a feeling-signal that all is not well in our relation to other persons or groups or to the world around us. Anger is a mode of connectedness to others and it is always a vivid form of caring.[59]

Anger, as Harrison suggests, not only may be grounded in love but may empower the work of love. Indeed, as she continues, "where anger is hidden or goes unattended, masking itself, there the power of love, the power to act, to deepen relation, atrophies and dies."[60] When a "dislocated" preacher enters the lives of marginalized people, listens to their stories, and begins to love them, anger at the powers of death that oppress them becomes an expression of that love. Love for the victims of the powers and anger at the powers of death belong together.

Second, the kind of anger I have in mind is anger directed at the *powers* rather than at individuals. While anger at individuals can be an appropriate expression of love, that anger has its place in contexts other than the sermon.[61]

---

57. Although she doesn't directly discuss anger, see Patterson, "Preaching as Nonviolent Resistance."

58. For a discussion of God's anger, see Abraham Heschel, *The Prophets*, vol. 2 (New York: Harper & Row, 1962), 59–86. For a different angle on both God's and Jesus' anger, see Carroll Saussy, *The Gift of Anger: A Call to Faithful Action* (Louisville, Ky.: Westminster John Knox Press, 1995), 65–100. Saussy examines the complexities of anger and argues, like Harrison, that anger can provide an impetus for constructive action in addressing injustice.

59. Harrison, "Power of Anger," 206. Harrison overstates the case by saying anger is *always* a form of caring.

60. Ibid., 207.

61. For example, anger at a spouse abuser can be an appropriate expression of love both for the abused woman, who has suffered at the hands of another, and for the abuser, whom one hopes will change.

The homiletical virtue of anger is directed toward the powers that hold people captive, rather than toward specific persons. When preachers direct their anger at individuals from the pulpit, the sermon usually becomes either an emotional outlet for the preacher or a means to verbally abuse the hearer, neither of which is an expression of virtuous anger.[62] When dealing with anger, the preacher does well to remember that our struggle is "not against enemies of blood and flesh" but against the principalities and powers.

With these qualifications in mind, one can affirm that anger is a critical virtue for resistance; it is a "sign of resistance in ourselves to the moral quality of social relations in which we are immersed."[63] Anger marks an end to the numbness—the demoralization—the powers seek to instill in people. It signals a stirring of the moral sense that the powers want to extinguish in order to maintain their dominion. Moreover, as Harrison argues, anger often provides the energy for action: "We must never lose touch with the fact that all serious human moral activity, especially action for social change, takes its bearings from the rising power of human anger. Such anger is a signal that change is called for, that transformation in relation is required."[64] No wonder the powers seek to make human beings numb! Once anger arises, the powers begin to lose their grip; their deadly ways have been discerned, and human resistance has begun. Preaching that seeks to resist the principalities and powers will be empowered by the virtue of anger.

Patience

Although patience has been viewed more positively than anger in the Christian tradition, it is no less dangerous, particularly for privileged people.[65] Counseling privileged people to be patient in the face of the havoc wreaked by the powers can seem like pronouncing a blessing on the status quo. In fact, the beneficiaries of the Domination System may not mind waiting patiently for its end. Those who enjoy many of the material and personal benefits of the System, and who would to some extent grieve its passing,

---

62. One may, of course, preach *about* the value of anger at another person in some situations, but that is a different matter from preaching out of anger at an individual or singling out an individual in the sermon.

63. Harrison, "Power of Anger," 206. For another discussion of the role of anger in a "spirituality of resistance," see Roger S. Gottlieb, *A Spirituality of Resistance: Finding a Peaceful Heart and Protecting the Earth* (New York: Crossroad, 1999), 172–75.

64. Harrison, "Power of Anger," 206.

65. For a helpful discussion of the virtue of patience, including its strong biblical warrant, see Philip D. Kenneson, *Life on the Vine: Cultivating the Fruit of the Spirit in Christian Community* (Downers Grove, Ill.: InterVarsity Press, 1999), 107–32.

might just as soon delay the reign of God. Amid the comforts of the present, patiently waiting for the coming of God's reign presents no problem. Indeed, in many privileged congregations the *lack* of urgency about the deadly ways of the powers is the more fundamental issue. "Thy kingdom come, O Lord, but not yet" may be their prayer. Counseling patience seems counterproductive.

That is why patience, truthfulness, and anger belong together. Truthfulness about the powers and oneself prevents patience from simply becoming comfort and complacency. When one is truthful about the deadly ways of the powers and one's own complicity in their work, the counsel to patience cannot become an opportunity for making peace with the status quo. Similarly, anger at the suffering caused by the powers of death, which generates the energy for action, prevents patience from becoming either inactivity in the face of the powers or resignation with the way things are. In fact, truthfulness and anger generate the need for patience. Once one becomes truthful about the work of the powers and angry enough to resist them, patience becomes necessary to keep the resistance from becoming violent. Patience helps shape the adjective—*nonviolent*—that necessarily modifies the noun—*resistance.*

At its root, patience is the ability to relinquish control.[66] As I have noted before, this desire for control often leads to coercion and violence. Consequently, our refusal to resort to coercion and violence in the face of the powers of death calls forth the virtue of patience. As Hauerwas writes, "A spirituality that acknowledges the tragic is one schooled in patience. Our unwillingness to use violence to make the world 'better' means that we must often learn to wait."[67] Patience in this sense is the opposite of resignation; it is rather the active refusal to be held captive by the myth of redemptive violence or to be resigned to the powers' means of violence. In this sense patience is a critical disposition that enables Christians to negotiate the world nonviolently; it is an essential virtue for breaking the cycle of violence in the world and moving toward the establishment of Shalom. This is one reason Jim Douglass argues that all acts of nonviolent civil disobedience must be accompanied by the prayer "Thy will be done," which turns control of the situation over to God.[68] Only through such prayer can the cycle of violence genuinely be broken. Patience is thus one of the critical virtues for preaching that operates out of an ethic of risk rather than an ethic of control.

Patience in this sense may be precisely the virtue that privileged people,

---

66. Ibid., 100, 110.
67. Hauerwas, *Peaceable Kingdom,* 145.
68. Douglass, "Civil Disobedience as Prayer," 149–52.

including preachers, need to cultivate.[69] For privileged people are accustomed to being in control. Waiting, whether in the grocery line or at a stoplight, frustrates us because the situation is out of our control. And this need to be in control may likewise explain why privileged people do not like being "patients"—to use the noun form of the word. Being a patient involves yielding control to another, in this case a health care professional.[70] No wonder Advent, the preeminent season of waiting in the Christian calendar, is so difficult to observe in privileged churches; the season requires the giving up of control that is inherent in waiting. In addition to the violence that results from this need for control, another consequence is a frenetic busyness, which diverts people from noticing the working of the powers, and a captivity to the spirit of efficiency and productivity, which shapes life according to the priorities of technology and consumerism.[71]

Preachers must deal with this need for control not only to resist violence and busyness but also to avoid demoralization in the face of the powers. As I mentioned in chapter 2, the powers seek to make people feel helpless before them. Because of the enormity of the powers, people often become demoralized trying to work for change. All too often in the face of the powers, it seems like there is nothing significant we can do. Deep down, this is an issue of control. Overwhelmed and frustrated by our lack of control over the powers, we either frenetically work ourselves to death trying to "change the world" or we give up and do nothing. In fact, this sense of "all or nothing" often drives us in relation to the principalities and powers. Either we feel we must do everything, which is impossible, or we feel we can do nothing, which ends up paralyzing us. In this way the powers use our own desire for control to overcome our resistance.

The virtue of patience is thus essential for ongoing resistance. Patience enables us to keep doing what we can—even if that is the foolish, puny resistance of preaching—without becoming demoralized about what remains to be done. For patience is grounded in a trust in God that constantly reminds us of this fact: just because there may be little or nothing constructive that we can do does not mean that nothing constructive is being done.[72] In Sharon Welch's terms, patience enables us to focus on creating the space for another step of resistance, rather than having to "transform the world" through our actions.

---

69. This virtue may not be one cultivated by oppressed and marginalized people who have little or no control over their circumstances. Certainly no privileged person can demand patience from oppressed people.

70. Kenneson, *Life on the Vine*, 109.

71. Ibid., 117–23.

72. Hauerwas, *Peaceable Kingdom*, 137. Hauerwas is developing an insight from H. Richard Niebuhr's classic essay "The Grace of Doing Nothing," *Christian Century* 49 (March 23, 1932): 378–80.

As Hauerwas has argued, patience enables us to live into the "grace of doing one thing."[73] Because of our need to "do everything" and control the outcome, we often ironically become caught up in the spirit of the Domination System—the spirit of control and violence. By patiently doing one thing that enables further resistance, however, we are led more deeply into God's peaceable reign. "For that 'one thing,'" as Hauerwas writes, "is just enough to remove us from the familiar world of violence so that our imagination might be freed to find yet one other thing we might do."[74]

In fact, the people who focus on "the grace of doing one thing" do seem to be the ones who persevere in resistance. Ed Loring, one of the founders of the Open Door Community in Atlanta, regularly reminds me that he focuses only on homelessness. He continually must resist the temptation to take up every cause in order to change the world. That is probably one of the reasons the Open Door Community has persevered in its ministry with homeless people for over twenty years. In a somewhat different way, Wes Howard-Brook and Anthony Gwyther suggest the need to begin taking small steps out of the empire of global capitalism. In addition to prayer, worship, and Bible study, Howard-Brook and Gwyther suggest starting a communal garden, ceasing to watch television, or sharing some possessions in community. Through such "little steps," they argue, our habits are changed, and we begin to move out of empire into the new Jerusalem.[75]

As Howard-Brook and Gwyther suggest, even seemingly trivial activities may be forms of resistance that shape our imaginations and point us in the direction of "next steps." Hauerwas concurs:

> Learning the discipline to wait, to be at rest with ourselves, to take the time to be a friend and to be loved, are all ascetic practices that are meant to free us from the normalcy of the world. Through them we are slowly recalled from the world of violence that we might envisage how interesting a people at peace might be.[76]

Such trivial practices both require and cultivate the virtue of patience. They train us to resist the violence, busyness, and demoralization the powers seek to work in us, and they prepare us for more dramatic acts of resistance, such as community organizing, public protest, and even civil disobedience. The people of Le Chambon, France, for example, provided sanctuary to Jews

---

73. Hauerwas, *Peaceable Kingdom*, 149.
74. Ibid., 150.
75. Wes Howard-Brook and Anthony Gwyther, *Unveiling Empire: Reading Revelation Then and Now* (Maryknoll, N.Y.: Orbis Books, 1999), 264–77.
76. Hauerwas, *Peaceable Kingdom*, 150.

during World War II in part because they had engaged in more trivial acts of hospitality throughout their lives. The dramatic act of resistance to the Nazis became a "natural" step growing out of their daily practice of hospitality.

The observance of the Sabbath is the primary liturgical context for the cultivation of patience. Sabbath rest affirms that the world can get along—at least for one day out of seven—without our work. It dispels our illusions of control. By resting on the Sabbath we gratefully receive the world as a gift, and we embody in our practice the recognition that human effort does not make the world turn.[77] Sabbath rest involves giving up control, ceasing the frenetic busyness whereby we seek to manage the future and secure ourselves. Moreover, on the Sabbath we recognize that the One we worship is a patient God, a God who can rest, a God who does not coerce human obedience but calls us forth in "steadfast love that endures forever." The God we worship on the Sabbath is a God whose power is manifest in patience, a God who "creates the time for us to learn that our lives are distorted as long as we think we, rather than God, rule the world."[78]

The Sabbath, then, is a primary liturgical practice within which the virtue of patience is cultivated. Although Christians worship on the Lord's Day rather than the Jewish Sabbath, the theological affirmations and practices of the Sabbath are certainly central to the Christian community's trust in God and life in the world.[79] To cultivate the virtue of patience, Christians, including preachers, need to develop a rhythm of Sabbath rest in the midst of the busyness of the week. For in resting together with the God who can rest, we begin to give up our need to control the future, and we cultivate one of the critical virtues that turns life from violence to Shalom.

The practice of dislocation also requires and cultivates patience in the sense of giving up control. In this practice, patience actually becomes a critical virtue for developing truthfulness and anger. As I suggested earlier, one way of cultivating truthfulness and anger involves sharing time with those people who are the most visible victims of the powers. It involves stepping out of the busyness of pressing pastoral work and patiently waiting while marginalized people tell us their stories, just as Jesus, even while hurrying to Jairus's house to heal his daughter, patiently listened while the woman with the flow of blood told him her story (Mark 5:33). Cultivating truthfulness and anger involves learning from the "other." It involves entering into a genuine relationship of

---

77. Dorothy C. Bass, "Keeping Sabbath," in *Practicing Our Faith: A Way of Life for a Searching People*, ed. Dorothy C. Bass (San Francisco: Jossey-Bass, 1997), 80, 86. See also Kenneson, *Life on the Vine*, 130.
78. Hauerwas, "Taking Time for Peace," 257.
79. In the next section I discuss Lord's Day worship.

hospitality, in which the privileged person no longer serves as the host but becomes the guest—the one welcomed into the other's space—and is changed in the process. In a similar way, the "stranger" on the road to Emmaus, who was invited as a guest to the disciples' table, became the host and opened the eyes of the disciples when they broke bread together (Luke 24:13–35).[80]

For privileged persons, the most difficult part of this process involves giving up control. All too often, privileged Christians approach marginalized people as "problems." And people in power usually deal with problems by taking control and fixing them. In the midst of a chaotic situation, powerful people almost immediately seek to impose an order of their own making. And this is how privileged people often deal with marginalized people. With the best of intentions, we often immediately try to impose our own order on their lives, to "rehabilitate" them according to our values, to force our solutions on their problems—all before we have taken the time to enter into their world and value them as "other," all before we have begun genuinely to stand with them in their space. The most visible recent consequence of this approach is a welfare-reform program based on the threat "Get to work or else!"

In developing the virtue of patience, then, preachers need to learn (patiently) to give up control in order to risk new kinds of relationship and new ways of attending to the world. Observing Sabbath and listening to the stories of marginalized people, preachers may begin to cultivate the virtue of patience as well as the virtues of truthfulness and anger. Preachers may begin to move beyond the need to control situations into a willingness to risk relationships of mutuality and reciprocity. They may, in short, begin moving beyond an ethic of control into an ethic of risk, which is essential for preaching as non-violent resistance to the powers.

Hope

The apostle Paul makes explicit the intimate relationship between hope and patience:

> We know that the whole creation has been groaning in labor pains until now; and not only the creation, but we ourselves, who have the first fruits of the Spirit, groan inwardly while we wait for adoption, the

---

80. In his book on hospitality, John Koenig repeatedly emphasizes that genuine hospitality involves a blurring of the roles of guest and host and a willingness to be changed by the stranger. See John Koenig, *New Testament Hospitality: Partnership with Strangers as Promise and Mission* (Philadelphia: Fortress Press, 1985). See also Christine D. Pohl, *Making Room: Recovering Hospitality as a Christian Tradition* (Grand Rapids: Wm. B. Eerdmans Publishing Co., 1999).

redemption of our bodies. For in hope we were saved. Now hope that is seen is not hope. For who hopes for what is seen? But if we hope for what we do not see, we wait for it with patience. (Rom. 8:22–25)

Hope, according to Paul, provides the ground for patience. Our hope in God's purposes for the world enables us patiently to resist the powers of death without becoming demoralized or having to control the future through acts of violence.

In fact, in the face of the powers' work, hope is the primary virtue that sustains the church's nonviolent resistance. Hope, in Stringfellow's words, "is reliance upon grace in the face of death; the issue is that of receiving life as a gift, not as a reward and not as a punishment; hope is living constantly, patiently, expectantly, resiliently, joyously in the efficacy of the Word of God."[81] In this sense, hope is a form of truthfulness; it is truthfulness about the redemptive work of God in the midst of the powers. Knowing that Jesus has already overcome the powers of death with the power of life, and living with the present assurance of the ultimate fulfillment of God's purposes of redemption, Christians can engage in the daily practices of resistance with patience and perseverance. Receiving both life and the future as a gift, we are set free from the idols of success and achievement, and we can remain steadfast along the way of discipleship.

The primary practice that nurtures the virtue of hope is Lord's Day worship. For Christians, every Lord's Day—every Sunday—is a "little Easter." In gathering for worship, Christians enter the new creation inaugurated by Jesus' resurrection from the dead. For this reason, Sunday has frequently been referred to as the "eighth day," the day that follows the seven days of the original creation and marks the beginning of God's new creation. Christian worship thus foreshadows that day when God's purposes will be brought to fulfillment and the new creation will be complete. And the Lord's Table, the central liturgical action on this day, likewise not only involves meeting the risen Christ, like the disciples on the way to Emmaus, but foreshadows the great banquet that will mark the fulfillment of God's reign in the world. Sunday, in short, is a day when Christians enter the reality and hope of Jesus' resurrection in the face of the powers of death.

Lord's Day worship thus equips Christians to face the fundamental threat of the powers: death. It sets Christians free from the fear of death, which is the ultimate strategy the powers use to keep people in conformity to their ways. In Walter Wink's terms, Lord's Day worship enacts the ultimate truth of the gospel in the face of the powers of death: "The good news to the world is that

---

81. Stringfellow, *Ethic for Christians*, 138.

we can stop living in thrall to the powers now, even under the conditions of death. The gospel is that God sets us free from the dread of death, the cajolery of death, and the seductiveness of death, even though we are complicit with death's power."[82] The practice of Lord's Day worship thus represents the fundamental Christian challenge to the powers of death in the world and provides the space in which believers develop the virtue of hope. Worshiping every Sunday in the reality of Jesus' resurrection, and being redeemed from the fear of death through which the powers hold us captive, Christians are nurtured in the hope that enables and sustains resistance to the powers and principalities. Although many churches today have lost the Lord's Day emphasis on resurrection hope, this emphasis was central to early Christian worship and needs to be reclaimed today as an act of resistance in the face of the powers of death. When this Lord's Day emphasis on resurrection is combined with the tradition of Sabbath rest, Christian worship nurtures the community in two of the fundamental virtues of nonviolence: patience and hope.

In addition to enabling worshipers to enter the reality of Jesus' resurrection, Christian worship also nurtures the community in the virtue of hope in another way: it provides the context in which the community rehearses the memories essential for hopefulness. Memory and hope are intimately related, for our hopes are shaped by our memories. As Jürgen Moltmann has written, "No real hope is ever born out of 'creative despair.' Hope must always be preceded by some positive remembrance."[83] The sacraments, the prayers, the hymns, the creeds, and the Scripture all nurture the worshiping community in the "positive remembrance" that forms the virtue of hope. We remember stories of a God who speaks an alternative future and surprises God's people with "new things." We remember stories of a God who makes and keeps promises and brings life out of death. We remember stories of a God who holds the world accountable for injustice but who loves the world with a steadfast love that endures forever. Worship reminds the community that Christian hope is not a general kind of hope or optimism that emerges naturally from human experience. It is instead a distinctive hope generated by peculiar memories.

If preachers are to cultivate the virtue of hope, then, they need to participate actively in the community's worship. On the one hand, this may seem easy. Preachers, after all, participate in worship weekly. Engaging with Scripture every week as they prepare for sermons, preachers have a unique opportunity to immerse themselves in the stories that nurture them as people of

82. Walter Wink, "Stringfellow on the Powers," in McThenia, ed., *Radical Christian and Exemplary Lawyer,* 20.
83. Jürgen Moltmann, *The Way of Jesus Christ: Christology in Messianic Dimensions,* trans. Margaret Kohl (San Francisco: HarperSanFrancisco, 1990), 8.

hope. The weekly practice of preparing the sermon and leading worship may be a blessing, helping form preachers in the virtue of hope.

On the other hand, preachers who lead worship each week face a danger. Worship can become a job, a burden that prevents the preacher from being nurtured within the worshiping community. How many worship leaders in fact feel that they themselves rarely get to worship? When this happens, worship can actually become a tool of the powers through which preachers become captive to the ways of death, rather than a practice that sets preachers free for lives of resistance. Worship can actually cultivate dispositions shaped more by the principalities and powers than by the biblical stories: efficiency, effectiveness, and control. Consequently, preachers need to find places and times where they can worship, where they can receive the gift of life in the power of Jesus' resurrection and immerse themselves in the memories that nurture hope. Only then will preachers themselves cultivate the virtue of hope that is essential for preaching as a practice of nonviolent resistance.

As Christians enter deeply into the communal memories of worship, however, we are reminded that hope cannot simply be nurtured within the safe religious compound of the church but must move "outside the gates" to the places of suffering (Heb. 13:12–13). As Paul's words from Romans make clear, hope has a "shadow side"; it lives in the midst of the creation's groaning for redemption. Hope is always hope in "things not seen," hope in the midst of a world in which the visions are not yet the full reality. Indeed, Paul himself proclaims that hope is not only a gift from God that frees us for resistance to the powers of death but also a virtue cultivated on the path of suffering discipleship:

> Therefore, since we are justified by faith, we have peace with God through our Lord Jesus Christ, through whom we have obtained access to this grace in which we stand; and we boast in our hope of sharing the glory of God. And not only that, but we also boast in our sufferings, knowing that suffering produces endurance, and endurance produces character, and character produces hope, and hope does not disappoint us, because God's love has been poured into our hearts through the Holy Spirit that has been given to us. (Rom. 5:1–5)

In the church's distinctive communal memories, suffering and hope are inextricably related. Hope does not belong to those who are comfortable and have secured themselves through the world's means. Rather, as Stringfellow reminds us, hope "is reliance upon grace in the face of death," and "any so-called hope is delusory and false without or apart from the confrontation with the power of death, whatever momentary or circumstantial form that may have."[84] In the church's story, hope cries out in the voices of slaves in Egypt. Hope sits in Babylon aching for home. Hope stands at the foot of the cross longing for an alternative to death. Hope looks for the city that is to come in the places of Jesus' suffering: at a mass grave in Kosovo; in a soup-kitchen line of homeless people; in a cell on death row; in a hospice bed. Hope, as Jürgen Moltmann writes, is always hope against hope: "The messianic hope was never the hope of the victors and the rulers. It was always the hope of the defeated and the ground down."[85] Here is the great challenge for Christian preachers: radical hope in the efficacy of the Word amid unflinching truthfulness about the suffering caused by the powers of death. Indeed, apart from such radical hope, preachers will not have the courage to be truthful about the deadly ways of the powers.[86]

The virtue of hope, like the other virtues I have discussed, requires preachers not only to enter the places of suffering in their ongoing pastoral work but also to "dislocate" themselves to the places of suffering among marginalized people. In these places of suffering, hope may surprise us. A man dying of cancer asks for his harmonica and, with what little breath he has left, plays a song of praise. A homeless woman gives testimony to the power and grace of God as she prays before the meal in the shelter. A man on death row shares the dramatic visions from God that sustain him in the midst of a seemingly hopeless situation. In places where death seeks to do its ugly work, the reality and power of hope may surprise us. And when it does, the power of death loses its sting, even if just for a moment.

In such places, hope becomes radical hope in God. It cannot be the shallow, more-of-the-same optimism of the privileged but becomes hope that is essential to sustain life from moment to moment. Such hope lives with truthfulness about the powers of death in the world, with lament over human suffering, and with anger at the forces of injustice.[87] In the places of suffering, the principalities and powers are unmasked for what they are—the powers of death, not life; the powers of despair, not hope. All the little false hopes and false promises are stripped away. When this happens, radical hope in *God* may be born among those who have been nurtured in the memories of the community of faith and cling to God's promises: a new heaven and a new earth; the

---

84. Stringfellow, *Ethic for Christians*, 138.
85. Moltmann, *Way of Jesus Christ*, 13.
86. In the New Testament, courage is not the alternative to fear. Rather, hope, which frees us from the fear of death, and "perfect love," which "casts out fear" (1 John 4:18), provide the ground for courage.
87. On the relationship between hope and anger, see Saussy, *Gift of Anger*, 56–58, 105–12.

new Jerusalem descending from heaven; a great messianic banquet where all God's children will sit together at table in Shalom. In the places of death, hope becomes radical hope in God, for no shallow, domesticated hope will do.

In the places of death, hope itself finally becomes a form of resistance—a defiance of the powers that pretend to rule the world. In the face of the powers, hope is no passive, wishful longing for a better day. Rather, it is a form of resistance to the principalities that masquerade as common sense; it challenges the closed definitions of reality that offer no alternative future. Where hope is present, the powers have lost control, and their reign has been broken. The future opens up, and life becomes possible even in the midst of death.

As preachers enter the reality of Jesus' resurrection, immerse themselves in the memories of the community of faith, and cultivate hope in the places of suffering, they are prepared to preach with hope on Sunday mornings. They are empowered to enter the pulpit and nonviolently resist the powers with the redemptive Word of the gospel. They are prepared to speak the Word that helps set the church free to live faithfully in the face of the powers of death. And grounded in such hope, preachers may even find themselves preaching with joy—the joy that comes with the assurance of God's redemption and the confidence that we are at least in the right struggle.[88]

---

88. Hauerwas, *Peaceable Kingdom*, 146–49.

Select Bibliography

Aristotle. *Nichomachean Ethics.* Translated by Martin Ostwald. Library of Liberal Arts. New York: Macmillan, 1986.

Arnhart, Larry. *Aristotle on Political Reasoning: A Commentary on the Rhetoric.* DeKalb, Ill.: Northern Illinois University Press, 1981.

Aulén, Gustaf. *Christus Victor: A Historical Study of the Three Main Types of the Idea of the Atonement.* Translated by A. G. Herbert. New York: Macmillan, 1931.

Bailie, Gil. *Violence Unveiled: Humanity at the Crossroads.* New York: Crossroad, 1995.

Bass, Dorothy C., ed. *Practicing Our Faith: A Way of Life for a Searching People.* San Francisco: Jossey-Bass, 1997.

Berkhof, Hendrik. *Christ and the Powers.* Translated by John H. Yoder. Scottdale, Pa.: Herald Press, 1977.

Blau, Joel. *The Visible Poor: Homelessness in the United States.* New York: Oxford University Press, 1992.

Bond, L. Susan. *Trouble with Jesus: Women, Christology, and Preaching.* St. Louis: Chalice Press, 1999.

Bourdieu, Pierre. *Outline of a Theory of Practice.* Translated by Richard Nice. Cambridge: Cambridge University Press, 1977.

Brueggemann, Walter. *Finally Comes the Poet: Daring Speech for Proclamation.* Philadelphia: Fortress Press, 1989.

———. *Peace.* St. Louis: Chalice Press, 2001.

———. "Preaching as Reimagination." *Theology Today* 52 (October 1995): 313–29.

———. "Preaching a Sub-Version." *Theology Today* 55 (July 1998): 195–212.

———. "Voice as Counter to Violence." *Calvin Theological Journal* 36 (2001): 22–33.

Butigan, Ken, and Patricia Bruno. *From Violence to Wholeness: A Ten Part Program in the Spirituality and Practice of Active Nonviolence.* Las Vegas: Pace e Bene Franciscan Nonviolence Center, 1999.

Buttrick, David. *The Mystery and the Passion: A Homiletic Reading of the Gospel Traditions.* Minneapolis: Fortress Press, 1992.

———. *Preaching Jesus Christ: An Exercise in Homiletic Theology.* Philadelphia: Fortress Press, 1988.

Campbell, Charles L. "Living Faith: Luther, Preaching, and Ethics." *Word and World* 10 (Fall 1990): 374–79.

———. "More than Quandaries: Character Ethics and Preaching." *Journal for Preachers* 16 (Pentecost 1993): 31–37.

———. *Preaching Jesus: New Directions for Homiletics in Hans Frei's Postliberal Theology.* Grand Rapids: Wm. B. Eerdmans Publishing Co., 1997.

———. "Principalities, Powers, and Preaching: Learning from William Stringfellow." *Interpretation* 51 (1997): 384–401.

Cannon, Katie G. *Black Womanist Ethics.* American Academy of Religion Academy Series, no. 60. Atlanta: Scholars Press, 1988.

Cone, James H. *God of the Oppressed.* New York: Seabury Press, 1975.

———. "Sanctification, Liberation, and Black Worship." *Theology Today* 35 (1978–79): 139–52.

Costas, Orlando E. *Christ Outside the Gate: Mission beyond Christendom.* Maryknoll, N.Y.: Orbis Books, 1982.

Craddock, Fred B. *As One without Authority.* 4th ed. St. Louis: Chalice Press, 2001.

Dawn, Marva J. *Powers, Weakness, and the Tabernacling of God.* Grand Rapids: Wm. B. Eerdmans Publishing Co., 2001.

Dawn, Marva Jenine Sandbe. "The Concept of 'the Principalities and Powers' in the Works of Jacques Ellul." Ph.D. diss., University of Notre Dame, 1992. Ann Arbor, Mich.: University Microfilms #9220014.

DeSilva, David A. *Perseverance in Gratitude: A Socio-Rhetorical Commentary on the Epistle "to the Hebrews."* Grand Rapids: Wm. B. Eerdmans Publishing Co., 2000.

Duff, Nancy J. "Atonement and the Christian Life: Reformed Doctrine from a Feminist Perspective." *Interpretation* 53 (January 1999): 21–33.

———. "The Significance of Pauline Apocalyptic for Theological Ethics." In *Apocalyptic and the New Testament: Essays in Honor of J. Louis Martyn,* edited by Joel Marcus and Marion L. Soards, 279–96. Journal for the Study of the New Testament: Supplement Series 24. Sheffield: JSOT Press, 1989.

Edwards, James C. *Ethics without Philosophy: Wittgenstein and the Moral Life.* Tampa: University Presses of Florida, 1982.

Ellul, Jacques. *The Humiliation of the Word.* Translated by Joyce Main Hanks. Grand Rapids: Wm. B. Eerdmans Publishing Co., 1985.

———. *The Meaning of the City.* Translated by Dennis Pardee. Grand Rapids: Wm. B. Eerdmans Publishing Co., 1970.

———. *The Presence of the Kingdom.* Translated by Olive Wyon. New York: Seabury Press, 1967.

———. *The Subversion of Christianity.* Translated by Geoffrey W. Bromiley. Grand Rapids: Wm. B. Eerdmans Publishing Co., 1986.

———. *The Technological Society.* Translated by John Wilkinson. New York: Alfred A. Knopf, 1964.

———. *Violence: Reflections from a Christian Perspective.* Translated by Cecelia Gaul Kings. New York: Seabury Press, 1969.

Eslinger, Richard. "The Homiletic Virtues: Explorations into the Character of the Preacher." *Worship Arts* 43 (July–August 1998): 8–11.

Evans, Patricia M. *The Verbally Abusive Relationship: How to Recognize It and How to Respond.* 2d ed. Holbrook, Mass.: Adams Media Corporation, 1996.

Florence, Anna Carter. "The Woman Who Just Said 'No.'" *Journal for Preachers* 22 (Advent 1998): 37–41.

Foucault, Michel. *Discipline and Punish: The Birth of the Prison.* Translated by Alan Sheridan. New York: Vintage Books, 1979.

Freire, Paulo. *Pedagogy of the Oppressed.* Translated by Myra Bergman Ramos. New York: Continuum, 1981.

Girard, René. *The Girard Reader.* Edited by James G. Williams. New York: Crossroad, 1996.

Gonzalez, Justo L., and Catherine Gunsalus Gonzalez. *The Liberating Pulpit.* Nashville: Abingdon Press, 1994.

Gottlieb, Roger S. *A Spirituality of Resistance: Finding a Peaceful Heart and Protecting the Earth.* New York: Crossroad, 1999.

Greider, William. *One World, Ready or Not: The Manic Logic of Global Capitalism.* New York: Simon & Schuster, 1997.

Hahn, Celia Allison. *Sexual Paradox: Creative Tensions in Our Lives and in Our Congregations.* New York: Pilgrim Press, 1991.

Hall, Douglas John. "Despair as Pervasive Ailment." In *Hope for the World: Mission in a Global Context,* edited by Walter Brueggemann, 83–93. Louisville, Ky.: Westminster John Knox Press, 2001.

Hallie, Philip Paul. *Lest Innocent Blood Be Shed: The Story of the Village of Le Chambon and How Goodness Happened There.* New York: Harper & Row, 1979. HarperPerennial ed., 1994.

Hamerton-Kelly, Robert. *Sacred Violence: Paul's Hermeneutic of the Cross.* Minneapolis: Fortress Press, 1992.

Harrison, Beverly Wildung. "The Power of Anger in the Work of Love: Christian Ethics for Women and Other Strangers." In *Feminist Theology: A Reader,* edited by Ann Loades, 194–214. Louisville, Ky.: Westminster/John Knox Press, 1990.

Hauerwas, Stanley. *After Christendom? How the Church Is to Behave if Freedom, Justice, and a Christian Nation Are Bad Ideas.* Nashville: Abingdon Press, 1991.

———. *Against the Nations: War and Survival in a Liberal Society.* Minneapolis: Winston Press, 1985.

———. *Christian Existence Today: Essays on Church, World, and Living in Between.* Durham, N.C.: Labyrinth Press, 1988.

———. *A Community of Character: Toward a Constructive Christian Social Ethic.* Notre Dame, Ind.: University of Notre Dame Press, 1981.

———. "Companions on the Way: The Necessity of Friendship." *Asbury Theological Journal* 45, 1 (Spring 1990): 35–48.

———. *In Good Company: The Church as Polis.* Notre Dame, Ind.: University of Notre Dame Press, 1995.

———. *The Peaceable Kingdom: A Primer in Christian Ethics.* Notre Dame, Ind.: University of Notre Dame Press, 1983.

———. *Vision and Virtue: Essays in Christian Ethical Reflection.* Notre Dame, Ind.: Fides Publishers, 1974. Reprint, Notre Dame, Ind.: University of Notre Dame Press, 1981.

Hays, Richard B. *The Moral Vision of the New Testament: A Contemporary Introduction to New Testament Ethics.* San Francisco: HarperSanFrancisco, 1996.

Hobgood, Mary Elizabeth. *Dismantling Privilege: An Ethics of Accountability.* Cleveland: Pilgrim Press, 2000.

Howard-Brook, Wes, and Anthony Gwyther. *Unveiling Empire: Reading Revelation Then and Now.* Maryknoll, N.Y.: Orbis Books, 1999.

Hunt, Mary E. *Fierce Tenderness: A Feminist Theology of Friendship.* New York: Crossroad, 1991.

Ignatieff, Michael. *Blood and Belonging: Journeys into the New Nationalism*. New York: Farrar, Straus & Giroux, 1995.

Kavanaugh, John F. *Following Christ in a Consumer Culture (Still)*. Maryknoll, N.Y.: Orbis Books, 1991.

Kay, James F. "Preaching in Advent." *Journal for Preachers* 13 (Advent 1989): 11–16.

———. "The Word of the Cross at the Turn of the Ages." *Interpretation* 53 (1999): 44–56.

Keck, Leander E. *A Future for the Historical Jesus: The Place of Jesus in Preaching and Theology*. Philadelphia: Fortress Press, 1981.

Kenneson, Philip D. *Life on the Vine: Cultivating the Fruit of the Spirit in Christian Community*. Downers Grove, Ill.: InterVarsity Press, 1999.

King, Martin Luther, Jr. *A Testament of Hope: The Essential Writings and Speeches of Martin Luther King, Jr.* Edited by James Melvin Washington. San Francisco: HarperSanFrancisco, 1986. 1st HarperCollins paperback ed., 1991.

Klein, Naomi. *No Logo: Taking Aim at the Brand Bullies*. New York: Picador USA, 2000.

Koenig, John. *New Testament Hospitality: Partnership with Strangers as Promise and Mission*. Philadelphia: Fortress Press, 1985.

Koontz, Gayle Gerber. "The Liberation of Atonement." *Mennonite Quarterly Review* 63 (April 1989): 171–92.

Lash, Nicholas. *Theology on the Way to Emmaus*. London: SCM Press, 1986.

Lewis, C. S. *The Four Loves*. New York: Harcourt, Brace & Co., 1960. Reprint, San Diego: Harvest Books, 1988.

Lindbeck, George A. *The Nature of Doctrine: Religion and Theology in a Postliberal Age*. Philadelphia: Westminster Press, 1984.

Lischer, Richard. *The Preacher King: Martin Luther King, Jr. and the Word That Moved America*. New York: Oxford University Press, 1995.

Lohfink, Gerhard. *Jesus and Community: The Social Dimension of Christian Faith*. Translated by John P. Galvin. Philadelphia: Fortress Press, 1984.

Lyon, David. *The Electronic Eye: The Rise of Surveillance Society*. Minneapolis: University of Minnesota Press, 1994.

MacIntyre, Alasdair. *After Virtue: A Study in Moral Theory*. 2d ed. Notre Dame, Ind.: University of Notre Dame Press, 1984.

Martyn, J. Louis. *Theological Issues in the Letters of Paul*. Nashville: Abingdon Press, 1997.

McClendon, James William Jr. *Systematic Theology: Ethics*. Nashville: Abingdon Press, 1986.

McClure, John S. *The Roundtable Pulpit: Where Leadership and Preaching Meet*. Nashville: Abingdon Press, 1995.

McClure, John S., and Nancy J. Ramsay, eds. *Telling the Truth: Preaching about Sexual and Domestic Violence*. Cleveland: United Church Press, 1998.

McThenia, Andrew W. Jr., ed. *Radical Christian and Exemplary Lawyer*. Grand Rapids: Wm. B. Eerdmans Publishing Co., 1995.

Meilaender, Gilbert. "The Place of Ethics in the Theological Task." *Currents in Theology and Mission* 6 (1979): 197–98.

Merton, Thomas. *Faith and Violence: Christian Teaching and Christian Practice*. Notre Dame, Ind.: University of Notre Dame Press, 1968.

Moltmann, Jürgen. *The Way of Jesus Christ: Christology in Messianic Dimensions*. Translated by Margaret Kohl. San Francisco: HarperSanFrancisco, 1990.

Morrison, Toni. *The Bluest Eye*. New York: Holt, Rinehart & Winston, 1970.

Murdoch, Iris. *The Sovereignty of Good*. London: Routledge & Kegan Paul, 1970. Reprint, London: Ark Paperbacks, 1986.

_____. "Vision and Choice in Morality." In *Christian Ethics and Contemporary Philosophy*, edited by Ian T. Ramsey, 195–218. London: SCM Press, 1966.

Murphy, Nancey C., Brad J. Kallenberg, and Mark Thiessen Nation, eds. *Virtues and Practices in the Christian Tradition: Christian Ethics after MacIntyre.* Harrisburg, Pa.: Trinity Press International, 1997.

Myers, Ched. *Binding the Strong Man: A Political Reading of Mark's Story of Jesus.* Maryknoll, N.Y.: Orbis Books, 1988.

_____. *Who Will Roll Away the Stone? Discipleship Queries for First World Christians.* Maryknoll, N.Y.: Orbis Books, 1994.

Nardi, Peter M. *Gay Men's Friendships: Invincible Communities, Worlds of Desire.* Chicago: University of Chicago Press, 1999.

Niebuhr, H. Richard. "The Grace of Doing Nothing." *Christian Century* 49 (March 23, 1932): 378–80.

Nisenson, Eric. *Ascension: John Coltrane and His Quest.* New York: St. Martin's Press, 1993.

O'Connor, Flannery. *Mystery and Manners: Occasional Prose.* New York: Farrar, Straus & Giroux, 1961.

Patterson, Barbara, "Preaching as Nonviolent Resistance." In *Telling the Truth: Preaching about Sexual and Domestic Violence*, edited by John S. McClure and Nancy J. Ramsey, 99–109. Cleveland: United Church Press, 1998.

Pincoffs, Edmund L. *Quandaries and Virtues: Against Reductivism in Ethics.* Lawrence, Kans.: University Press of Kansas, 1986.

Pohl, Christine D. *Making Room: Recovering Hospitality as a Christian Tradition.* Grand Rapids: Wm. B. Eerdmans Publishing Co., 1999.

Porter, Jean. *The Recovery of Virtue: The Relevance of Aquinas for Christian Ethics.* Louisville, Ky.: Westminster/John Knox Press, 1990.

Postman, Neil. *Amusing Ourselves to Death: Public Discourse in the Age of Show Business.* New York: Viking/Penguin Books, 1985.

_____. *Technopoly: The Surrender of Culture to Technology.* New York: Alfred A. Knopf, 1992. Vintage Books Edition, 1993.

Rader, Rosemary. *Breaking Boundaries: Male/Female Friendship in Early Christian Communities.* New York: Paulist Press, 1983.

Resner, André. *Preacher and Cross: Person and Message in Theology and Rhetoric.* Grand Rapids: Wm. B. Eerdmans Publishing Co., 1999.

Richard, Pablo. *Apocalypse: A People's Commentary on the Book of Revelation.* Translated by Phillip Berryman. Maryknoll, N.Y.: Orbis Books, 1995.

Rose, Lucy Atkinson. *Sharing the Word: Preaching in the Roundtable Church.* Louisville, Ky.: Westminster John Knox Press, 1997.

Russell-Jones, Iwan. "The Real Thing?" *And Straightaway* (Fall 1993): 3–4.

Saunders, Stanley P., and Charles L. Campbell. *The Word on the Street: Performing the Scriptures in the Urban Context.* Grand Rapids: Wm. B. Eerdmans Publishing Co., 2000.

Saussy, Carroll. *The Gift of Anger: A Call to Faithful Action.* Louisville, Ky.: Westminster John Knox Press, 1995.

Sawicki, Marianne. *Seeing the Lord: Resurrection and Early Christian Practices.* Minneapolis: Fortress Press, 1994.

Scott, James C. *Domination and the Arts of Resistance: Hidden Transcripts.* New Haven, Conn.: Yale University Press, 1990.

Smith, Christine M. "Preaching as an Art of Resistance." In *The Arts of Ministry: Feminist-Womanist Approaches*, edited by Christie Cozad Neuger, 39–59. Louisville, Ky.: Westminster John Knox Press, 1996.

————. *Preaching as Weeping, Confession, and Resistance: Radical Responses to Radical Evil.* Louisville, Ky.: Westminster/John Knox Press, 1992.

Smith, Luther E. *Intimacy and Mission: Intentional Community as a Crucible for Radical Discipleship.* Scottdale, Pa.: Herald Press, 1994.

Soskice, Janet Martin. *Metaphor and Religious Language.* Oxford: Oxford University Press, 1985.

Steinbeck, John. *The Grapes of Wrath.* Penguin Great Books of the Twentieth Century. New York: Penguin Books, 1999.

Stendahl, Krister. *Paul among Jews and Gentiles, and Other Essays.* Philadelphia: Fortress Press, 1976.

Stringfellow, William. *An Ethic for Christians and Other Aliens in a Strange Land.* Waco, Tex.: Word Books, 1973. 3d paperback ed., 1979.

————. *Free in Obedience.* New York: Seabury Press, 1964.

————. *A Keeper of the Word: Selected Writings of William Stringfellow.* Edited by Bill Wylie-Kellermann. Grand Rapids: Wm. B. Eerdmans Publishing Co., 1994.

————. *My People Is the Enemy: An Autobiographical Polemic.* New York: Holt, Rinehart & Winston, 1964.

Stroupe, Nibs, and Inez Fleming. *While We Run This Race: Confronting the Power of Racism in a Southern Church.* Maryknoll, N.Y.: Orbis Books, 1995.

Stuart, Elizabeth. *Just Good Friends: Towards a Lesbian and Gay Theology of Relationships.* New York: Mowbray, 1996.

Tompkins, Jane P. *Sensational Designs: The Cultural Work of American Fiction, 1790–1860.* New York: Oxford University Press, 1985.

————. *West of Everything: The Inner Life of Westerns.* New York: Oxford University Press, 1992.

Toole, David. *Waiting for Godot in Sarajevo: Theological Reflections on Nihilism, Tragedy, and Apocalypse.* Boulder, Colo.: Westview Press, 1998.

Volf, Miroslav, and Dorothy C. Bass, eds. *Practicing Theology: Beliefs and Practices in Christian Life.* Grand Rapids: Wm. B. Eerdmans Publishing Co., 2001.

Wadell, Paul J. *Friendship and the Moral Life.* Notre Dame, Ind.: University of Notre Dame Press, 1989.

Warren, Michael. *At This Time, in This Place: The Spirit Embodied in the Local Assembly.* Harrisburg, Pa.: Trinity Press International, 1999.

————. "Culture, Counterculture, and the Word." *Liturgy* 6 (Summer 1986): 85–93.

Weaver, J. Denny. "Atonement for the Nonconstantinian Church." *Modern Theology* 6 (July 1990): 307–23.

Webb, Stephen H. "A Hyperbolic Imagination: Theology and the Rhetoric of Excess." *Theology Today* 50 (April 1993): 56–67.

Welch, Sharon D. *Communities of Resistance and Solidarity: A Feminist Theology of Liberation.* Maryknoll, N.Y.: Orbis Books, 1985.

————. *A Feminist Ethic of Risk.* Minneapolis: Fortress Press, 1990.

Wink, Walter. *Engaging the Powers: Discernment and Resistance in a World of Domination.* Minneapolis: Fortress Press, 1992.

————. *Naming the Powers: The Language of Power in the New Testament.* Philadelphia: Fortress Press, 1984.

————. *The Powers That Be: Theology for a New Millennium.* New York: Doubleday, 1998.

————. *Unmasking the Powers: The Invisible Forces That Determine Human Existence.* Philadelphia: Fortress Press, 1986.

_____, ed. *Peace Is the Way: Writings on Nonviolence from the Fellowship of Reconciliation.* Maryknoll, N.Y.: Orbis Books, 2000.

Wylie-Kellermann, Bill. "Listen to This Man! A Parable before the Powers." *Theology Today* 53 (October 1996): 299–310.

———. "Not Vice Versa. Reading the Powers Biblically: Stringfellow, Hermeneutics, and the Principalities." *Anglican Theological Review* 81, 4 (1999): 665–82.

———. *Seasons of Faith and Conscience: Kairos, Confession, Liturgy.* Maryknoll, N.Y.: Orbis Books, 1991.

Yoder, John Howard. *He Came Preaching Peace.* Scottdale, Pa.: Herald Press, 1985.

———. *The Politics of Jesus: Vicit Agnus Noster.* Grand Rapids: Wm. B. Eerdmans Publishing Co., 1972.

Zink-Sawyer, Beverly. "'The Word Purely Preached and Heard': The Listeners and the Homiletical Endeavor." *Interpretation* 51 (October 1997): 342–57.

Index of Biblical Passages

197

Index of Names and Subjects

Printed in the United States
210061BV00002B/193-225/A

9 780664 222338